EFFECTIVE STRATEGIES FOR PROTECTING HUMAN RIGHTS

Effective Strategies for Protecting Human Rights

Prevention and intervention, trade and education

Edited by
DAVID BARNHIZER
Cleveland State University

DARTMOUTH
Aldershot • Burlington USA • Singapore • Sydney

Published by
Dartmouth Publishing Company
Ashgate Publishing Limited
Gower House
Croft Road
Aldershot
Hampshire GU11 3HR
England

Ashgate Publishing Company
131 Main Street
Burlington, VT 05401-5600 USA

Ashgate website: http://www.ashgate.com

British Library Cataloguing in Publication Data
Effective strategies for protecting human rights :
    prevention and intervention, trade and education. - (Law,
    justice and power)
    1.Human rights
    I.Barnhizer, David
    323

Library of Congress Cataloging-in-Publication Data
Effective strategies for protecting human rights : prevention and intervention, trade and
education / edited by David Barnhizer.
        p. cm. -- (Law, power and justice)
    Includes bibliographical references.
    ISBN 0-7546-2207-X
        1. Human rights--Congresses. I. Barnhizer, David, 1944-II. Symposium on Practical
    Strategies for Human Rights Protection (2000 : Cleveland, Ohio) III. Series.

JC571 .E43 2001
323--dc21

                                                                        2001046266

ISBN 0 7546 2207 X

Printed and bound in Great Britain by MPG Books Ltd, Bodmin, Cornwall

Contents

Notes on the Authors

David Barnhizer, LL.M, Harvard, J.D. *summa cum laude*, Ohio State, A.B., Muskingum, is Professor of Law at the Cleveland State University College of Law where he teaches courses in environmental law, international trade, strategy, philosophy and trial advocacy. He is also Senior Advisor to the International Program of the Natural Resources Defense Council, a member of the Board and General Counsel of Earth Summit Watch in Washington, D.C.; General Counsel to the NRDC-based Shrimp Sentinel; and a member of the Steering Committee of the Industrial Shrimp Action Network (ISA Net), a global network of more than twenty grass roots and community organizations in Latin America, Asia and Africa that have come together to resist the destructive expansion of ⸱shrimp aquaculture in tropical developing countries. He has taught and worked on environmental and human rights activities in a diverse range of countries, including Russia, Mongolia, Thailand, Ecuador, Honduras, Bangladesh and Colombia, as well as most European nations. He is author of *The Warrior Lawyer* (Transnational 1997) which applies Japanese and Chinese strategic thinking to law practice, and *Strategies for Sustainable Societies* (Global Tomorrow Coalition 1988), as well as numerous articles on topics including Agenda 21, environmental protection, judicial decision-making, natural law, history, judicial corruption and the adversary system.

Ilias Bantekas, J.D. Athens; LL.M Liverpool, *Distinction*; Ph.D. Liverpool, *magna cum laude*. Senior Lecturer and Director, International Law Unit, School of Law, University of Westminster, and Barrister. Co-author of *International Criminal Law* (Cavendish, 2001), and *Principles of Direct and Superior Responsibility in International Humanitarian Law* (Manchester UP, 2001). Editor, *International Criminal Law Review*.

Susan Bazilli, B.A., LL.B., International Women's Rights Project, York University, Toronto, Canada. Susan Bazilli has worked internationally as a lawyer, consultant, activist, advocate, researcher and writer on issues of human rights, women's rights, and information technology for the past 25 years.

Eric Stener Carlson is pursuing his Ph.D. in Political Science at the University of California, Santa Barbara, where he is a Doctoral Scholars Fellow. He is currently based in Geneva, Switzerland, where he works for the International Programme for the Elimination of Child Labour as an official for the International Labour Organisation (United Nations ILO). He is a former Fulbright Scholar to Argentina and former Expert-on-Mission for the International Criminal Tribunal for the Former Yugoslavia based in the Netherlands. He is the author of *I Remember Julia: Voices of the Disappeared* (Temple University Press, 1996), and has written a number of articles on human rights advocacy, torture and civil-military relations in Latin America.

Jason W. Clay studied at Harvard, the London School of Economics and Cornell University. He received his Ph.D. in anthropology in 1979. Clay is the author of more than a dozen books and 400 articles. Dr. Clay was founder and editor of *Cultural Survival Quarterly* and Director of Research at Cultural Survival from 1980-1992. Since 1993, Clay has worked as a consultant and a Senior Fellow with World Wildlife Fund. He has conducted research on indigenous people and human rights violations in more than two dozen countries. Clay's research methodology has been applied in eight countries and in each instance has changed the policies of multilateral and bilateral organizations as well as those of foundations and NGOs.

Brian Concannon, Jr., Georgetown University Law Center, J.D. 1989, Middlebury College, B.A. History and French, 1985. Brian has managed the *Bureau des Avocats Internationaux* (BAI) in Port-au-Prince, Haiti, since 1996. The BAI helps the Haitian justice system and victims pursue human rights cases and trains new lawyers in a clinical setting. The BAI's most prominent case, the *Raboteau Massacre*, is considered the best and most complex trial of any kind in Haiti's history. Brian is interviewed regularly for Haitian, U.S. and European press, radio and television reports and documentaries on human rights and justice in Haiti. He first came to Haiti as a Human Rights Observer with the United Nations/Organization of American States International Civilian Mission to Haiti in 1995. He is author of "Beyond Complementarity: The International Criminal Court and National Prosecutions, a View from Haiti," 32 Columbia Human Rights

Law Review 201 (2000); and "Justice in Haiti: The Raboteau Trial," *Human Rights Tribune*, V. 7 No. 4 (Dec. 2000).

Ann Cooper is Executive Director of the Committee to Protect Journalists. She worked as a reporter in the former Soviet Union, Africa, and Washington, D.C., before joining CPJ in July 1998. Her voice is well known to radio listeners in the United States from her nine years as a correspondent for National Public Radio (NPR). She has also reported for *The Louisville Courier-Journal*, the *Capitol Hill News Service*, *Congressional Quarterly*, *The Baltimore Sun*, and *National Journal* magazine. Appointed NPR's first Moscow bureau chief in 1987, Cooper spent five years covering the tumultuous events of the times, including the failed coup attempt in Moscow. She co-edited a book of first-person accounts of that siege, *Russia at the Barricades*. NPR also sent her to Beijing to cover the Tiananmen Square pro-democracy movement. Based in Johannesburg, South Africa, from 1992-95, Cooper's coverage there won NPR a prestigious Alfred I. duPont-Columbia University Award in broadcast journalism. She traveled throughout Africa, writing features and analysis on a range of subjects, including the famine and international intervention in Somalia, the 1994 Rwandan refugee crisis, and the cholera epidemic in Zaire. Returning to the United States in 1995, she studied refugee policy issues as a fellow at the Council on Foreign Relations in New York and also traveled in Kenya, Rwanda, Zaire, Bosnia and Haiti to produce a series on refugee policy for NPR. She has taught radio and international reporting at the Columbia University Graduate School of Journalism, and is a journalism graduate of Iowa State University.

D. Christopher Decker, LL.M. in International Human Rights Law, University of Essex; J.D. University of Buffalo School of Law; B.A. Purdue University. Mr. Decker is the Legal Adviser on Human Rights in Law Enforcement for the Organization for Security and Co-operation in Europe's (OSCE) Mission in Kosovo. He also served as an Adviser to the Ombudsperson Institution in Kosovo for the OSCE. Mr. Decker was the Administrator of the European Court of Human Rights Litigation Support Unit at the University of Essex Human Rights Centre and a Legal Officer for the International Crisis Group Humanitarian Law Documentation Project in Kosovo. He has recently published an article with Lucia Fresa, "The Status of Conscientious Objection under Article 4 of the European Convention for Human Rights," 33 *NYU J. INT'L L. AND POL* 379 (2001).

Frank J. Garcia is an associate professor of international and comparative law at the Boston College Law School. His principal research interests include the link between international trade law and global social issues such as development and human rights; and the process of regional economic integration in the Americas. A member of the American Society of International Law since 1993 and past vice-chair of its International Economic Law Interest Group, Professor Garcia is currently collaborating on the ASIL Human Rights and International Trade research project. He also serves on the advisory council and editorial board of the Procedural Aspects of International Law Institute. A 1989 graduate of the University of Michigan Law School, Professor Garcia has taught and researched at a variety of institutions in the United States and abroad.

Anne Tierney Goldstein has been the Human Rights Education Director for the International Women Judges Foundation since 1993. In that capacity, she has designed and run training programs for judges and judicial trainers in nine countries on four continents, one isthmus and an archipelago. A graduate of Princeton University and Harvard Law School, Ms. Goldstein spent three years as an attorney with the United States Department of Justice and two years with the Washington, D.C. office of Hogan and Hartson before entering the non-profit world. As an adjunct professor at Georgetown University, the Georgetown University Law Center, and now George Washington University National Law Center, she has taught courses on *Women and the Law* and *Human Rights of Women*, and is currently preparing a course on *International and Comparative Family Law*.

Edward F. Halpin, MA, MIInfSc. He is Reader in Information Management in the School of Information Management, at the Leeds Metropolitan University. His research interests include human rights and the Internet, privacy, surveillance and the technologies of political control, and information warfare. His publications include "Children's Rights and the Internet" (with Hick) *Annals of the American Association of Political and Social Sciences* 575, May 2001, *Human Rights and the Internet* (with Hick and Hoskins, MacMillan, 2000), "Through the Net to Freedom" *Journal of Information Science* (with Brophy, Bowker Saur, 1999), and *The Use of the Internet by the European Parliament for the Promotion and Protection of Human Rights* (with Fisher, European Parliament, 1998).

Shulamith Koenig is a human rights activist, Founder and Executive Director of PDHRE (the People's Movement for Human Rights Education), an organization promoting worldwide human rights education for social transformation at the community level with a special focus on gender and economic issues. She served as an officer in the Israeli Army, worked as a volunteer at the Alfred Adler Institute in Israel and is one of the founders of Peace Now. She has also worked with New Outlook, seeking a two-State Solution to the Israeli/Palestinian conflict. She is a graduate of Columbia University's schools of Engineering and Management, specializing in water systems and irrigation. She has published extensively in various human rights and human rights education anthologies, and is a lecturer and sculptor.

Malini Mehra is founder-director of the Centre for Social Markets based in India and London. Ms Mehra has also served as Director of the People's Decade for Human Rights Education (PDHRE); trade and investment policy adviser for Oxfam UK, and international campaigns officer for Friends of the Earth International. She is an experienced campaigner at a variety of international *fora* such as the World Trade Organization, the OECD (MAI campaign coordinator), European Parliament, and the UN Commission for Sustainable Development. A lifelong activist, she has initiated campaigns and organized efforts in social justice movements around the world. Her academic training has been as a political scientist and gender specialist at Smith College (USA), the Institute of Development Studies, University of Sussex (UK), and the Institute of Development Research, at the University of Amsterdam (Netherlands). She is editor of *"Human rights and economic globalisation: Directions for the WTO"* and has published on issues including trade and investment policy, economic liberalisation and poverty reduction, sustainable development and local authorities, new indicators for sustainability, human rights and corporations, and gender and reproductive rights. Contact information is (www.centre-socialmarkets.org).

Marianne Møllmann is the Executive Director of the Network in Solidarity with the People of Guatemala (NISGUA), a Washington-based grassroots organization working for justice and human rights in Guatemala. She holds a Bachelor degree in Political Science from Copenhagen University, a Masters in Business Administration from the Ecole des Affairs de Paris, and an LL.M. in International Human Rights Law from Essex University.

Marianne worked for several years in international advertising brand strategy planning and development, before deciding to dedicate herself exclusively to human rights work. She joined NISGUA in February 2000 from Public Citizen's Global Trade Watch, where she helped research and edit a groundbreaking book on international trade, Wallach and Sforza: *Whose Trade Organization?*

Peter Takirambudde is Executive Director for Africa at Human Rights Watch. Before joining Human Rights Watch in 1995, he was Professor of Law (corporate and tax law) and Dean of Social Sciences at the University of Botswana. A graduate of Makerere University (Uganda), he earned his doctorate (J.S.D.) degree in international business transactions from Yale University. At Princeton University, Peter was a Compton Fellow. He has also been a University Consortium Fellow in international relations and human rights (Princeton, Harvard, and Yale), a Ford Foundation Fellow, and a visiting professor/scholar at the universities of Edinburgh and Lund. Peter played a pioneering role in the design, inauguration, and management of several important human rights initiatives in Africa, including the creation of the Botswana Human Rights Center, Botswana Childline, Labor Lawyers Network of South Africa, Africa Association for Human Rights Development, the First All Africa Law Conference, and the Southern Africa Network for Criminal Law and Human Rights. Active for more than twenty years in the human rights movement, he has written extensively on human rights in Africa.

Jorge Varela Márquez is a biologist, with international studies and works related to the environment, marine biology, fishing and aquaculture. He is director of a community-based, grassroots organization named the Comité para la Defensa y Desarrollo de la Flora y Fauna del Golfo de Fonseca (CODDEFFAGOLF) in Honduras, which has received three international environmental awards for its work. His main activity has been in defense of coastal wetlands of the world, and mainly the Gulf of Fonseca, where he and others have fought against the chaotic and uncontrolled expansion of the shrimp farming industry on the coastal wetlands. He also works to expand people's respect for human rights, education and equitable development in local communities. His principal contributions with CODDEFFAGOLF have included the negotiation of two national moratoriums on shrimp farming expansion during 1996 and 1998; working to have a significant portion of the coastal wetlands of the Gulf of Fonseca designated as a protected "Ramsar Site 1000," and working with the government to dedicate a System of Protected Areas of the Gulf of Fonseca. At the national level in Honduras Mr. Varela has worked along with other leaders to resist against international trends such as the importation of sludge, wastes, and used tires from industrial countries, and has also fought against grants of forest concessions and efforts to modify constitutional laws in ways that would harm local communities and the Honduran environment. At the international level he is participating in an awareness campaign around the world against the shrimp farming expansion in tropical and sub tropical zones, serving as a founding member of ISA Net. In 1999 he was awarded the prestigious Goldman Environmental Prize, granted by the Goldman Foundation in recognition of his important contributions to protecting the environment.

Preface

The two volumes on effective strategies for protecting human rights are derived in part from a conference on human rights sponsored by the Cleveland State University College of Law and the Washington, DC-based organization, Earth Summit Watch. Held April 13-15, 2000, the *"Symposium on Practical Strategies for Human Rights Protection"* brought together leading human rights activists and scholars who had devoted their energies and hearts to human rights causes and organizations.

As Coordinator of the conference and editor of the two books on practical strategies for protecting human rights I have been incredibly fortunate to work with the contributors to this process. The significance of the work being done by every contributor and their willingness to elaborate and share their experiences and insights has made the entire process one of the most rewarding and gratifying of my career. I personally have learned so much from the people involved with both the conference and as contributors of the chapters that it is difficult to express the extent of my respect for what they are doing and my appreciation of their contributions. I hope the work done in editing the books reflects that respect and appreciation, and that they will feel that as an editor I have done justice to their vital work.

I also want to express my regard for the contributions made to this process by Peter Fitzpatrick and to Austin Sarat. Although Peter was unable to contribute to the books, he nonetheless made a substantial contribution to the conference and to the design of the books and I am extremely grateful for his help. Austin Sarat, as Series Editor of Ashgate's *Law, Power and Justice* series, demonstrated encouragement and intellectual excitement for this project from the beginning and made it somehow seem an easy process. I, and the other contributors, will always appreciate his support and his interest in having these two books appear in his series.

Finally, I want to thank Eric Domanski, Holli Goodman, and April Mixon, each of whom worked "above and beyond" to assist in the production of the books. Without their professionalism and continual commitment and good humor this project could never have been completed within the time frame and at the level of quality that I feel was achieved.

1 Human Rights Strategies for Investigation and "Shaming," Resisting Globalization Rhetoric, and Education

DAVID BARNHIZER

A strength of the approach taken in this volume involves the combination of a strategic perspective with the concrete knowledge offered by people who are living their lives to oppose and end torture, genocide, denials of freedom and basic equity, and violation of women through forced subservience and sexual brutality and exploitation. This volume concentrates on three primary areas. The first involves strategies for monitoring and investigating potential human rights violations, along with the power offered by information technologies to improve these strategic functions. A part of this analysis is contained in the reminder by Ann Cooper, director of the Committee to Protect Journalists, in her analysis of the lengths to which human rights violators both within and outside governments will go to prevent journalists' *witnessing* of their actions and reporting what they see to the world—to the extent that journalists are frequently murdered, tortured and imprisoned. A second major area of concentration examines the compelling and difficult intersection of the globalization of trade, including its tendency to produce violations of human rights, anti-democratic repression, and environmental harm. Finally, a diverse range of educational strategies is considered. The educational analyses focus not only on the continuing need to educate a wide range of people whose moral indignation is essential to building the relentless political will required to support decisive action to prevent violations and to apprehend and punish violators when prevention does not succeed—but on actors such as judges and prosecutors who must apply the law, and potential violators of human rights such as the military and the police.

1

The guiding premise of the book is that we have now had significant experience with human rights violations—and the limits of our often feeble and tardy attempts to prevent violations and to inhibit actors from committing even worse atrocities than they would if completely unafraid of possible sanctions. From these wide-ranging experiences we are now at a point where lessons can be extracted as to which approaches work and which do not. This strategic analysis includes the need to realistically understand how the system can be made more effective in preventing human rights violations, and ways in which the worst effects can at least be mitigated even if they can not be fully prevented. Along with this humanitarian mission is the need to identify the best strategies for sanctioning violators.

Human rights protection—including prevention and detection, and humanitarian responses to aid victims and assist in the rebuilding of societies devastated by atrocities—requires clear focus, strong action, and sustained and powerful political will to provide continuing support for action and to pressure political decision-makers. It also requires the dedication of resources at levels adequate to the various tasks that are required to protect against human rights violations, rebuild shattered societies and sanction violators. Protecting human rights requires the ability and willingness to impose intelligent and appropriate sanctions, and to stimulate the political will needed to demand and sustain the implementation of those sanctions. The inability to "stay the course" with appropriate sanctions weakens the entire system of non-military sanctions. Of course, the initial selection of inappropriate or inappropriately targeted non-military sanctions is itself a serious strategic problem—as is the use of sanctions such as in Iraq where the consequences fall on ordinary people who are incapable of creating enough opposition to influence the actual target—Saddam Hussein.

When specific and detailed actions and strategies are required, lofty pronouncements allow political leaders to proclaim their commitment to high ideals in international *fora* while their domestic behavior doesn't change. Insistence that national actors encounter some strong consequence for their abuses of others can be viewed as naïve or a nuisance. It is therefore important to go behind the "paper systems" many countries and private sector actors have created in order to manufacture the appearance of a national commitment to human rights. Penetrating the veils that mask governments' "apparent compliance" with the terms of human rights treaties, and overcoming governmental disinformation strategies such as are described by Peter Takirambudde is vital. So is being honest about the inability of voluntary codes and soft law norms to shape the behavior of potential human rights violators.

Detection, Monitoring, and "Shaming"

Achieving the essential degree of strength in human rights protection requires increasing our capabilities on many levels. These include improving our ability to monitor and investigate violations. These critical functions are described by Peter Takirambudde, Ann Cooper, Jason Clay, Christopher Decker and Edward Halpin. But strong protection of human rights also necessitates insisting that human rights considerations be placed centrally into the rules of the inexorably expanding international trading regime that is currently under attack for trampling on humanitarian concerns to achieve increased trade efficiencies. Chapters by Marianne Møllmann, Malini Mehra, David Barnhizer, Frank Garcia and Jorge Varela focus on these concerns. If globalization and the free market are inevitable forces—as they appear to be—it is time to hold them to the rhetoric of openness and of enhanced democratization that their advocates often use to justify the shift to a large-scale market economy. It is appropriate to demand that the trading regime use the power and influence that accrues to its institutional actors from the expansion of economic activity and increased financial integration as mechanisms through which victims of human rights abuses are protected and violators deterred or punished. Otherwise globalization rhetoric is nothing more than warmed over and repackaged "trickle down" propaganda of the kind that has long characterized political discourse in the United States.

There are several keys to building an effective human rights system. Early warning and detection of violations is critical. Takirambudde and Halpin offer strategies on how this can be done. It is vital to begin the process of intervention and putting pressure on emerging violators before the worst of the violations arise. This is obviously difficult in many instances because we may not know that there are going to be problems at an early enough time and by the time it is obvious the momentum may be too great. But given the tragedies in Cambodia, Rwanda, Kosovo, Bosnia, Chechnya and far too many other countries we are no longer entitled to innocence. In the Rwandan context, the analysis by Rawson and Drumbl in volume one make it painfully obvious that we knew what was happening at a relatively early point but simply didn't make any serious move to stop the killing. As Richard Goldstone observes from the perspective of his being an African, the great powers didn't move until genocide revisited Europe. The time to investigate, monitor and create pressure—even to the extent of using military force—is before the Kosovos and East Timors get started. This requires that we anticipate what could happen and initiate measures before the violations get going. Taking anticipatory action to preempt the potentially unfolding crisis is, however, one of the things we do poorly in virtually everything we do. Instead our political systems wait for a problem to become a crisis and for crises to become tragedies before political leaders are willing to act.

The Internet provides an intelligence gathering system far beyond what has historically been possessed by virtually any government, not to mention ordinary citizens. It provides a means of real-time communication, free publicity and information dissemination, and intra and inter-organizational networking. Intelligence gathering, information dissemination and networking have created an enlarged scale of action for the public interest community. A result is that the competitive "game" between human rights activists and those they challenge has changed immeasurably. This is noted by Takirambudde's description of the use of satellite photos in monitoring, Ann Cooper's discussion of the work of the Committee to Protect Journalists, and Jason Clay's analysis of the changed conditions under which human rights monitors work with the new information technology. But human rights workers have much more to do in order to take full advantage of their new information capability. Some paths are described in depth by Edward Halpin's elaboration of case studies demonstrating how communications technology and the Internet have been used in human rights contexts, and by Christopher Decker's work using information technology to build and maintain a detailed record of violations in Kosovo.

One important way information technology has changed the rules relates to the behavior of powerful international institutions and governments. Institutions such as the World Bank, the World Trade Organization and the International Monetary Fund are accustomed to behaving without transparent processes. As with many national govern-ments, they reach their desired decisions behind closed doors or through decision-making processes that allow participation by only very carefully chosen interests. They have long expected their goodwill and expertise to be taken as a given. The Internet has stripped much of the "smoke and mirrors" away from such decision-makers. It has increasingly allowed activists to make early interventions into the institutions' planning and decision-making processes in ways that challenge their assumptions and force other concerns onto their agendas.

Globalization, Trade, and Human Rights

Globalization, trade and protection of the human rights of local people and small communities tend to be in conflict. In large part this is caused by the very different interests that are served by what might be called the "real-government-in-interest" of any country. At best there is a schism between the elites with capital who nearly always control most countries and the local people found in more rural areas and along the coasts. In many nations and particularly in many developing nations, the finance, foreign trade, and economic development agencies are considerably more powerful and influential than those responsible for environmental protection and social issues. But the inequality is driven also by the fact that foreign trade, finance, exploitation of natural resources and economic development are where money can be made and deals brokered. Those who seek to preserve existing wealth or have access to opportunities to expand their resources are much more likely to gravitate to those ministries that control money and financial opportunity than to ministries charged with responsibilities for environmental enforcement or social welfare. The gross disparity in the power and influence of the different types of agencies means that laws will be applied or ignored mainly according to the power of the interests affected. Poor people lack voice, training, and representation. Their interests will almost always be subordinated to those of the groups who run the country.

Much has been made of the transformational shift to an information-based economy and to a global scale of economic competitiveness. Invisible economic actors are endowed with powers beyond that possessed by many national governments. Through information technology and the economies of scale they allow there has been a quantum shift in the ability of vast and powerful institutions to concentrate and mobilize resources. They can use their global power to manipulate national policy-making, to influence both corrupt and honest political leaders, and move their resources and bases of activity freely if they see better deals elsewhere or are resisted in their efforts to gain concessions. These changes in the scale, speed, and mobility of capital activity have transformed economic actors to such a degree that they have in many ways become largely unaccountable for their actions. This transmutation through information systems and the mobility of capital means that for those countries desiring to participate fully in the global marketplace, the traditional forms of national sovereignty have become quaint artifacts.

Rather then democracy being advanced, as advocates of "free-market globalization" argue, the very concept of democracy is threatened by the scale on which such enormously powerful and unaccountable economic leviathans operate and by the equivalent scale of institutions such as the World Bank, the International Monetary Fund, and the World Trade Organization. This shift to a globalized economic/political system does, however, have mixed implications for human rights. On the one hand, market-driven behavior has no intrinsic core of positive values. It functions for its own ends and those are to achieve profit and competitive power while molding the environment within which it operates in order to achieve its goals. Left to its own ends the free market will automatically abuse human rights. To make it do otherwise requires strong countervailing incentives that buffer and shape the behavior of market participants. This demands strong public and private institutions designed to resist the anti-democratic behavior of governments, corporations, and multilateral institutions.

Such strong countervailing institutions become critical in defending against a globalized economic system and shaping the system to act in a way that advances social goods. This is necessary because the powerful public and private institutions of the global economic system operate outside the ability of any nation's citizens to control. They take decisions, create policies, and implement actions that have never been agreed to by the citizens of a particular nation. Even the elected representatives of a country such as the United States have little voice in the decisions of the international institutions—other than through the formalistic and tenuous threads legally spun through legislative consent to the terms of a particular treaty by which the entity is established and empowered. The result is that the mechanisms of citizen participation and political control over decisions that impact their lives in the most fundamental ways are becoming increasingly remote. This is discussed in various ways by Garcia, Møllmann, Varela, Barnhizer, and Mehra.

No equivalent set of public and regulatory organizations has been allowed to arise to balance these massive private and public forces. The Internet has to some degree offered hope that it can evolve into such a device. But the Internet's potential is to enhance the investigation, information sharing and mobilization capabilities of non-governmental organizations (NGOs) and individual citizens rather than governments and multilateral bodies. It has become an important means of increasing the transparency of decision-making by such institutions.

A consequence of increased economic investment and development in poorer countries has supposedly created less favorable conditions for inefficient, corrupt, or undemocratic governments that are now argued to be operating under greater international scrutiny. To some extent this argument is an illusion. There has been heightened pressure on governments of developing countries by powerful industries, particularly those engaged in extractive and manufacturing activities. These countries typically have weak laws and poorly funded and less-capable governmental institutions. As globalization progresses there has been greater degradation of biological diversity and frequent disruption of indigenous societies as a direct result of commercial activity encroaching into previously remote, undisturbed areas. Rather than making life better for all, there have been increasing disparities in relative wealth and income, in health, and in access to information technology between "haves" and "have nots" both within nations and between the developed and the developing world.

As suggested above, one of the most important consequences of globalization has been the growing power of big business enterprises relative to governments. This shift in relative power has resulted in pressures on financially weak governments from the financial markets and from international financial institutions. These pressures are argued by many to have resulted in the reduction or unfair constraint of essential social spending in the affected countries. It is clear that social safeguards have lagged behind trade liberalization. This is characterized at least symbolically by the inaccessible and undemocratic procedures at the WTO and other major economic and financial institutions.

Even with its intrinsic flaws and numerous injustices globalization is in many ways inevitable. The challenge is therefore how to shape its institutions so that they are fairer and more inclusive, and how to understand globalization's dynamics sufficiently to use its terms and conditions as a means of pressure to prevent human rights abuses and to impose sanctions against violators. Properly understood globalization presents new opportunities to address human rights problems. It represents expanded capabilities for human rights cooperation among governments, as well as among far-flung non-governmental organizations. It allows the enhanced flow of information and technology needed to identify and respond to human rights threats. Through this information flow is emerging far greater transparency in which human rights violators have much greater difficulty suppressing information about what they are doing.

One of the most important opportunities offered by globalization is that it has created unprecedented leverage to harness consumer power in the marketplace to influence corporate behavior (e.g., South Africa). If it can not be stopped then a wise strategist must come to understand globalization, trade and finance, and learn how to use its levers of power. A significant part of this new power relates to the capabilities of information technology. NGOs now have instantaneous communications capabilities well beyond that of many national governments today. Acts done that would have traditionally been invisible to the world are now discovered within days or even hours. A vital part of strategies to protect human rights must therefore involve the use of the Internet as a tool for investigation, organizing and advocacy.

Educational and Training Strategies

Educational and training strategies are also particularly important aspects of effective protection of human rights. This thread runs through both volumes but is brought out most explicitly in volume two. The lack of any real deterrent power generated by human rights laws and norms becomes even clearer when we accept that few scholars can agree on the effectiveness of crime deterrence strategies even in the context of a self-contained national system of criminal law. This connection becomes far more blurred and attenuated when we shift to the international arena and expect internal national actors to comprehend and be deterred by the potential application of war crimes and crimes against humanity liability by coalitions of other nations. This suggests that, although potentially useful, deterrence strategies are last-ditch options that pale in utility in comparison with anticipatory and early intervention approaches—as well as education to prevent violations in the first instance.

These educational and training strategies are, however, not simply directed at the general education of people regarding the importance of human rights ideals. At least as important is the need to focus education and training strategies on a diverse range of distinct constituencies that either nurture or inhibit our ability to protect human rights. These distinct constituencies include potential violators, monitors, investigators and relief providers. An important example is found in Eric Carlson's description of his experience in training soldiers at the U.S. Army's controversial School of the Americas.

The aim of some of the human rights education is to convince potential violators to behave in more humane ways—either because it is the right thing to do or, more likely, because there is a high probability that there will be serious consequences to them for their inhumane behavior if they pursue that path. Carlson's discussion of self-interested and morality-based strategies for human rights education of the military from Latin American countries at the School of the Americas offers insights. Jason Clay outlines important strategies that are basic to effective monitoring and investigation as well as protecting human rights monitors and investigators. The educational "targets" also include judges, defense lawyers and prosecutors, as well as journalists and academics. Anne Goldstein offers insights on judicial training through the International Women's Judges Association. Brian Concannon's description of the work of the *Bureau des Avocats Internationaux* in Haiti relates to the training of judges, prosecutors and police as a critical part of efforts to bring Haitians to justice who had played important roles in tortures and massacres in that country. Ilias Bantekas demonstrates how public opinion can be enhanced in ways that increase public awareness of human rights and indignation at violations. Shulamith Koenig's compelling description of her work to educate people in the values of human rights—and helping them understand that human rights are *their* rights—serves as a powerful reminder of the vital role of human rights values supported by a fair and just system of law.

2 Building the Record of Human Rights Violations in Africa—the Functions of Monitoring, Investigation and Advocacy

PETER TAKIRAMBUDDE

The mandate of the program of Human Rights Watch (HRW) I direct is to monitor the human rights environment in Sub-Saharan Africa, which contains about 50 countries. This is quite a tall order. The principal goal is to gather strategic information, particularly relating to the various levels of a nation's activities. But information gathering is inherently risky to the investigator and his contacts. Depending on country specific contexts, this has varying degrees of risk both to ourselves, and to local human rights activists and our sources. Each country poses a different challenge. In many African nations we don't have major problems, we can come and go without difficulty. But there are countries like Angola, Sudan, Rwanda, Burundi, Sierra Leone, Liberia and the war-torn Democratic Republic of Congo where there is significant danger.

The defense of human rights has increasingly become a "motherhood and apple pie" issue—that is, it is a set of values and mission that no one can afford to disagree with, at least publicly. Now that the human rights records of governments in Africa and elsewhere have become a widely used yardstick for measuring the legitimacy of a government (though not always with any consequences resulting from the measurement), government officials have all learned to talk the right talk. But to avoid human rights becoming simply a largely empty discourse that all use and no one takes seriously, observers who want to improve the situation in a country must have the hard and detailed data on which to base their assessments. This information is important both in evaluating the behavior of a government at any given point in time, but also in establishing a base

11

line (as in satisfaction of conditionality arrangements) against which to judge subsequent behavior. With the factual foundation based on hard data, those pressing for reform of the human rights behavior of governments can do so more effectively. On the other hand, if activists and other reformers show no grasp of the concrete information of the actual situation, no one will listen seriously to them.

Investigation

Depending on context, investigation can be done with varying degrees of transparency. As a result the primary operational principle for our people is that you have to know a country pretty well. You have to know how sophisticated the security system of that country is. How is the security system organized, how does it work? Telephone and other communications services are critical and potentially dangerous. Are telecommunications monitored and bugged? Are the organizations we talk with infiltrated, and are they or we under surveillance? Do the authorities plant taxi drivers? Is there an extensive network of secret police like in Zaire under Mobutu, for example? Will the act of making contact with a source put them or you in danger at some later point?

In instances where it is important to mobilize public opinion to press for action, activists and the media will have their greatest success if they can provide the detailed data needed to present the victims of human rights abuses as human beings. This is an essential strategy that allows others to empathize more strongly with the victims' plight and be moved to action. This movement to action must be the goal of human rights workers. The data gathered by a research organization like HRW give life and depth not only to print stories but also to film and video reports.

Advocacy

The functions of investigation must be followed up with advocacy on both the national and international levels. At both levels, information gained from monitoring is strategically deployed to put pressure on relevant decision-makers and insisting they put human rights protection on the top of their agendas. Hard data and monitoring information are used to confront double standards, to insist that human rights considerations be taken seriously when looking for political solutions, and when evaluating the success of those solutions.

Part of our job at Human Rights Watch involves not only working in the daily trenches in which some of us find ourselves in a fight against human rights abuses but also reflecting on the implications and uses of the information explosion as it applies to protecting human rights. As a human rights organization the principal goal of HRW is to bring about change. In the short term it is to bring about improvements in the human rights conditions of people in Sub-Saharan Africa. My task particularly relates to the means through which we can generate sound, reliable and targeted information and then strategically use that information to create pressure on key decision-makers in Africa.

But human rights activity is part of a complex system. An important part of our strategy is that we also want to put pressure on other key decision-making centers in Europe and North America. This includes the important financial institutions from which African governments often seek funds and concessional development terms. We seek to target those institutions that have the most influence over the recipient countries in terms of foreign aid. Part of the strategy is obviously that we seek to shame those who commit the primary abuses. But we also seek to shame those who support them, those who cooperate with them, and those who give them financial and other means of assistance. With this pressure on national and international decision-makers we seek to change abusive practices and also avoid new abuses.

HRW's Strategic Goal

In the long term HRW's strategic goal is to obtain sustainable long-term improvements overall in terms of human rights, and in the acceptance of the rule of law and expanded democratic involvement across the African continent. We have devoted an increasing amount of resources to investigating human rights conditions in Sub-Saharan Africa. Our job is to use that information as strategically as possible to bring about better outcomes. But to do so requires an extremely high level of efficiency. It is vital that we are able to strategically release information on a timely basis. But even that is not enough. The information must be accurate. It must be information that is clearly expressed. It must be information that allows effective communication to the centers of power one is seeking to influence. And it is very important that it is information that places the organization ahead of the occurrence-curve of the abuses.

Of late, there has been improvement in some areas of the African continent. Ten years ago it was a period primarily of denial, deception and rejection regarding the reality of extensive human rights violations. But the political environment in a substantial part of Africa has changed and there now appears to be more support for the protection of human rights. There even appears to be something of an emerging consensus about the need to defend human rights. The danger, however, is that the improvements may lead us to confuse rhetoric with reality. As I remarked at the beginning of this chapter, protection of essential human rights seems to have become a sort of rhetorical "motherhood and apple pie" issue. In terms of the donor agencies it has become an issue about which no one seems to disagree or disapprove. The right bureaucratic words are all in place. Human rights assessments have become widely used as a yardstick against which the legitimacy of a government seeking to receive assistance is measured. Governments all over the African continent have learned to *talk the talk*, and are increasingly giving the impression that they have set out to outdo even me in terms of the chapter and verse of the various international conventions. But the question is whether they are also willing to *walk the walk* required in the actual protection of their peoples' human rights.

High Quality, Timely and Concrete Information

The challenge for us is to continue generating high quality and timely information and the hard data, the concrete information that is the best possible way to establish a baseline against which to hold governments accountable for their actions. If you want to be able to hold governments accountable for what they have done and to influence their future behavior that is the best way—through having baseline information. This allows you to measure a country's behavior over time and this can only be done through creating a baseline to measure progress or regression. Having baseline data available makes it possible to demonstrate that some countries are merely making an appearance of difference but that there is no real difference in their actual behavior.

We have major networks of sources of information, traditional and untraditional. Traditional sources have always included diplomats, military leaders, political leaders, civil society groups, business leaders and academics. But we find that many of those sources are drying up, evidently due to a vested interest in not reporting abuses or for fear of reprisals if they were discovered to have supplied information to us. So there are a number of countries where we are now using less traditional sources of information. This includes sources such as market vendors, and bus and taxi drivers, street kids—people who have lots of time to watch and talk—small business people and traders, local doctors and nurses at both large and small clinics who have turned out to be some of our best informed and reliable sources in a number of countries. Small merchants and business people who are able to move between town and country end up both providing us with invaluable information and helping to distribute our messages.

The local media is a valuable source of information but we have to carefully watch out for distortion due to governmental pressure on media in many countries. While newspapers are useful, their stories sometimes tend to be exaggerated, sensationalized and based on questionable tips. It is important that we do our own independent investigation. In many countries where we work we find that priests and nuns tend to be more protected from local pressures, less suspect when an international researcher goes to visit them, and they also tend to be more objective. They also have a good understanding about the culture. If you can find a nun or a priest who has been working in a country for 20 years or more you are going to end up with an extremely knowledgeable person. Of course they are usually better protected against reprisals than are a country's nationals, so it is much easier to get them to talk. They also have opportunities to witness crimes or are told the details by their parishioners. Likewise humanitarian workers or personnel attached to development projects often witness or are told of human rights abuses but are unable to publicize the information for fear of compromising their continuing work under their own mandate. Thus HRW has found in recent years a growing willingness by such workers to hand over data to HRW for further investigation, if need be, and then for subsequent publicity or other action.

Coping with Increasingly Sophisticated Government Propaganda and Cover-up

We increasingly find that governments have become extremely sophisticated at the control and use of information. Because governments are more aware of the possible public relations costs of being identified as abusers, they have become better at devising strategies for hiding abuses. During the genocide in Rwanda, when Rwandan authorities learned that the killing was costing them international goodwill and impeding promised French military aid, they altered their tactics. A few days after the French suggested that renewed assistance might follow on improvements in the Rwandan image, Radio Mille Colline broadcast the news that the French would be willing to help the government, but that people must no longer stand and laugh at the barriers when Tutsi were slaughtered there by having their throats cut; and it was broadcast that cadavers should no longer be left on the road, but removed to the banana groves. From large-scale massacres, the government moved instead to extracting a few dozen victims at a time from churches and so forth and killing them under cover of night.

Similarly Rwandan government troops are reported to have burned the bodies of victims, both in Rwanda and in the Democratic Republic of Congo. In addition to hiding evidence, the violators attempt to prevent discovery by simply refusing to allow observers into zones where crimes have recently been committed. Thus we saw such methods used as obstruction of the UN investigation team in the Democratic Republic of Congo, and confiscation of their list of witnesses. Furthermore, abusive governments have learned how to exploit the media to present themselves well. Rwanda's leader, Paul Kagame, thus told a British journalist, "There is a new way to make war through the media. And we do it better than anyone else."

The increasing sophistication of abusers—e.g., putting obstacles in the way of getting to the sites of their crimes, creating clouds of favorable propaganda and hiding evidence—requires researchers to always search for new methods themselves. For example, we now have networks to locate witnesses and bring them to us when we can't go to the sites—either because they are placed off limits by government order or because seeing witnesses on the site would place them at risk.

Technology and Investigation Strategies

New technology promises to greatly circumvent many of these obstacles. We regularly use encrypted e-mail to protect our information and sources. High technology now provides key information through satellite images. During a recent investigation of abuses in Sudan, we were able to access detailed images with super resolution, which can give much information about specific locations. Where there are massive abuses, and slashing and burning, satellite technology is capable of providing images of the scene that can filter out virtually everything but the flame and the smoke. If we were to pick a date on which there was an attack, the image could confirm the burning! An academic who had obtained satellite photos for another purpose offered them to us for use in locating and checking conditions in Burundi regroupment camps.

But even in cases when the witnesses are accessible and apparently safe, they sometimes do not talk. Part of the reason they don't speak is because they have no permission to do so from the village chief. It pays to sit down with a chief. If he wants a bit of whiskey you might want to give him a quart of whiskey, and then you will get his permission. After you get permission from the chief, you can literally do anything you want. But you may still be unable to investigate some abuses. The chief's permission does not necessarily cover all contingencies. For example, you may not make headway in investigating sexual abuses as part of the circumstances of a conflict. The victims will not speak to you despite the chief's permission. You still have to go to other leaders, women's leaders, who are the ones who have to investigate this female.

Pressuring External Power-Brokers and Mobilizing Public Opinion

The United States, the EU, and any other donor institutions should show that they will not take any African government seriously unless they demonstrate that they have a fine grasp over the human rights situation on the ground and that they have dealt with the problem that is reflected in the information provided by rights organizations such as HRW. Our information plays a crucial role. When we provide this information to key decision-makers outside Africa it is taken seriously by those concerned. It plays a special role in their discussions of conditionality arrangements for financial negotiations.

But that information provided to the financial decision-makers will not be considered credible or useful unless it is given in timely fashion, is accurate, and is particular and clear. We spend a great amount of time within my organization ensuring that the information we collect and communicate fits these criteria. Beyond the provision of the best information, we devote the most part of our time in mobilizing public opinion and in organizing a powerful constituency through which we are trying to create support. This public opinion and constituency-building work is aimed at being able to reach and influence key decision-makers through our provision of information.

The most critical condition for the effective organization of public opinion, especially through the press, is to be able to go beyond what the press normally prints. There is already a great deal of available information in the media of human rights conditions in Africa and in many other countries. But that information and stories are not important ways of moving people to action unless the information is presented in such a way that the victims are perceived as human beings. Another role *vis-à-vis* the media, therefore, is to generate data in the form of detailed stories which add life and depth, and which present victims as human beings. When this is done we are then often able to move people to action.

Until recently monitoring has involved gathering and presenting data about a current situation primarily with the intent to influence policy. With the Rwandan genocide and other egregious abusive situations such as Sierra Leone and the Democratic Republic of Congo, HRW felt the need to move in a slightly different direction—that is, to thoroughly document a past crime. This has become an important part of our ways of focusing on strategies to bring about change. We allocated significant resources, especially in Rwanda, that included supporting two and sometimes three researchers over a period of five years to produce the definitive account of the 1994 genocide. This is turn has led to another development—the role of researchers in judicial proceedings. We have provided expert testimony as well as considerable documentation to the international tribunal for Rwanda as well as to courts in Canada, Belgium, and Switzerland.

Human rights must be lived, not simply taught. Informing people about the various conventions and local laws is useful but does not show them how to put these regulations to work for their own defense. That is shown only through systematic monitoring and consistent public use of monitoring data to demand improvement. At HRW, we also seek to use our offices and capacities to empower local NGOs and activists in Africa. To the extent that human rights are shown to be actually lived as opposed to only being taught, we have witnessed the experience of a population that is increasingly seeking enforcement of their rights within the African continent itself. We seek to reinforce this development through capacity building projects and joint monitoring, investigation and reporting projects with local groups and individuals.

Armaments Trade, Refugees and Forced Migration

As arms flows to Africa escalate and conflicts increasingly target civilians as part of a military strategy, refugee and internally displaced populations are growing on the African continent. These refugee and internally displaced populations who seek refuge by taking flight are often subjected to continuing abuses after being displaced. HRW is compelled to increasingly focus on issues of arms acquisition by abusive forces and the plight of these forcibly displaced persons.

Arms research is even much more difficult than is the regular reporting of human rights abuses. It is sensitive work and the risks involved are far greater than those involved in ordinary human rights investigations. There is also an increasing tendency for libel actions in courts if suppliers are named and shamed. The result often is that it takes much longer to undertake arms related investigations, thus costing enormous resources.

With respect to forced migration, we have focused a considerable amount of our time on the issue of refugees. We have documented violence, forced deportations, forced round-ups, harassment of urban refugees, rape and domestic violence against refugee women, and refugee children's rights abuses in Tanzania, Ethiopia, the Democratic Republic of Congo, Kenya, Guinea, and South Africa. We have also documented the gaps in international protection for internally displaced persons and the lack of an effective international protection regime for those forcibly displaced in their own countries, including in Kenya, Burundi, Rwanda, and the Democratic Republic of Congo.

HRW has also continued to call attention to the disparity in the international response to refugees as opposed to internally displaced populations that are often forgotten. Additionally, we have pointed out the discrepancy in the international assistance provided to refugees in Europe as compared to those in Africa. A refugee in Macedonia and Albania in 1999 received ten times the daily allowance than did a refugee in Africa.

Although investigative and documentation work on the refugees and the internally displaced persons (IDP) is very similar to most other human rights investigations, there are some distinct differences in the methodology used. Firstly, refugees and internally displaced persons are often located in extremely remote and underdeveloped areas, often close to insecure borders. Travelling to these populations to obtain first-hand testimonies frequently requires several days. Since displaced populations are often confined in camps, permission is required by the government or controlling authority to obtain access to the displaced. Within the campsites, the issue of confidentiality is key. Often we have to rely on other refugees to serve as interpreters. If not done carefully, this may hinder the safety and privacy of those interviewed. Factors such as the political situation, or the ethnicity or gender of the interpreter as well as other factors can make a significant difference in whether people feel comfortable talking about their experiences.

Refugee camps are often run by the UN High Commissioner for Refugees. In some cases, our ability to access refugee populations is dependent on the cooperation of UNHCR to provide logistical and other assistance. For internally displaced persons, the problem of access is frequently exacerbated by the fact that there is often no single international agency responsible for assisting them that can help to facilitate access.

Advocacy work on refugee and IDP rights issues is often focused on the international actors. In many places, host governments are either unable or unwilling to provide assistance to refugees. In other places, it is the government that is actually responsible for the displacement. In cases such as these, a vigorous advocacy role by UN agencies and other humanitarian actors can play a key role. HRW has increasingly begun to scrutinize the role of UN agencies in refugee/IDP protection. We have issued reports that point out not only the violations occurring, but also the negligence or limitations of the UN in providing protection and assistance.

© Peter Takirambudde and Ashgate Publishing Company, 2001. Peter Takirambudde is Director of the Africa Program for Human Rights Watch.

3 Targeting Journalists to Prevent the Dissemination of Knowledge of Human Rights Violations

ANN COOPER

The Committee to Protect Journalists has been in existence since 1981. Our basic work is to take reports of abuses of journalists from all over the world, and do research to document what has happened. When we determine that an attack has happened because of a journalist's work, that becomes a case for us, and we take action. Peter Takirambudde described the need to get information about human rights issues into the media and journalists certainly are crucial in terms of reporting on human rights issues. But journalists are themselves often embroiled in their own human rights issues involving the suppression of freedom of the press. That is where my organization, The Committee to Protect Journalists, comes in. We are based in New York and we do our work around the world. We document all kinds of abuses and attacks on the press. The CPJ works on everything from journalists who are killed because of their work to those in prison because of their work.

We also monitor more broadly the press freedom situation in about 120 countries around the world. All of that is put into our annual book, *Attacks on the Press*. CPJ is based in New York, but we are a lot better known in places like Peru, Turkey, Algeria, and Belarus than we are in much of the United States. The reason that we are better known in these other areas is because the people on the ground—the local journalists—are the most vulnerable. They are almost always more vulnerable than foreign correspondents dropping in to cover a crisis or controversy. So that is where we concentrate our resources—outside the United States, although we occasionally do take a case in the U.S.

This is something that our board of directors has periodically debated when considering how we can best use our resources. It is a very conscious

21

decision that, while there are certainly abuses and cases in the United States involving journalists, there are also other organizations here that work on freedom of expression issues. But there is nobody who is doing this outside the United States and every time this has come up the board's decision has been that that is where we need to put our resources.

The Importance of Journalists' Reporting of Human Rights Abuses

In the U.S., people joke, "The Committee to Protect Journalists? Shouldn't that be 'The Committee to Protect People *from* Journalists?'" Even some of our journalist-colleagues say, "So what is it you actually do—pass out flak jackets to people?"

Obviously we don't. We strive to protect journalists with journalism. We believe attacks on the press must be exposed as widely as possible, because until you get the word out about press freedom violations, nothing is going to happen. You are never going to see somebody brought to justice without evidence and exposure. You are never going to see a country pressured to change its behavior. Obviously it is not always effective. Sometimes it is only effective in the very long term, but sometimes it is effective immediately.

There is really very little in the way of official protection for journalists. They are covered under the Geneva Conventions, which consider journalists to be civilians in war situations. In many of the countries where we work there are extremely repressive laws used against the press all the time. In Cuba, we have four journalists currently in jail. In one of our cases last year, Jesus Joel Diaz Hernandez, was convicted of the crime of *dangerousness*. In Yugoslavia, Slobodan Milosevic had an information law that among other things, outlaws creating "fear, panic and defeatism." You don't get thrown in jail for violating that law, but you are subject to very heavy fines and that is exactly what Milosevic did for about a year and half, trying to drive the independent or opposition media out of business by essentially fining them into bankruptcy. That may be less dramatic than using assassination or jail to silence the media, but if you succeed in shutting them down financially, that can be just as effective.

When we hear about an attack on the press we document what happened and determine whether the action was taken in reprisal for the journalist's work. We document about 500-600 such cases every year— journalists killed for their work, or thrown in jail, or physically assaulted, or censored.

Suppression and Harassment of Journalists

There are all kinds of bureaucratic control devices that are used against the media. Often the steps are not obvious and it takes investigation to identify the ties and connections between journalism and reprisal. Governments may use tax laws to harass journalists. In many places the state controls newsprint or controls access to printing presses and transportation and distribution. Maybe the action taken against a paper was because of something a journalist wrote that the government didn't like. It is harder to prove those kinds of cases, but we do investigate and try to make those connections. I can't document this statistically but, as suggested with Milosevic we do feel that there are some leaders who have become more sophisticated in the way that they go about controlling the media and are not using violence but instead using fines and laws to intimidate and punish journalists and publishers.

These leaders are using a variety of tactics to suppress the media. This includes laws used to impose heavy fines for violations by the media. Or it can be done through the use of tax laws, state-controlled advertising, state-controlled newsprint, or state-controlled printing presses. These are techniques that can be used against the media generally or to punish or intimidate a particular journalist who writes something against the powers that be or some armed forces leader or whomever it might be who does not like or does not want to see the criticism in print.

Killing and Imprisoning Journalists

But inevitably we pay the most attention to the documentation of those journalists who are killed or put in prison for no reason. In 1999 the most dangerous country in the world for journalists was Sierra Leone. Out of the 34 cases of journalists who died because of their work, 10 were in Sierra Leone. And eight of those were killed in a 10-day period when rebels entered the capital of Freetown, literally hunting down journalists who had written about atrocities committed by the rebels. Some were hunted down and assassinated in their homes.

Why pay special attention to the journalists when there are many other human rights violations occurring? It is because journalists are the *witnesses*. They are the ones who are there on the scene and in the midst of the violence and who are recording and exposing the violators and violations. This is particularly true for the local journalists. They are there when it happens, or they get there right after it happens before international monitors come in. They are particular targets because they are witnesses with access to media sources and they can tell the world about the crimes that are being committed. There is also a broader issue. When there is no free press, there is no free expression in that country. There is not a free public forum which is a critical part of countries being able to solve their problems, or being able to deal with country-to-country disputes. Of course it is not a guarantee that there will be peace and harmony and great democracy even when a free press exists. But without the fundamentals of free press and freedom of expression it is almost certain you will not get democracy.

The ten journalists who died in Sierra Leone in 1999 represented a very extreme case, but the killing of journalists is not unique. In Sierra Leone there was very little that we could do. The ten journalists were killed very quickly, and it was a very tragic situation. But subsequently we did help several journalists come out from Sierra Leone into exile. Some of them have not gone back to their country. But there is nothing that we can do about the journalists who were killed there.

Examples of the CPJ's Pressure for Press Freedoms

But I was struck by Richard Goldstone's observation that we need to take a step back and take a longer view of things. The truth is that not that many years before the *Pinochet* case came up who would have thought that his arrest would happen? Who would thought he could be arrested in another country? I try to remind my staff and myself that you can never stop because no matter how hopeless situations appear, things always change. I have been the director at CPJ for two years. When I started, one of our very worst situations was in Nigeria, where 17 journalists were in prison. They were being held in a jail with terrible conditions and had been held for years with no signs that they were going to get out. We had already done a lot of publicity about their cases and we were quietly helping with each of their families if they needed help. But it certainly was not achieving the goal of getting the journalists out of jail.

Things could have gone on that way indefinitely, but then something happened. Sani Abacha died, and he was the dictator who was responsible for imprisoning so many journalists in Nigeria. Even then they were not immediately let out of prison. But as I saw when I covered the Soviet Union for National Public Radio and Gorbachev came to power, he was looking for a high profile public way to demonstrate his sincerity as a compassionate and democratic leader. Mikhail Gorbachev wanted a way to say, "Hey I'm different, I want you to think of me as a good guy." The first thing Gorbachev did was to start releasing some of the prisoners who had been put away by other people.

When the new generals came to power in Nigeria they were also people of a different mindset from Sani Abacha. They talked about elections and democracy. And to try to overcome the deep skepticism they could reasonably anticipate, they started releasing political prisoners. Among the first to be released were the journalists. I believe that an important reason they released the journalists was the publicity that we gave to the imprisoned journalists, and that other groups also gave to the journalists and to other political prisoners in Nigeria. This publicity sent out the message to the new leaders that, if you want to prove that you are something different from the prior regime, then let those people out of jail. They did.

Sometimes all we really do is give people moral support. That can be important because the imprisoned journalists tell us that it is important to know that people are out there and that somebody still cares. They say that "I just needed to know that other journalists felt this way and this helps me to know that I was right." To have an entire state government condemning you and saying that what you wrote was against the law and harmed the country's interests can be a heavy burden. It is important to know there are other people who believe in that principle of freedom of expression and who support you. Even in places like Cuba and China, there are people continuing to try to practice independent journalism. They are increasingly figuring out ways for using the Internet to obtain information. So it is important to continue sending the message of press freedom and the importance of freedom of expression to those people.

Elsewhere we exploit whatever leverage we can. We have seen the people of Turkey's desire to end that country's suppression of press freedom. Human rights groups in Turkey are campaigning and saying to the European Union that Turkey lacks fair standards and real press freedom and limits freedom of expression. They are saying to the Turkish government that if you want to be part of the European Union, you need to behave as do the other people in the EU. There is some sensitivity there and we have succeeded in having two journalists released who are part of at least 11 journalists in prison in Turkey.

But what is needed is much broader legal reform, and we expect to keep working at it until the results are achieved. We use a variety of tools. This includes our advocacy reports and sending protests to governments. Sometimes you look at the protest and know this president at whom it is aimed will never see it or will throw it in the wastebasket, and you ask, "what's the point?" But often the point is that we give local journalists an excuse to write about a case that they otherwise might be too intimidated to write about. The local journalists may also be our sources for a lot of our reporting. They may go out and document that "this newspaper was firebombed two days after it published such and such an article on government corruption" or some other provocative topic. But because of the intimidation it may be difficult for them to publish that exposé on their own.

I want to end with one very recent example of how an international campaign can work to apply pressure. That example involves Russia's imprisonment of Andrei Babitsky, a Radio Liberty reporter who was one of the few people doing some real investigative work in Chechnya. Russia has made it almost impossible to know the truth of what is happening in Chechnya. To be allowed down there you have to be registered with the Russian military. Once you have registered with them, they take you around and show you what they want you to see. They tell you "don't write about what you see over there." If you don't do what they tell you, you are in trouble.

When the Russian government detained Babitsky, he might well have disappeared—except that CPJ and other press freedom organizations sent out protests, turning his disappearance into something of an international incident. Eventually the Russian Government did bring him back to Moscow, although he cannot leave Moscow, and he still has charges against him. As far as we know the government is still considering charges against him for allegedly collaborating with Chechen rebels. I don't know whether those charges will actually be prosecuted but he is still sitting there waiting to see whether this case will go forward. We will be watching closely. The success in finally getting the Russian Government to at least bring him out of captivity and back to Moscow is a lesson to all of us.

Of course the most dramatic statistic is the number of journalists who are killed every year. But we document about 500 cases of attacks on journalists every year. Of that number about 34 journalists were killed last year because of their work. We do, however, have a number of other cases that we call our "unconfirmed cases" where we strongly suspect that the journalists were killed because of their journalistic activity. We are still working on those cases until we can feel comfortable saying that the person was killed for journalism. Not only were these 34 journalists writing about human rights issues, journalists have been writing about drug trafficking in Colombia for years. Colombia is one of the most dangerous countries in the world. A number of journalists are choosing to go into exile instead of living in a state of constant threat.

Government corruption is a topic that lands journalists in trouble in many countries. Reporting human rights violations is clearly one of the most dangerous topics for journalists. The two countries in which the danger became abundantly clear were Sierra Leone where eight journalists were killed in a period of only ten days when forces came in to Freetown in

January 1999. The journalists were deliberately targeted and they were reporting on rebel-committed violations against civilians. The other country was East Timor where two journalists were killed. But there were many more journalists who were beaten and intimidated both before and after the independence. As Noam Chomsky points out in discussing citizen responsibility regarding human rights, the violence of these people began long before the independence effort in East Timor. In April 1999 the militia attacked the local newspaper, gutted it and burned it to the ground. They put the newspaper out of business for a time. Many journalists coming into East Timor during the early part of 1999, and covering events that eventually led up to the independence vote, were frequently attacked. By the time of the independence there were many more journalists who were covering the events, and they were constantly attacked. Things got so violent that as the people were fleeing to escape the violence and killing, journalists were fleeing as well. By September 3rd, 1999 when the independence vote results were announced there were almost no members of the media left in East Timor. Most of the local journalists fled along with their countrymen and the very few foreign journalists who were left retreated to the U.S. compound.

Why were these journalists targeted with so much violence? It is because they were the people who reported about the effort to move a whole population out of the country. We are convinced that there was a deliberate strategy to target journalists implemented by the militia backed by the Indonesian military, just as journalists were very deliberate targets in so many other places over the last ten to fifteen years. When the Australian peacekeeping force entered the country there were two journalists killed in the very early days. One was a Dutch reporter and one was a local reporter. The UN has said that it appears that soldiers from an Indonesian Army battalion killed the Dutch journalist and it is also believed that they are also the same soldiers who killed the local journalist, and also harassed and attacked other journalists. In this case with this specific Indonesian battalion, they were wearing uniforms and there is some reasonable degree of certainty about whom the killers actually were. This does not mean that they will be brought to justice.

As we found in so many of our cases, it is extremely rare that anyone is brought to justice in these countries for killing a journalist. Sierra Leone in 1999 was obviously the deadliest country for journalists. Several journalists, with some assistance from the Committee to Protect Journalists and other various groups, left Sierra Leone to go into exile after the worst of the killings. One of them was a journalist who worked for the state broadcasting system and he is seeking asylum in the United States. He was assigned to do programs on abuses and he went out and pulled together his documentaries, and they were broadcast on TV. Then they were used as evidence in treason trials that ended in the executions of 24 rebel officers. In October of 1998, the journalist began to receive death threats and those threats began to intensify in July 1999 after peace agreements were signed and more rebels were coming into Freetown, Sierra Leone. Those threats were so severe that we believed that the only safe thing to do was for him to leave the country.

Conclusion

There is no question that the deliberate targeting of journalists has increased, and some of that is due to journalists' role in reporting on human rights violations. There are, as we have seen in the post Cold War world, more civil conflicts. At the same time, journalists have much better access to information than they have ever had before. In the time that I worked in the Soviet Union, when something happened there was state control of information that was very effective. It was impossible for a journalist in Moscow to write about the problems. Nowadays we complain to the Russian government about the steps that they take to control access to information and journalistic content. But it is nothing compared to what they did in the days of the Soviet Union. And there are still some journalists who are able to get around the present-day Russian controls on information and report independently on what is happening in places like Chechnya. But it is a very dangerous situation. They have more opportunities to report.

Some people have training courses for journalists. This is now done routinely for BBC correspondents. Unfortunately the journalists are at risk because they are the ones who are there all the time on the front lines. While there are some efforts to develop training courses for the local journalists in trouble spots there are not nearly enough. Jason Clay comments about what human rights activists and journalists have to learn to do is to protect themselves. His points are absolutely right. Journalists must be smarter about the dangers they face because the risks really are greater. They have to use common sense. When people call me and ask me about going into a particular area I always remind them that there is no point in going in to a place so dangerous that it is almost guaranteed you will be kidnapped or where it is very likely you will be shot. Because if you are kidnapped or shot you are not going to be able to tell the story or write about it.

4 Investigating Human Rights Violations: Some Lessons from the Field

JASON W. CLAY

During the 1980s, I spent much of my time investigating and analyzing human rights violations against indigenous peoples and ethnic minorities. This work was undertaken at an organization called Cultural Survival where I was director of research and was building the organization's research capacity and its ability to analyze and respond to urgent situations such as genocide, famine, and refugee crises. In order to present these analyses to a wider audience, I founded and edited the organization's magazine, *Cultural Survival Quarterly*.

At Cultural Survival, I organized and undertook a number of research projects in response to crisis situations, both in refugee and displaced people camps in Central America, the Horn of Africa and Southeast Asia. While our teams' findings were often controversial, they were never disproved and over time the approach became the standard by which such data were judged. Consequently, I was increasingly asked to advise other NGOs, individual researchers, and bilateral and multilateral agencies on the best techniques and strategies for the collection of reliable data in crisis situations.

The protection of human rights activists and journalists requires first and foremost that they take wise steps to help themselves. The better they get at this and the more they do it, they are going to be able to get in and out of difficult situations much more easily. Learning from others, and being parts of teams when you are first starting out in this field of work is very important. Human rights organizations also need materials that they can give to the people that work for them. It is very clear who the human rights activists are. They tend to be young people. They don't tend to be people in their forties or fifties with families because they can't afford to do that kind of work anymore and raise a family. Or, they have become so good at what they do that they assume other responsibilities in their organizations. Consequently, it is a constant battle to keep people with skills that are needed who can share their accumulated knowledge and act as guides and mentors for newer activists. In addition, it is important to team them up with local people so that they will always have a learning exchange back and forth with each other.

Most of my work involved documenting human rights abuses in Third World countries. With that in mind, there were, however, also activities done in the U.S. For example, we interviewed refugees who had been relocated to the U.S. in order to obtain ideas about what was going on in their countries and to identify good contacts back in those countries. We also interviewed aid and development workers who could often tell about things going on in countries or even particular locations or refugee camps. Like many people being debriefed about their experiences it turned out once we interviewed them they knew things that they didn't even know they knew. Some assistance agencies asked us to interview their people after they returned from assignments to find out what they weren't learning on the ground that they should know in order to be more effective. Finally, much of what I did—at least once a week for about ten years—was write affidavits in U.S. immigration cases for people trying to seek political asylum in the U.S. based on having a reasonable fear of persecution as a member of a threatened group.

I have been arrested, expelled from refugee camps, and deported. Over time I have found that there are some basic lessons that can protect those who would investigate human rights violations. Ten lessons are listed below.

Ten Basic Steps to Protect Activists

There are at least ten ways to reduce the risk of attack and persecution and to increase the chances of survival for human rights activists and journalists. It needs to be emphasized that there is no universal solution that allows anyone to give a checklist of things that need to be focused upon. There are many cultural differences and we are looking at so many different situations—past, present and yet to come—that it is very complicated.

There are certainly other steps than those described below that can be taken to increase journalists' and activists' survival probability. But, these ten strategies for survival are important actions to remember when you go into dangerous situations. Of course the reality is that the individuals doing this work are already trying to protect themselves. The bottom line is that if you are picked up on the street by plainclothes policemen the best thing to do is just act natural—although it is much easier to say this than to do it. The problem is that at that point there is no one who is going to help you. So it is extremely important to figure out what you can do to prevent getting picked up by the police and tortured or killed. There are some *do's and don'ts* of your behavior that can at least reduce the risk.

- *Don't travel alone* Never do this kind of work by yourself. There is strength in numbers, at least a pair. Whether you are an activist or a journalist trying to get a story, take someone else along—a photographer, translator or guide journalist. You will at least have somebody.
- *If at all possible, do everything by the book* That means enter the country legally, and say exactly what it is you are doing there. There are times, however, when this "going by the book" approach doesn't work if you have to cross borders into areas of conflict. But many times having a legal basis for doing something versus entering a country under false pretenses can be the difference between survival, or even the success of a mission.
- *It is extremely important to talk to all sides of a conflict* No one has a corner on the truth of what has transpired or what might set it right. Try to remain as objective as possible in your pursuit of reality. Don't just go into a situation intending to prove a point or to prove something you have already decided before you even hit the ground.
- *Make sure that your movements in a conflict zone are known to people you trust* Whether they are friends, religious leaders, sympathetic officials, embassy staff or others, someone should know where you are and when you can be expected to be at specific locations.
- *One thing that has changed considerably about human rights work in the past 20 years is the proliferation and use of electronics* In the mid-1980s, we had human rights monitors on the Mexican border near Guatemala to talk to Mayan Indian refugees about what was happening inside Guatemala. The monitors were able to write up to five or six page stories and send them out as electronic bursts over local telephone lines. One of those stories was the basis for an article in the *New York Times*. That kind of publicity creates transparency and is a way to protect both monitors and refugees and to bring pressure against the perpetrators. Once a story has been covered, it's part of a public record. Human rights violators try to keep information about what they are doing out of the public eye. This is, in fact, the most dangerous time for people trying to expose them. The use of cell phones with the ability to send e-mail and faxes is now very important in this work.

But because many human rights organizations and researchers are underfunded, advanced electronics are almost totally unused.

There are other ways that more advanced technologies can be used to document human rights abuses. For example, in the early and mid-1980s, during the Ethiopian famine, there was a large resettlement program and an even larger *villagization* program which involved the movement of some 10 million people and the burning of many houses. With current technology, one can document those kinds of human rights violations. Satellite surveillance systems allow one to prove that homes have been built in specific locations. When you can use the technology to read license plates or count the number of ears on a stalk of corn, you can certainly tell where a house has been burned. This is not rocket science.

- *There is almost always an issue of language* One role of monitoring human rights violations is to give the victim a voice. Their voice is not the only important one, but inevitably it is the one least heard.

- *Isolated indigenous peoples and minorities often do not speak the "national" language. In fact, the national language was often the language of the oppressors. For such groups it is important to interview them in their own language* Since no one speaks all these different languages, monitors must rely on translators. This is a very important but sensitive issue. It should be approached with caution. The most important thing is to identify and hire the translator yourself. Do not leave this up to anyone else. Then, tape record all the interviews so that they can be independently translated to make sure that you are not being misled. The interviews should be conducted in a way to protect the anonymity of those being interviewed.

- *During a crisis, get on the ground as quickly as possible* This includes trying to get a medical team on the ground within 24 hours to deal with the victims and document the abuses. Action must be taken as quickly as possible. After security and control systems are established it is much harder to gather reliable information about what has happened. Outsiders have far less unsupervised access. The task of interviewing people also becomes more difficult over time because the victims begin to talk among themselves and create a more homogenized version of what occurred. To obtain raw data, which is really what you are looking for, it is very important to try to obtain unfiltered responses. This gives you the most reliable insights into the nuances of what happened.

- *Have a convincing explanation for what you are doing in a crisis area* For example, I was on the border of Ethiopia and Sudan. I was there to interview refugees in order to find out why they left in order to predict how many more would flee and to determine how long they would stay. And I did that. But what I really wanted to do was to document systematically what had caused the people to flee in the first place. However, my cover role gave me access that allowed me to go into the camps and ask all kinds of questions. In the late 1980s, we tried to organize a conference on research methods that different organizations had learned during crises. People who collect information on topics from different fields can and should learn from each other about how to do their work better. Amnesty International, for example, has people go into prisons. They can tell by looking at fingernails, clothes, and various other things about the conditions of a person they are interviewing. Likewise the Center for Disease Control in Atlanta has doctors who go into crisis situations to gather reliable information in order to predict population flows and medical needs of masses of people moving across borders. They have gotten very good at it. We need to be able to learn from that. How do they do it? What can we learn from each other? We need to take these lessons and incorporate them into our own activities. It simply works better than only talking to those who want to talk to you. In my own work, I have found that random samples are key to the collection of reliable information in large populations of displaced people.

- *Human rights activists and journalists need to know much more about the lives of the people they're trying to help before they hit the ground* One of the curiosities that I have found is that most of the people who are doing a lot of the human rights activist work were urban, middle class or even wealthier individuals. Yet, they ended up interviewing primarily rural poor people. They didn't know the relevant questions to ask. They could not communicate even though they talked to a lot of people. They simply did not understand the importance of someone interrupting the planting season, stealing seeds or taking oxen when it is time to plow—or somebody taking ropes and straps needed for harnesses. In these instances, the human rights activists didn't know what a two week delay in planting meant in an agricultural society. So this information was never recorded, and the extent of such violations in the creation of famine was never documented.

The Difficult Role of Human Rights Activists

A useful focus for our concern about these issues is the role of outsiders as human rights workers. An important issue relates to how human rights organizations and other types of charitable and religious service organizations, of which there are thousands in the field, can effectively work through the various and often conflicting cultural issues to achieve the necessary goals without alienating the intended recipients of the assistance. There is also the question of what happens when the human rights workers from outside all leave. This is particularly important in terms of what appears to be a process of reconciliation where there has been a constitutional legal arrangement reached on paper and somebody has the bright idea that the people will therefore eventually live together in harmony because all the paper solutions are in place. The reality is unfortunately that the people who live there will not be ready to live in an harmonious relationship for three, four, five, or even six generations. It takes peacetime and a strong economy to forget what has gone before. Unfortunately, continuous or even intermittent conflict tends to reinforce the memories of the earlier atrocities.

From my point of view the thing to remember is that it is never as hard for us to react to crises as it is for the people we are trying to help in their own countries and those who have been the victims of violence and human rights violations. That point is my overriding perspective. That is what the reality of the situation on the ground is for the victims and for us who feel in good faith and with the best intentions that we are trying to help them. With activists and journalists it is always hardest for those who are national actors acting and reporting in their country. They remain after everyone else goes away. There is much more protection for international people coming into a human rights crisis from outside. I worked with a human rights group in Brazil where ten of the eleven founding members were tortured in the 1970s by the military government. This is the reality on the ground. It has become much better because of the power and speed of communications. Improved communications have changed the ability and speed with which information can be transmitted around the world. This greatly increases the pressure that can be brought to bear and the ability to intervene earlier in conflicts.

Work needs to be undertaken with local NGOs and people who live in a country. For example, religious leaders and workers who have lived in the country for twenty or more years will often be integrated more into the society and can make significant contributions. Or, and this is talking just about Westerners such as those who have left organizations such as the Peace Corps and remained in the country, people like this can also be helpful. But the local NGOs can play particularly important roles during transitions that facilitate "cooling off."

In using metaphors of good and evil in human rights situations there is a flip side to the image of the monstrous human rights violator we are supplanting. That flip side imagery involves our tendency to view ourselves as cultural heroes and playing our role as the powerful outsiders coming in to say, "Here we come to save the day!" We have achieved an incredible degree of mobility that we didn't have even fifty years ago and can now move human and material resources from one corner of the world to another with relative ease and great speed. This means that we can intervene (some would say interfere) almost anywhere. But there is a danger to our walking into another culture about which we have little knowledge and suggesting that, "I'm here to help—I'll leave computers; I'll do whatever it is that I can do." There is a serious risk of damage, much less simply that of harmless disconnection from the culture into which we are intruding. The question is also one of physical resources as well as one of human resources. The strategic question is what are the best ways for us to structure responses to crises and to help cultures to rebuild that have been devastated by inhuman brutality?

Activists who go into these situations are usually young and idealistic. They want to change the world and address wrongs, but it is hard to control their emotions. Many times, the problem is that they do not have enough training or experience. They just want to change it all and "make it all better." The result can be that many of the well-intentioned activists do more harm than good. This is not just a problem for younger people. Think about this in a context when a worker from one culture interviews a person from another culture based on a questionnaire seeking to identify post-traumatic stress syndrome. It is a problem when people go into this kind of troubled and tragic situation without the right preparation and cultural understanding. They may be trained in psychology but they are often not trained in the cultural psychology applicable to the specific people they interview, and they are not trained in how to go in and talk to people. They just have their formalized checklist, and it is based on the simplistic assumption that *in my society*, if you *have these symptoms* then you have *post-traumatic stress syndrome*. This then leads to the conclusion that since you fit my profile of post-traumatic stress syndrome, "we will *treat* you *this* way and we will put you in *this* category." It is a very difficult issue and I wish there were some real answers across the board.

I have worked with several organizations that pride themselves on being non-interventionist. The operating premise should be that when you go into such situations you don't do anything that locals could be doing on their own behalf. I think that is a very good philosophy, although it is not entirely valid because just by working in human rights you have already decided that there are some things that are okay to do and contrarily that some things are not okay. You are already making value judgments. So, by saying that we are going in but we are not making a value judgment, is false. However, with non-intervention as the underlying principle, it is less likely that you will step over the line. At least that is what I have found.

You still have to make that horrible decision of whether to do this or not, and who to work with or not. But at least you have an assumption to begin from that will make it easier to make the "right" decision.

In these situations people often acknowledge there is a problem. It is not as if, because you are going in as a human rights actor, a light goes off and says, "oh you're condemned to fail because this is a *human rights problem.*" The real issue is to identify the conditions that allow a local society, particularly societies that are multinational or multicultural or multi-religious, to fill the moral vacuum that exists after atrocities have taken place. I don't think outsiders have any role in that decision-making process. The tendency of anybody who wants to help in this direction should be to hold back and allow the people who ultimately have to learn how to heal, forgive, and live with each other to make the decisions. As soon as outsiders try to fill that vacuum it is full and nobody else can get in there. Then the outsiders start identifying who comes into the process and that is not only wrong—it will ultimately fail.

We have to set up a protective space and capability that allows violent and humanitarian situations to be dealt with. But we can't do it ourselves. It involves creating the space for local people to come forward because it is those people who are going to have to live there after we outsiders are long gone. And it is those people who need to set up the leadership and to reestablish connections on whatever terms they can negotiate, both initially and over time. It is similar to grafting back onto a tree all the different branches that have to be there for the tree to survive. It may never be a perfect tree but it is *their* tree and *their* business, and no one can do it for them.

There are two guiding principles that I would like to communicate to activists about human rights investigations. Don't ever forget why you are there. First and foremost it is to give a voice to the victims. It is not to say that their voice is the only one that counts, but rather that their voice regarding what happened to them is the sound most often ignored.

The second point is to constantly question your assumptions. Preconceived and preformed ideas get in the way of our really understanding what is going on in any situation. All of us have blinders. The trick is to try to loosen them even a little. One of the groups that I worked with off and on over many years is the Oromo of Ethiopia. They have a saying that goes something like, "You can't wake a person who is pretending to sleep." Many people would choose to interpret the relevance of this saying as applying only to the violators of human rights or those who directly or indirectly support them. However, the shoe fits equally on activists who go into crises knowing exactly what they have to prove before they even arrive on the ground.

5 The Use of Information and Communication Technology, especially the Internet, for the Promotion and Protection of Human Rights, including Detection, Early Warning and Prevention[1]

EDWARD F. HALPIN

The growth of the Internet and other new information and communication technologies (ICTs)[2] has had a profound impact on society, to the extent that those of us living in the western world regard them as ubiquitous; with the vision of a computer in every household and the arrival of a wired society. This perception appears to be supported by good evidence, with one survey estimating the global number of Internet user in December 1996 as 60 million and in November 2000 as 407 million.[3] Another source suggested that the, "Total number of Internet users worldwide by 1999 was ... between 150 and 180 million..." with estimates that the "... expected numbers would rise to one billion by 2005."[4] Whilst there is little agreement on the exact number of Internet users, and care is required in using or accepting any of the estimates, the trend presented is of rapid growth, though the global nature of this growth is uneven. Of the 407 million users identified in the first survey 167 million were in North America, 113 million in Europe, 105 million in Asia/Pacific, 16 million in Latin America and only 3 million in the whole of Africa.[5] This picture, of variable growth in Internet access or usage, might be worthy of reflection from a human rights perspective, giving rise to questions about the utility of the Internet as a global tool for human rights activism and perhaps to questions about global economic exclusion.

The exponential growth in ICTs has also provided a plethora of new descriptive words and phrases; most of which invest great worth in them, creating an image of other-worldliness or of some forthcoming Utopia. Terms such as the "information superhighway," "cyberspace," and even "Digital Democracy"[6] are readily used and the presumed benefits of ICTs are accepted almost without question. Are such descriptions a reality or merely image and hype? The technologies provide us with a means for instant or almost instant communication; they provide the images of war and human rights atrocities to more homes, and do so faster then ever before. But is this simply becoming a new form of entertainment, a new sort of "fly on the wall" experience, or does it help in the battle for human rights by raising awareness and consciousness?

The human rights world has readily adopted the Internet and other new communication technologies, employing them to prevent and monitor human rights abuses and to promote and protect human rights. It is fundamental to recognize that the nature of human rights abuses requires rapid responses, clearly "... oppressive regimes do not wait for the international community to register a complaint, or for human rights workers to launch a campaign. The faster human rights organizations can respond, the more likely it will be that illegal detention and other abuses can be reduced or stopped."[7] As a means of communication the Internet provides a tool for both rapid and effective responses to human rights abuses around the world, supporting the work of those who fight for justice and fairness.

Why is Quick, Accurate Information Important to Human Rights Work?

Metzl describes the importance of information to the work of human rights, commenting that "... accurate and timely information is an indispensable tool and an essential precondition for effective responsive action and the promotion of human rights, whether by organizations, individuals, governments or international institutions."[8] Information used in responding to human rights violations must be accurate, timely and verified, and then must be used with care. The major human rights NGOs apply rigorous thresholds in checking the reliability of information, even if on occasions this might cause a little delay. The failure to apply such care to information gathering and usage creates a credibility problem, which can have both short and long term consequences. Arguably if credibility is lost human rights abusers can respond to any allegations made against them by referring to previous errors or inaccuracies, in the short term leaving the individual victim at risk and in the long term leaving the whole organization vulnerable and weak. The protection of individuals at risk, subject to arrest, torture and often under the threat of summary execution, is reliant upon the ability of organizations and individuals to campaign on their behalf, with credibility, acting quickly and using accurate information.

The Internet provides human rights NGOs and activists with the ability to promote and protect human rights, with web sites as campaigning tools and email a means of instant communication. It also aids detection by providing an immediate means of gathering information as situations develop, a mechanism for ensuring early warning, and tools to enable decision-making. Through these mechanisms preventative action can be initiated using rapid response networks, campaigning and by the provision of reports to governments and the mass media.

Metzl describes the Internet as a quicker and cheaper way for human rights groups to exchange messages, a significant factor being the ability to send a message to multiple recipients by one action, rather than sending them one at a time.[9] He also contends that information can be obtained more quickly. The Internet allows interactive communication between various parts of the human rights movement, with local groups being able to directly contact international groups without the need for intermediaries, sometimes leading to the development of new communities of interest or changes in organizational structure. He further suggests that the relationship between local groups and national/international groups is changing, with local groups becoming less reliant upon national groups for information. Metzl concludes that the Internet is "... having enormous consequences for the human rights movement as an aid to its efforts to collect, interpret, and disseminate information and to push for appropriate action in response to violations ..." and that "... electronic communication can play an essential role in developing issue networks which pressure governments and others to act."

As a preventative tool the use of modeling and identifying trends can be undertaken, an issue that the American Association for the Advancement of Science, Human Rights Program, has worked.[10] The utility of databases should allow the mapping of human rights violations and the identification of trends and types of abuse. If done properly this would allow political intervention. However, this would rely upon the standardization of information in the human rights world. Ball[11] refers to the problems and the misunderstandings that can occur, noting the need for careful database design, which should reflect an understanding of the information being collated and ensure that its presentation on the database does not distort the analysis and comparison that can be undertaken. Ball also outlines the difference between "representative standards and exchange standards", providing a detailed explanation of the problems faced in the management of information and the problems associated with sharing it between organizations. The need for standardized controlled vocabularies, which ensure that when organizations share information they are all describing the same things, remains a difficult problem to resolve.

Human Rights Internet Users?

The human rights world consists of a global spread of organizations, ranging from major international organizations to the single-person-single-issue campaigner, with the individual activist often playing more than one role in the system. Deibert (in Alexander and Pal)[12] describes the growth and extent of human rights movement from 1950 onwards, when approximately 38 NGOs were identifiable, to 1994, when some 14,500 existed. The vast majority of these organizations participate in networks and coalitions, with the Internet now providing a significant communication tool.

The use of the Internet by human rights activists, perhaps not surprisingly, tends to mirror the picture of Internet usage found within society generally, with greatest usage found in North America and Europe and more limited access in Africa, Latin America and parts of Asia. The networks of human rights organizations based in North America and Europe work in concert with related organizations in what is often described as the developing world. The human rights world has long relied upon the ability to share information about abuses, using links, relationship and networks as a fundamental tool in the process. The development of the Internet as a mode of communication has been embraced widely by human rights NGO's with support provided in developing Internet access, as well as in fighting human rights violations, across the networks of organizations. A combination of the existing human networks, coupled with the experience of activists, has become an effective means for spreading the use of ICTs into less developed regions and in supporting capacity building.

There are two major groups of human rights players using the Internet; the organizations which work on human rights and are using the Internet as a tool for their professional activities, and individual human rights activists who use the Internet to fight against abuse directly. Because of the dispersed nature of the activity and the myriad organizational models that can be found, it might at first glance appear that the human rights activism is as anarchically organized as the Internet. However, on closer examination, it is possible to discern both formal and informal networks which are used by all of the various actors or players. One consequence of the use of the Internet that has been observed is the change in organizational structure, with new communities of interest being formed. These new communities often focus on their own specific interest or a single issue, without the need to participate in a general human rights NGO in their country or region.

A Survey of Human Rights Activity on the Internet[13]

The nature of use of the Internet for human rights activism was the subject of a survey undertaken in 1997/98, as part of a research project funded by the European Parliament Scientific and Technical Options (STOA) Unit. The questionnaire was distributed by the *Organisation Mondial Contre Torture* (OMCT) by electronic mail and in hard copy (paper), and through the Amnesty International World Wide Web (WWW) site. In total 551 questionnaires were returned and analyzed. In view of the medium used it was not possible to control the sample or to know how many other people viewed the questionnaire but chose not to respond. As a result the survey returns cannot be regarded as a complete or fully representative sample and no attempt is made to draw quantitative conclusions about the extent of Internet usage among human rights activists.

Questionnaires were completed by respondents from over 50 countries around the world, the majority coming from the developed world where, as we have seen, there is a higher recorded level of access to and usage of the Internet. The distribution of respondents by region is shown in Figure 1.

Figure 1: Regional location of respondents

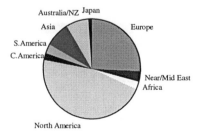

Responses were made in all three formats, although the most popular, which itself is indicative of the power of IT, were World Wide Web versions distributed and returned over the Internet.

Figure 2: Number of returns by format

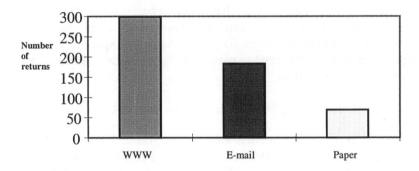

Not surprisingly the largest numbers of questionnaire returns were from individual activists. Perhaps more surprising was the finding that the second largest group were interested visitors to WWW sites. That people who would not describe themselves as active in the human rights world should visit the sites demonstrates the potential of the Web as a campaigning tool, their active participation showing that interest can be translated into action and involvement. The findings also demonstrate the potential of IT to support a broad range of human rights activity.

Figure 3: Respondents' involvement in Human Rights activities

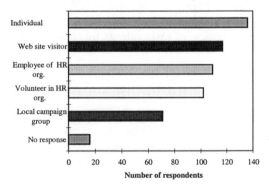

Respondents were asked to indicate what they already used the Internet for, and what they would use it for if they could. The most frequent existing use was "searching for information," which was significantly more important than the next most frequent uses, i.e. "responding to appeals," "publishing information" and "posting appeals." The greatest potential, as opposed to actual, uses were for "posting appeals for action" and "responding to appeals for action" and "publishing information." Clearly responses to this part of the questionnaires would be influenced by existing usage.

Figure 4: Existing and potential uses of the Internet

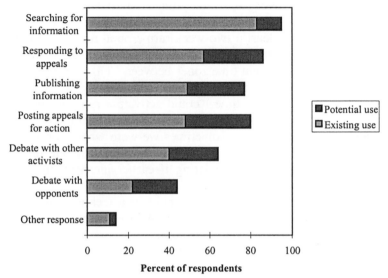

The primary reasons cited for using the Internet in human rights work were because it is quicker, more convenient and that it facilitates collaboration.

Case Studies

Much of the following case study material can be found in the book *Human Rights and the Internet*.[14]

Amnesty International—A User Case Study[15]

In this first case study Marty Langley, a long time Amnesty International member, describes the process from a volunteer point of view:

Since 1983, I have served as a member of the Aegean Country Co-ordination Group of the United States section of Amnesty International. Along with three other Amnesty volunteers, I co-ordinate the work that members of our section do to promote improvement in human rights in Turkey, Greece, and Cyprus. In that capacity, the four of us must communicate on a regular basis not just among ourselves but also with staff members in Amnesty office around the country (primarily in Washington, D.C., and New York) and with Amnesty members throughout the United States. We must also stay in touch with our International Secretariat in London, and we have a responsibility to stay abreast of the political situations in the three countries named above.

During my first years in this position, these tasks were carried out either by the exchange of letters and printed materials through regular mail or by making phone calls. The former required trips to copy machines and the post office and at least a two-week turn-around time (internationally a month or more); the latter meant not just a large phone bill but also having to deal with all the different time zones between California and London. It was, to say the least, expensive and inconvenient; at worst, it was frustrating because, by the time I could activate a response to news of a possible torture case or a disappearance, the information was already a minimum of two weeks old. Sometimes we were writing on behalf of an individual already released; all too often we were pleading on behalf of someone already dead and wondering if earlier intervention might have produced a different outcome.

Fifteen years later, we are functioning in a technologically different world, and it is an exciting improvement. As a volunteer, I do most of my work in the evenings after returning home from my paying job. At that time, I can send email messages and files to our other co-group members (in Ohio, Washington, D.C., and New York), to London, or to other sections in Europe, and often by the next evening I have a reply waiting for me. Our London office has many times sent email requesting that we respond immediately to a detention, and we can usually accomplish that within 48 hours of the time that the individual has been taken into custody. On at least two occasions we have actually responded ahead of the fact when there was information that an individual would be detained.

With the assistance of a former co-group member who culls the Internet for information on Turkey, Greece and Cyprus, I am able to maintain an up-to-date background on the situation in those countries that far surpasses anything I could have managed when I had to rely on U.S. media and libraries alone, and it takes one-tenth of the time. Through the World Wide Web I can monitor the daily editions of the *Turkish Daily News* (a subscription in the U.S. was beyond the means of our co-group's budget) and other web sites that have invaluable information. I am on the e-mail distribution list of various organizations, which supply relevant information on a regular basis, and I relay that to other co-group members simply by clicking the "send" button. We have a plethora of information, actually more than we can fully use, but that is a wondrous gift compared to the days when we had virtually none. A specific example is the situation of the refugees who have recently begun migrating in large numbers from Turkey to Europe. Were I restricted to information available in the U.S. media, I would have been aware of events only about a month after stories began to appear in the European press. Instead, I have been receiving reports from the outset of the story.

One facet of our work is to co-ordinate with staff in Washington, D.C. to supply Amnesty International information to members of the United States Congress and the Administration. Preparing such information is handled through exchange of e-mail and is completed in two or three days where it used to take two or three weeks. Often in the past we simply did not do the work because, by the time we were aware of the need, it was too late to meet a deadline. Now we rarely miss an opportunity to inform officials about our concerns.

I would not hesitate to say that, since our co-group has become an "online" group, we have increased our human rights work output by at least five times what it was prior to the use of the Internet. The ability to exchange information rapidly and to respond immediately to human rights violations is a giant leap forward in this arena, and it is one that I hope will as quickly as possible be available to human rights defenders worldwide. Amnesty International has from its beginnings stated that the best weapon against human rights violations is spreading the news that they are happening and holding the violators responsible in front of the whole world community. The Internet makes it possible to do this virtually instantaneously. For those of us who do that work, it means a morale boost from stepping out of our isolated little rooms. For the victims of those violations, it can mean the difference between life and death.

This case study provides a good example of the traditional mode of operation for an Amnesty International group, prior to the introduction of the Internet, with heavy reliance placed on exchange of information between countries, traditionally undertaken by snail mail and telephone, and later by fax. The problems encountered included a long turn round time for mail (often weeks), costly telephone calls, and the bridging of global time zones. The mode of action was expensive, inconvenient and frustrating, with action sometimes being too late to be worthwhile.

The advent of the Internet has resulted in communication by email, saving time, costs and allowing instantaneous communication across time zones. It has also provided the activists with the capability to respond immediately to detentions, and additionally the ability to obtain and monitor international news and politics via the Web to provide background information vital to the analysis of daily events in the countries being monitored.

The technology provides a very substantial weapon to the armoury of the human rights activist in this case study, providing a network of skilled activists with the tools to successfully carry out their work.

A Case for the Internet: The Former Yugoslavia—The Zamir Network[16]

This case study is the product of the experiences of Djurdja Knezevic, founder and director of the Zenska Infoteka, a Women's Information and Documentation Centre in Zagreb. Djurdja was the initiator of the women's e-mail network, Zamir (for peace), in the countries of the former Yugoslavia. The following paraphrases her thoughts and words on the development of the Zamir network.

The Internet not only assists the human rights community in organizing its work; it also plays a crucial role in ensuring the free flow of information in crisis situations. During a crisis it is critical to quickly disseminate information around the world. For example, the Internet was a vital part of human rights work in the Former Yugoslavia. In 1991, when the war started in the Former Yugoslavia, communication became extremely limited, propaganda from the machinery of the state was divisive and information was difficult to share both internally and externally. One response was the creation of new communications structures by the people, with many organizations and individuals becoming members of a network called ZaMir. Subsequently this became ZaMir Transnational Net (ZTN).

Through the network, non-governmental organizations—humanitarian, peace, human rights and women's groups, among others, communicated filling the void left by the war. Through an exchange of information, they were able to mobilize resources for humanitarian aid. At the forefront of this development were women's groups, and many women acting individually. To quote Djurdja directly:

There are a number of reasons for their enthusiastic reaction. First, feminist and other women's groups in the former Yugoslavia, especially those from Zagreb and Belgrade, were already very much connected, co-operating on many issues, and many were closely related personally as friends.

With the outbreak of the war these relationships were jeopardized by the lack of communication on one hand, and by the fierce nationalistic propaganda on the other. One has to be aware that it was incredibly difficult to stay sane and objective when nationalistic propaganda had polluted the public sphere and discourse. There were many misunderstandings and mutual suspicions about groups or individuals. Many were wondering if others—those on the other sides of the front lines—were affected by their respective nationalism. As a result of the ensuing hostilities, there was a sudden break in communication between women's groups in Zagreb and Belgrade. Where formerly these groups enjoyed open and friendly discourse, a level of suspicion arose between them that temporarily froze any contact. The need for communication was funda-mental, so ICTs were greeted enthusiastically. Many relationships between groups, and many more on a personal level, were re-established. It was a sort of new beginning, as new forms of co-operation emerged among women in the region.

Secondly, the war called for an urgent reaction: first to try to stop the fighting, although this was unfortunately a rather utopian goal at that time, and, more realistically, to organize and give immediate help. On this latter point in particular, women are usually much faster to react. This might be explained by the general attitude of women regarding politics. Since women are traditionally not, for patriarchal reasons, involved in politics as much as men are, politics in turn does not hold as great an importance for them. Therefore, they have greater political flexibility. Moreover, women in particular suffer far more, and more immediately, from the atrocities of war. Therefore, women were not only the first who organized help for refugees and other displaced persons, but when the huge scandal of mass rape in Bosnia and Herzegovina broke out, women's groups took immediate action to turn international attention to the matter. Although the issue should be analyzed more thoroughly, it is likely that computer-mediated communication (CMC) played a fundamental role in making it a high-priority political cause. Thousands of messages from women activists and eye-witnesses—protests, calls for actions and the like—were sent via e-mail all over the world, to surprisingly great effect. In later wars where similar atrocities occurred, women, and the public in general, spoke out against the issue and were ready to face it openly. Additionally, international law has now officially recognized rape in war as a war crime; the Internet provides a tool to ensure that this crime is immediately visible to the international community.

This testimony to the importance of communication provides an important perspective, not only did the Zamir Women's Network provide a means to unite and to overcome the divisions of war, but it also provided a means by which a light could be shone on the atrocities of war. In this case adding strength to the campaign to ensure that rape was recognized as a war crime. A significant factor in this case study is the role of the technology in acting as a bridge between networks disrupted by war. Whatever the propaganda the reality of human contact, even though mediated through the technology, provided a means for human trust to develop and activists to campaign together.

B92—A Free Voice in War[17]

The following case study was presented by Graham Lane, the then Director of Information Technology at the International Secretariat based in London. It presents a brief sketch of another use of technology used to campaign against human rights abuses, often in the face of strong government intervention.

"Radio B92 (formerly www.b92.net and now at www.freeB92.net) is a broadcast and publishing organization based in Belgrade. Founded in 1989, it undertook a wide range of activities including: radio broadcast; the production of radio and television programmes; the publishing of books, magazines, and CDs; and the operation of a cinema and cultural centre for alternative arts with a cyber centre for electronic arts and Internet training. The editorial policy of B92 is based on the Universal Declaration of Human Rights, the protection of all minorities and an anti-war stance. In April 1999, shortly after the start of NATO air strikes, Radio B92 was taken over by the Serbian authorities and the Director was replaced. Staff and journalists refused to work for the government-controlled Radio B92, eventually re-grouping around the Free B92 web site.

As one of the most prominent independent voices in Serbia, Radio B92 made extensive use of Internet technology. In November 1995, B92 started an ISP called OpenNet, as an extension of its established activities, aimed particularly at providing free Internet access for independent media and NGOs. For six months OpenNet was the only service provider in Serbia.

During the winter of 1996 and spring 1997, Radio B92 played an important role in providing independent reporting of demonstrations in Belgrade and other parts of Serbia, protesting against the government annulment of local election results, and carrying announcements and statements made by the demonstrators. As a result, in early December 1996 the Serbian authorities banned transmissions by Radio B92. In response, Radio B92 broadcast its programs across the Internet using RealAudio. These were downloaded and re-broadcast by Radio Free Europe and Voice of America resulting in more people than ever before listening to the station. Additionally, the English news service staff updated the Web site several times a day. Within 51 hours the ban was lifted and Radio B92 was back on the air.

The Association of Independent Electronic Media (ANEM), a network of 33 local radio stations, developed following the success of this 'Internet Revolution' and in recognition of the victory of the opposition parties in the disputed local elections. By early 1999 the association was broadcasting to seventy percent (70%) of the Yugoslavian population, each day carrying four hours of material produced by Radio B92. In the words of the B92 Web site: 'We can say, without fear of contradiction, that together we have successfully broken the state information monopoly, especially in the electronic media...'

It is important to note that the ANEM project is based on true technical innovation and is completely the brainchild of the radio station's young experts. It is a combination of the Internet and satellite relay, something undertaken here for the first time in Europe. In this way we have jumped the hurdle of the state ban on the use of the existing ground repeaters and have opened up a space for even broader application of the satellite relay.

Despite such successes, the activities of B92, OpenNet and, indeed, all independent media in Serbia, remained under intense pressure from the Serbian authorities. In October 1998 a draconian 'Law on Information' was brought into effect, though Internet technology continued to support the free flow of information. At the beginning of 1999 the Serbian authorities backed moves to block access to OpenNet from the Serbian academic computer network, thereby denying students, professors and researchers throughout the country access to information produced by B92. It was, however, easy for B92 to circumvent the blockade by establishing numerous mirror sites which could not, in turn, all be blocked. As a result the blockade was partly lifted.

The Free B92 web site, hosted by XS4ALL in the Netherlands, is now an important focus for information about the status of the independent media in Yugoslavia. The site is edited and published by the B92 team of journalists and associates, working from various parts of the world. Free B92 also works on projects to support journalists and media at risk in other areas of the world.

The overall aim of the Free B92 project is to 'preserve the spirit of professionalism which has been stripped from everyday communication in Yugoslavia through the Belgrade regime's banning and take-over of Radio B92.' The Free B92 site has already hosted three 24-hour NetAid music and art events on the Web using audio and video to link worldwide soundspots with Belgrade, including a dedicated streaming session from Bosnia-Herzegovina to Belgrade."

In this case study the activists regularly faced the intervention of the state and censorship, however through imaginative use of the available technologies and the fortitude to continue they prevailed. Not only did they survive, but they also provided the focus for the battle for democracy.

East Timor—The International Internet Campaign [18]

This case study is based on the work of Sharon Scharfe, Director of the International Secretariat, Parliamentarians for East Timor (PET). PET is an international organization with support and membership in all parts of the world, who were united by concern for the human rights violations perpetrated by Indonesia on the people of East Timor.

As an element in the campaign activists concerned with human rights abuses in East Timor used the Internet as a major means of promoting awareness of the problems faced by the East Timorese however, their political opponents also became adept at using the Internet. The Indonesian government used the Internet to promote its own position on the issue of East Timor, for example, through the Indonesian Army (ABRI) web site Http://www.mil.id, the campaigners for freedom for East Timor responded by finding their own freedom for East Timor.

"The Internet is such an effective human rights tool that it is generally viewed as a threat by the government being challenged. One example of such a challenge is that independence movements can declare 'virtual' sovereignty by registering their own unique country code domain name on the Internet. In the case of East Timor, this declaration of sovereignty was met with a severe electronic attack by Internet hackers opposed to East Timor's independence. The hackers successfully shut down much of Ireland's Internet service in their effort to combat the East Timor Ireland Solidarity Campaign's (ETISC) web site.

The ETISC, with the help of Ireland's main ISP, Connect Ireland, created the top level domain name for East Timor, '.tp.' Each country has a designated top level domain name, for example, Ireland is 'ie,' Canada is 'ca,' and so on. Previously, East Timor had not been registered ..., so ETISC did so in the name of Xanana Gusamo, the jailed independence leader of East Timor.

"The use of an offshore domain service is not unusual. There are a number of countries whose top-level domain is serviced outside their territory. The registration of the domain meant that, at least in cyberspace, East Timor was recognized as independent. This symbolic victory was not unnoticed by the Indonesian government, which reacted swiftly.

On January 19, 1999, the '.tp' domain site was attacked by hackers in the most sophisticated hacking ever recorded in Ireland. It is believed at least 18 hackers worked simultaneously in a concerted effort to break into Connect Ireland's high-security system. Connect Ireland director Martin Maguire said that as soon as breaches of the system's security were detected, the company immediately shut down its operations. "Our assumption is that the attack was so well organized, so deliberate and so skilful that whoever was doing it must be getting paid. The value to them is not one of 'kudos,' said Maguire."

"The assault on virtual East Timor was the cyberspace equivalent of a military invasion. It demonstrates the power of the Internet as a human-rights tool, and the lengths to which those opposed to such sites will go to combat the Net's success. It also has broader implications, for as human rights organizations become increasingly dependent on the Internet, they may also become more vulnerable to this new brand of information terrorism."

In the East Timor case it is possible to see how the Internet can be used to create a clear political statement, the creation of a "virtual sovereignty" providing a vision of freedom for a people controlled by their neighbours. However the might of the neighbors is equally apparent in the crushing of the "virtual sovereignty." This provides a useful reminder that whilst the Internet can be used to campaign for human rights, it can equally be used by the oppressor, perhaps in ways that the human rights activist has not yet imagined. Certainly at one level the Internet can be controlled and censored, but at another level it might be used to fake campaigns and discredit the human rights activists.

Another example from East Timor of the role of the Internet is provided by Amnesty International Chile, in their Indonesia campaign, which involved the use of both email and the WWW. The technology allowed information, which would not otherwise have been allowed into Indonesia, to enter and then to be circulated widely, quickly and relatively cheaply by NGOs inside the country. This flow of information amongst human rights activists and other interested individuals created pressure on the government to cease or desist from human rights abuses. This campaign provided access to a full text document of some 90 pages, including photographs, in a range of languages including English, French, Spanish and Indonesian, via the Internet.[19]

Some Concluding Thoughts

The case studies provided serve to show how the Internet has become a key tool in campaigning for human rights, and can be described as a quick and cheap way for human rights groups to exchange messages. One significant factor being the ability to send a message to multiple recipients by one action rather than sending messages one at a time. The Internet allows interactive communication between various parts of the human rights movement, with local groups being able to contact international groups directly without the need for intermediaries, and thus encourage the development of new communities of interest. The many applications and utilities available on the Internet seem to make it the 'killer application' for the human rights world, but a more balanced approach to it is required. The following bullet points are deliberately not answered here, but are provided as food for thought about the nature of the Internet and perhaps its value.

Some Positives

- Speed of response.
- Growing access.
- Difficulty for oppressive regimes to control.
- Exciting media, providing the opportunity to reach a new audience?

Some Negatives

- Poor quality of information.
- Western, male origins—reinforcing traditional power relations.
- Domination of the Internet by Western values, culture and language.
- Information overload—desensitizing people to the issues.
- Unequal access and economic questions for the developing world.
- Co-ordination—or rather the lack of co-ordination that the Internet provides.
- Hate/Extremism, pornography, paedophilia, trade in children and women.
- Freedom of speech and control—some governments still seek to control access.

The Internet has grown rapidly and its role within human rights organizations has become commonplace. Guzman[20] describes information technology as a positive force, where "the simple accessibility of the Internet makes it possible for people worldwide to join forces in existing human rights organizations and to form new organizations. Recruiting membership, communicating, researching issues, and mobilizing for action are facilitated by the Net."

However, when one considers the misuse of ICTs, as mechanisms of surveillance, to deny privacy and to control populations, it becomes necessary to temper one's enthusiasm. Recent work by the European Parliament,[21] for example, has identified the large-scale use of technologies for political control and the use of technology as tools of torture and repression; some of these are the very tools that in other hands are used to fight against abuses. The Report "*Silencing the Net*"[22] details the extent to which governments worldwide seek to control and manage the flow of information.

Patti Whaley, Deputy General Secretary of Amnesty International, passed this to me a little while ago. It is from a "Bluffer's Guide to the Internet" from a South Africa newspaper,[23] and it explained alternating options for predicting the impact of the Internet:

"The world will be a better place! By 2006, everyone in the world will be online. The Internet will make shops, offices, and business travel entirely unnecessary. This will save so much money that everything will be free! Wars will end! Everyone will be happy!

The world will be a worse place By 2006, everyone *in the West* will be online, but the growing billions outside developed capitalist society will still live in poverty. The resulting instability will cause worldwide war, or someone will finally use the nuclear bomb recipe—available over the Internet. Everyone will die.

People will take over the Internet By 2006, the sheer volume of Internet traffic will mean that government control will be impossible. Self-governing little societies will spring up with people living in 'virtual villages'. Everyone will be free.

Government will take over the Internet By 2006, Big Brother will really be watching you. All your e-mails, all your bank details, all your personal schedules and purchases—everything will be recorded and scrutinised. Internet computers will be fitted with cameras that will monitor you 24 hours a day. Totalitarian regimes will be in power everywhere. Everyone will be oppressed.

The Internet is a passing fad By 2006, the novelty of cyberspace will fade. Everyone will go about their business, just as they always did. It will save you a lot of money to ignore it—it will go away.

The Internet is here to stay By 2006, everyone in the world will be connected to everyone else at least twice. You will socialise through your computer screen, go on holiday without leaving your living room, and have arguments with thousands of people you've never met before. The Internet will be so pervasive that your only chance for economic survival is to invest heavily and reorient your entire strategy around the Net."

Patti went on to say that:

Although tongue-in-cheek, the article illustrates the bewilderment that many of us feel when we try to assess the impact of the Net on our lives. Human rights NGOs are not immune from that bewilderment; we tend to swing between unbridled enthusiasm for the Net's potential for activism, and dire warnings of the ruination of public discourse that will result from meddling regulators and commercial interests.

It is perhaps better not to imagine or believe that the Internet and current technological developments provide us with a digital Utopia for human rights activism. Rather than invest too much faith or belief in the Internet it is perhaps better to view it as a tool, to be used when appropriate and useful. The Internet must therefore be valued for its utility, not an answer to all the world's ills, creating new opportunities and raising new questions for the human rights world.

The important factor in human rights work remains the individual activists—it is only through their intervention and action that we know about the abuses and violations of human rights. As Justice Richard Goldstone pointed out, as Chief Prosecutor to the United Nations International Tribunals for the former Yugoslavia and Rwanda, the weight of traditional mail he received from activists and victims ensured that he was fully aware of the extent and nature of war crimes. The people's voice prevailed.

Notes

© Edward F. Halpin and Ashgate Publishing Company, 2001. Edward Halpin is Reader in Information Management in the School of Information Management, at the Leeds Metropolitan University.

1   This chapter results from work and publications undertaken over the past three years and relies upon the following published works. *The Use of the Internet by the European Parliament for the Promotion and Protection of Human Rights.* European Parliament, Luxembourg 1998 (with S. Fisher), "Through the Net to Freedom: information, the Internet and human rights," *Journal of Information Science* (with P Brophy), and *Human Rights and the Internet* (with S. Hick and E. Hoskins). I wish to record here my appreciation of their work, thanks for their collaboration and recognition of their contribution to this chapter through my research and publications with them.
2   The wider term Information and Communication Technologies (ICTs) is used here, as the   Internet is only one of a number of technologies used by the human rights world. The Internet,   however, will be the primary technology considered.
3   Http://www.nua.net/surveys/how_many_online/ (site visited 21st March 2001).
4   J.Slavin *The Internet and Society* (Polity Press, Cambridge, UK, 2000).
5   Http://www.nua.net/surveys/how_many_online/ (site visited 21st March 2001).
6   B. Hague and B. Loader, *Digital Democracy: Discourse and Decision Making in the Information Age* (London, Routledge, 1999).
7   P. Brophy and E. F. Halpin 'Through the Net to Freedom: information, the Internet and human rights,' *Journal of Information Science* 25 (5) 1999, PP 351- 364
8   J. Metzl, 'Information technology and human rights,' *Human Rights Quarterly*, 18 (1996) 705-746.
9   Metzl, *id.*
10   Available at: http://shr.aaas.org/program/
11   Ball P., et al, "Information Technology, information management and human rights: a response to Metzl," *Human Rights Quarterly* 19 (1997) 836-863.
12   Pal L. and Alexander C. J. (chapter by Deibert), *Digital Democracy*, Toronto, Oxford University Press (1998).
13   Halpin E. F. and Fisher S. M., *The Use of the Internet by the European Parliament for the Promotion and Protection of Human Rights.* European Parliament, Luxembourg 1998.
14   Hick S., Halpin E. F. and Hoskins E., *Human Rights and the Internet.* Macmillan, Basingstoke 2000.
15   Guzman D., Unpublished paper from work on the history of the Internet in human rights work.

16   *Human Rights and the Internet, supra,* n. 14, chapter by Djurdja Knevic.
17   *Human Rights and the Internet, supra,* n. 14, chapter by Graham Lane.
18   *Human Rights and the Internet, supra,* n. 14, chapter by Sharon Scharfe.
19   Halpin E. F. and Fisher S. M., *supra,* n. 13.
20   Halpin E. F. and Fisher S. M., *supra,* n. 13.
21   European Parliament Scientific and Technological Assessment (STOA) Unit, *The Technologies of Political Control,* European Parliament, Luxembourg, 1998, PE 166.499.
22   http://www.epic.org/free_speech/intl/hrw_report_5_96.html.
23   R. Ainsley, and A. Rae, *Bluff Your Way in Computers* (Ravette Pub Ltd 1996).

6 The Information Technology Revolution and Gross Human Rights Violations: Justice for the Masses or "Fast-Food" Human Rights?

D. CHRISTOPHER DECKER

The events leading up to the NATO bombing of Kosovo in March of 1999 are well-documented in newspaper accounts, documentaries and books. However, the world is still attempting to piece together what occurred in Kosovo when the Organization for Security and Cooperation in Europe's (OSCE) Kosovo Verification Mission (KVM) pulled out of Kosovo a few days prior to the NATO bombing. The International Criminal Tribunal for the Former Yugoslavia (ICTY) has the jurisdiction to prosecute violators of International Criminal Law and International Humanitarian Law for the conflict in Kosovo.[1] As of April 2000, there are only five persons indicted by the ICTY in association with the alleged humanitarian law violations in Kosovo.[2] The ICTY is still working in Kosovo to create further indictments and to obtain evidence in view of potential war crimes trials to be held in the future. This chapter explores the work of one organization that aided the ICTY in gathering information through the use of a database. The chapter discusses the project, not simply on a theoretical basis, but describes the actual logistics and functioning. Lastly, the chapter discusses the positive and negative implications of documenting human rights and humanitarian law violations using databases.

The International Crisis Group Humanitarian Law Documentation Project

The International Crisis Group Humanitarian Law Documentation Project (the Project) had its roots in other organizations. No Peace Without Justice (NPWJ) is an Italian non-governmental organization (NGO) which is a campaign of the Transnational Radical Party that is lobbying governments to ratify the International Criminal Court Statute. Between the summer of 1998 and February 1999, NPWJ twice sent a six-person team comprised of mostly former ICTY personnel into Kosovo "to prepare a dossier on violations of International Humanitarian Law."[3] The NPWJ report was prepared for Justice of the Supreme Court of Canada, Louise Arbour, then Chief Prosecutor of the ICTY. After completion of this report, the group felt that something additional must be done.

Amidst the NATO bombing of Kosovo and the floods of refugees heading into neighboring countries revealing stories of atrocities being committed against the civilian population, the idea to create a database that would document the crimes committed in Kosovo was born. The group decided that greater reporting of violations of humanitarian law in Kosovo must be achieved. Some members of the group decided to carry out an assessment concerning the creation of a project to document violations of humanitarian law. The group met with local NGOs, the Prosecutor General of Albania, representatives of the OSCE, and the ICTY Representatives in Tirana. After these meetings, a funding application was forwarded to the European Commission Humanitarian Office, and the International Crisis Group (ICG) agreed to sponsor the Project. One point that should be emphasized is that the Humanitarian Law Documentation Project was completely separate and unique from the usual work of ICG.[4]

The purpose of the Project was "to identify violations of international humanitarian law—often termed 'the laws of armed conflict' or 'laws of war'—and record direct evidence of these violations" from victims and witnesses.[5] "All of the evidence thus gathered was to be handed over" to the Office of the Prosecutor of the ICTY, for use in the investigation and prosecution of persons responsible for committing such violations.[6]

The Project had three main goals: first, to aid the ICTY "by providing an extensive list of witnesses whom its investigators could subsequently interview in a more in-depth manner" through the creation of a database which would give basic information about the witness or victim and the incident(s).[7] Second, a report was to be drafted focusing on the events during the conflict in 1999 in an attempt to reconstruct, as fully as possible, the sequence of events that took place during the NATO bombing campaign. Third, there was an element of capacity building in the project because the idea was to work with local partner NGOs in the collection of witness statements, and upon completion of the project to distribute the Project's equipment to local NGOs to assist them in their work.

The Project began in Tirana on 28 May 1999 with only four international staff members, but over the duration of the Project it grew exponentially. The basis of the project was simple: conduct interviews of witnesses and victims of violations of humanitarian law, including minorities, and put these interviews into a uniform database that would be easily searchable. While sounding practical and simple, it turned out to have numerous logistical and technical problems. But in the end the difficulties were overcome.

The Logistics

Offices and Staff

The Project required a large secure area where translating and analyzing data could take place. In Tirana, most interviews were taken in the refugee camps by local partner organizations. Therefore with only a small staff, office space was not an issue. As the refugees flowed back across the border to their homes after NATO troops moved into Kosovo, the Project decided to move its base to Gjakove/Djakovica.[8] However, in Djakovica a much larger facility was needed because of an increase of Project staff and the number of visitors who came to give statements. Furthermore, the Project also allocated space to the War Crimes Trauma Unit of Medecins du Monde (MdM) Sweden so that they could counsel victims and witnesses interviewed by the Project that suffered from Post-Traumatic Stress Syndrome (PTS). MdM held training and counseling sessions on PTS for staff and other mental health professionals in the area.

The Project eventually employed 46 international staff including information technology experts, logistics and finance staff, and international lawyers. The Project also employed 123 local personnel as interpreters, data entry personnel, drivers, security and other miscellaneous staff during the duration of the Project.

Communications and Electricity

Communications were the most difficult aspect of the Project. This was a problem in two spheres, both internal and external. Internally, the International Legal Officers (ILOs) needed to coordinate their activities with the partner NGOs. However, land telephone lines worked only locally within the municipalities. Therefore, in Djakovica work could only be coordinated with the partners in the Djakovica AOR (Area of Responsibility). In order to arrange working hours and meetings, the ILOs would need to drive around and locate people. One can see the obvious problems if weather or automobile problems caused an ILO to be late or miss a meeting. It could take several days before the ILO could get in contact with the person again. Because of constant security concerns such as mines, robberies, and the possibility that a situation may arise requiring an evacuation the ILOs were required to check in every two to three hours. While each person on the Project carried a hand-held very-high frequency radio for communication, often they did not work in the more distant AORs. The Project had six satellite phones, two were fixed in the office and the ILOs used the other phones in the field.

External communications had to be conducted with the satellite phones or e-mail. Since all these means of communication relied heavily on electricity and on satellites not being "down," communication was a constant concern. Electricity was sporadic at best and it became a critical logistic issue. Because the Project required the use of computers and other electronic equipment, the lack of electricity rendered them useless. Although difficult, the Project obtained a generator. Unfortunately this generator was only able to run a minimal number of computers and lights in the office. Moreover, the generator was stolen which caused a scramble to purchase a generator large enough to run all the computers and office equipment necessary to complete the Project.[9]

Computer Hardware

Considering that the Project was in the field and in a post-war situation it had an extensive computer system. Two servers networked between 30-35 desktop and laptop computers. One server was designated for Internet use and was attached to a satellite connection. The other server contained the database and was not connected to the satellite link as a security precaution to prevent anyone from trying to e-mail the database. The database was also encrypted every night and at least one staff member knew how to detach the hard drive from the computer used to store the database in case rapid evacuation was necessary. The Project also utilized compact disc (CD) technology. The Project had CD writers so that CD ROMs containing the database could be periodically turned over to the ICTY. Each AOR had access to digital cameras and Global Positioning Satellite (GPS) equipment in order to give accurate coordinates to the ICTY of bodies, potential or actual gravesites, and other evidence. Lastly, the Project used scanners to make digital copies of the interview forms. This was done for space concerns and security. It was physically far easier to transport and turn over three CD ROMs that contained database entries with photos and the scanned statements attached rather than 20,000 plus pages of documents.[10] Furthermore, in the case of evacuation it was much easier to take a set of CD ROMs and the database hard drive rather than cumbersome volumes of statements on paper.

The Primary Goal of Human Rights Databases

Although the Project was unique in creating a database during a post-conflict situation to be used by a prosecutor's office, the theories concerning its design and the methodology used to collect data are comparable to other projects. Human rights databases are generally used to gather data to support allegations of abuses or to establish a history of an area that has suffered from gross and/or systematic human rights violations. The end goal is to create an official record. Ball and Spirer suggest that: "The official record is derived from the collective memory, and the collective memory is based on information and data. The systematic arrangement of the information and data is the basis of the information management system."[11]

Since information is coming in from numerous areas, data must be merged together in order to create a picture that allows the database's target audience to understand what has occurred. The aim is that:

The information management system provides a collective memory and the ability to relate information from different sources. By so doing, it allows anyone in the organization to access information collected by any investigator, without restriction. An information management system used for these purposes is a process by which information is collected, standardized, represented in a database, and then analyzed by a variety of methods.[12]

The goal for most human rights databases is to create and utilize an information management system that will generate statistics based on the data that is collected and entered into the database. The statistics are used to derive an analysis that, hopefully, recreates the history of the period that the data reflects.

The Project had, however, slightly different goals than those of more traditional human rights databases. The goal of the Project's database was to assist the ICTY in locating witnesses and victims. In order for the database to be of any value, the ICTY had to know what the witnesses and victims had seen and experienced. The ICTY also needed to be able to locate these witnesses again in case they needed depositions. The ICTY also needed the ability to sort and search the data in an efficient way so that they could locate the best witnesses for their purposes. Otherwise the goal of creating the database would not be realized.

One major critique of human rights databases is "that the chosen interview subjects are not representative of the population of all victims. Even if a group has taken testimonies from many thousands of subjects, there are probably many others who were victims or witnesses of human rights violations but were not interviewed."[13] This was a critique of the report published by the Project after its completion. The report was accused of being biased and of focusing only on the violations of humanitarian law committed by Serb and Federal Republic of Yugoslavia forces.[14] Certainly there were NATO briefings on the targets they had chosen. There were also plenty of independent news stories that could have been used. However, the data that was analyzed by the Project came only from witness' and victims' statements. The purpose of the database was "to provide basic information about these witnesses and the types of crimes they had experienced, or seen, in a manner that was readily searchable by computer."[15] The report written by the Project was not the primary goal in itself, nor was the goal one of creating statistics.

Due to the political and security realities in Kosovo, there are an extremely small number of people who are willing to discuss humanitarian law violations committed by NATO or the Kosovo Liberation Army (KLA). In the case of NATO, bombs hit civilian targets and witnesses were able to tell interviewers about this. But people were reluctant to blame NATO because the people saw NATO as a "savior." Very little reliable data can be received from these accounts because many of the bombs and missiles were fired from miles away. Most potential witnesses willing to speak about violations committed by the KLA (i.e., Serbs) have left Kosovo and moved to Serbia or Montenegro, and were out of the reach of the Project's teams. The Project did have a "minorities" team that was not assigned to a specific AOR. The team went to enclaves and other areas where minorities are concentrated. In many instances people were unwilling to discuss KLA involvement in violations. Moreover, many Albanians are unwilling to discuss the KLA either. Even in October 1999, the KLA was collecting "taxes" and were involved in "community policing" in some municipalities.[16]

Therefore, in order to have a full understanding of the Project one must look at the process of data collection and data processing and come to their own conclusions concerning any potential bias of the data. It is important for groups who wish to replicate documentation projects to study other projects and learn from their mistakes.[17]

Data Collection

The partner NGOs and ILOs were primarily responsible for the collection of data. The Project divided Kosovo into AORs that were congruent with the municipalities in Kosovo.[18] The Project worked with local partner NGOs like the Council for the Protection of Human Rights and Fundamental Freedoms. These local NGOs actually conducted the interviews while the ILO offered support, guidance and instruction. This meant that every day ILOs drove to the AORs and picked up the local NGO partners and then drove to villages throughout the municipality. The ILOs had interpreters that translated as the interviews were conducted. This allowed the ILOs to elicit more details or clarify issues brought up by the witnesses. The interviews always started off with questions concerning whether the witness had been previously interviewed by anyone, whether they were willing to allow the Project to turn over the information in their interview to the ICTY, or in the case of minorities, to the United Nations High Commissioner for Refugees (UNHCR) and the Organization for Security and Co-operation in Europe (OSCE).

The questioning of witnesses and victims followed a form that was supplied to them by the Project. After noting the witnesses' personal data, the interviewers were encouraged to take the interview in the form of a narrative rather than asking specific questions. At the end of an interview specific questions were asked regarding the status of witnesses documents[19] and, if the witness was forcibly expelled or displaced from Kosovo which routes they took.[20]

Leading scholars in the field report that: "The narrative is often complex because each narrative can contain from one to many victims, violations, and perpetrators, and they may be related to each other through complicated relationships."[21] Because some of the local NGO partners did not have staff that were experienced in conducting interviews, the ILOs were often required to ask follow up questions in order to illicit or clarify pertinent information. The interviewers wrote detailed notes on paper kept separate from the interview form. After the interview concluded the interviewer generally wrote a chronological narrative on the form. This procedure was done so that the data processors could more easily input the data. For example, a witness might start their story relating how their village was shelled, then discuss the death of a relative at a checkpoint, and then return to discussing other people who were killed in the village during the shelling. If the interviewer wrote the story directly onto the form the data processor had a very difficult time in reconstructing the sequence of events from the statement that was given in a temporally disjointed manner. A further complication to the collection of data was the language barrier.

All the interviews were taken in Albanian or Serbian thereby requiring translation.[22] As everyone who has studied a foreign language knows, some words do not translate well. This was the case with some key words. Furthermore, most witnesses would use words that had an English equivalent, but did not accurately reflect the situation. For example, the use of the word *masakër* in Albanian translates into "massacre" in English. People being interviewed used this word constantly to describe anyone killed during the war. The difficulty is that in English massacre implies the killing of a number of defenseless people or when one army is far larger than another and destroys its opponent rather than the killing of a single victim. Another example of this linguistic difficulty was the use of the word *bombë*. Although Albanian contains distinct words for "shell," "mortar," and "grenade," witnesses still generally only used the word *bombë*.

What makes narrative interviewing a difficult form of information gathering is that the data processor must make decisions about which details in the story to include in the database. "Data processors receive the essentially raw data from the interview narratives and prepare it to be entered into the database. In so doing, they extract the names of victims, perpetrators, and organizations, and apply standard definitions of violations and geographic locations."[23]

Data Processing

This section discusses the data processing of the interviews from the form as they were input into the database and the steps that were taken to create uniformity. When the interviews for the day were completed the forms were brought back to the office where bilingual staff would input the data into the database. In many cases the person that interpreted for the ILO would actually input the interview into the database. After the interview form was entered into the database, the interview form was electronically scanned and attached to the record.[24]

The data entry procedures consisted of seven steps. First, the ILO brought in the completed forms from the field. Second, an ILO supervised the data processing staff and answered questions related to grammar and classification of crimes. Third, the interview forms were entered into the database and the alphanumeric reference number was written at the top of the interview form. Fourth, the ILO supervising the data processing reviewed part of the entry to correct errors. Fifth, the data processor gave the interview form to the person in charge of scanning the forms. Sixth, the permanent data entry supervisor or an ILO carried out a second translation check. Seventh, the interview forms were sorted according to AOR and the

ILOs performed a final check of the database as compared to the interview forms.

The database is essentially an Excel database with an Access 97 search interface. Each interview accounted for one record. Every record had a unique 10 digit alphanumeric reference. The record included information about the witness, his or her movements, status, and details of up to five specific incidents.[25] The database consisted of an interface for data entry that was designed with a number of pull-downs. Because an objective of a database is to create uniformity, it was essential to limit the latitude a data processor had in inputting data. For example, a complete list of all villages and municipalities was put in a pull-down list. This eliminated the chance of misspelling of place names. The interface had an initial screen where the personal data was entered. Subsequent screens dealt with incidents, loss of documentation, and the route of displacement.

The core of the database involved the strategy to break a witness' story into separate incidents. There were five screens where the data processor would break the narrative interview down into separate incidents. This section also had boxes that could be "ticked." All the incident screens had a free text area, which allowed for greater detail to be stored in the database. There was a section of each incident screen where perpetrators were identified. The choices for perpetrators included "VJ/JNA," "paramilitaries," "police," "KLA," and "other." Each of these incident screens had a choice of "crimes" the data processor could chose from. The "crimes" included killing, destruction (theft) of property, forced displacement, sexual assault, torture/ill-treatment, harassment and other. The free text area and the "crimes" portion of the database were the most problematic parts of the data processing. These sections required the data processors to make judgments about what constituted critical information that needed to be included in the free text area and whether the facts presented supported one or more of the "crimes" listed.

The data processors are the people in the organization who take each story and decide whether the evidence is sufficient to classify the acts described in the story as violations according to the agreed definitions of the organization. . . . The data processors apply the organization's rules and classifications to make this decision. By applying these rules and standardizing the disparate information, the data processors create an organizational memory that can be accessed by any member or part of the organization.[26]

The organizational memory that is created allows the organization to analyze the data in a coherent way and facilitate projects, such as compiling a report. Section VI will discuss some of the problems the Project faced concerning standardization in more depth. The interface also had screens that tracked other information. There were boxes to trace the path taken by the refugees and internally displaced in Kosovo in order to ascertain where checkpoints were and where Serbian/FRY troops or KLA were stationed. Another screen provided boxes regarding different types of identification or documents that had been taken from the witness. Even with all this planning there are still issues that arouse concern regarding the methodology, language, and the database itself.

Data Issues

As successful as the Project was its drawbacks and difficulties should be addressed, especially problems that arose in the use of information technology (IT) both in general and particular to databases. While this new technology empowers those seeking to use it, there are lessons to be learned from the Project that have both specific and general application to projects that document violations of human rights and humanitarian law.

In retrospect, it appears the Project encountered many of the same challenges that scholars have discovered among other efforts to document human rights violations. In a 1996 article, Dr. Jamie Metzl, looked at how IT could be used by NGOs, governments, and the United Nations to promote human rights and facilitate the work of these groups.[27] He defined IT broadly to include email, Internet, and online-databases. In a discussion concerning several such databases,[28] Dr. Metzl noted, "[t]he establishment of effective databases . . . requires uniformity of database design and reporting standards so that information from different regions and sources can be compared and trends analyzed."[29]

In practice, the problem is that those who create and use the databases are generally not people with the expertise to create such uniformity. They are lawyers and researchers and grassroots organizers and so on, each with their own way of perceiving and presenting information. The vocabulary and design of a database must keep this factor in mind. The vocabulary and design of a database are not problems of information technology as such, but rather ones of information management.[30]

As was the case for the Project, a key point in the system is where, as Ball and others describe it, data is "rendered in a standardized form according to the organization's controlled vocabularies."[31] At the Project, this process included classifying acts as killing, harassment, ill-treatment, destruction of property and sexual assault, etc. This vocabulary, however, was imprecise and using it sometimes led to imprecise and perhaps inconsistent entries. Take the following scenario, for example. Perpetrators fired at several victims at once in an apparent summary execution. A bullet hit the witness in the shoulder and bodies fell on top of him. Clearly, this was an attempted killing with respect to the witness. The

Project classified it, however, as a "killing" which captured the fact that the perpetrator performed an act that he intended to result in the death of a human being. But this definition does not capture the fact that the perpetrator's acts did not accomplish what was intended. At the same time, there was a box for "other" crimes; perhaps other projects used this box for attempted killings, which would be an inconsistency.[32]

This problem illustrates the need of what Patrick Ball and others refer to as a "controlled vocabulary." Ball et al. discuss the controlled vocabulary problems in terms of a more theoretical issue concerning databases; the difference between representation and exchange databases.

[A]nalysts within a large-scale human rights project need to know that all of the interviews administered by the project were conducted in a standard way so that trends found in one area can be compared to trends in another area. However, merging raw data—the organizational memories and products of investigations—from different organizations is quite another matter.[33]

Each organization that creates a database, even on the same issue, will have a different controlled vocabulary. Unless there is a high degree of coordination at the outset and as the project progresses, unanticipated issues arising in the field will result in such differences.

Each human rights group has its own particular substantive focus, political context, and defining mandate. The combination of human rights groups' focus, context, available financial and human resources, technical depth, and especially their mandate, guides how each organization's leadership understands the nuances of "human rights." Defining an organization's controlled vocabulary means defining what the organization thinks.[34]

In short, different projects will compile data differently. This is precisely the problem that the ICTY will now encounter with attempting to merge the data of projects that worked separately with only a limited degree of coordination. While giving the same database to different projects should have settled some of these problems, the lack of a common controlled vocabulary will lead to discrepancies. In essence, the language will be the same, but not the definitions applied to that language.

The notion of a controlled vocabulary is also important in that should the ICTY ever use the database for purely statistical purposes, it would be an inaccurate or ineffective tool.[35] With ambiguous or alternative definitions, a search for all instances of "killing," say, would bring up more kinds of incidents than the searcher had in mind. While those with scientific or statistic backgrounds could easily discern the data's true value, a lawyer or judge might not have such a background, and may read more into the results of a search than is proper.

Yet as long as the users in The Hague understand the language that the field people are using, there will be no problem. It does not matter what definitions we chose for classifying crimes as long as the users understand that in the Project database, a particular attempted killing, say, is classified as a killing. As might be expected, however, this understanding is not first-hand knowledge for researchers and prosecutors in The Hague; they were not involved in the collection or classification of that information.

For this latter reason, ILOs who *did* have intricate knowledge of the workings and foibles of the database wrote a manual setting out how acts were to be classified. After having read the manual, hopefully, a user who wanted instances of people maimed but not killed in the shelling of a village, for example, would know to call up all instances of "killing." Of course this means that the researcher is required to perform extra work because in order to find injured survivors of a shelling attack she is required to sift through records of those killed in addition to those maimed. With the clarifications that the database manual makes, users have the tools necessary to accurately interpret search results and individual records.

Closing Issues—"Fast Food" Human Rights

One can imagine in the not so distant future a situation where mobile teams armed with laptops and satellite/wireless telephone technology can be out in the field taking statements. Small digital cameras can photograph the witness or victim, the scene of the incidents, and evidence. All this information can be sent directly back to a central database in another part of the world. While the Project has some similarities to the scenario described above, it was not quite that advanced. For example, another project in Kosovo by an American lawyer, Michael Stechow, took digital photographs of families that had missing relatives in the hopes that they could be matched up by using a web site.[36] This project functioned in the refugee camps while the bombing was still occurring.

One concern about making human rights documentation so technologically advanced is that we may be de-humanizing human rights. While it is probably not the intention of the creators and human rights workers on these projects, there is a certain amount of "sterilization" of the witnesses' and victims' stories. For instance, when a witness describes a killing, there is no way for a database to reflect the detail that a witness gives during their interview. Logically, however, "sterilization" must happen in order for there to be uniformity of a database.

In essence, human rights organizations that create databases must be careful not to "package" or "prefabricate" human rights violations. This is a "fast food" approach to human rights documentation. Fast food is all made the same way, each hamburger has the same toppings. However, human rights violations do not necessarily occur in the same way or with the same severity. For example, there are numerous types of torture. Some forms of torture are more brutal and vicious than other forms of torture. If human rights groups' emphasis is placed on getting as much information as possible and relying too heavily on "ticking" boxes on data forms rather than reflecting accurately and completely the detail of the torture, there is a great risk that human rights violations will lose the grotesque uniqueness that makes then so repugnant. Cataloging violations will simply become like ordering fast food where everything is packaged the same way. If reporting of violations becomes so uniform, nondescriptive, and sterile, we risk allowing violations to become more palatable.

There appears to be two methods that allow human rights database creators to avoid a fast food approach or resist the "sterilization" phenomenon. If a free-text area is added to a database, this incorporates the uniqueness of the witnesses' or victims' story. Free text, however, defeats the purpose of making the data uniform. A second approach may be to adopt an extensive list of violations and details concerning the violations. The Human Rights Information and Documentation Systems, International (HURIDOCS) is on the cutting edge concerning standard setting. HURIDOCS has developed a list of 48 categories.[37] These 48 categories are each broken down into sub-categories. These sub-categories are broken down yet further. For example, category 4 is "Types of Acts." *Violations of the right to life* are coded as 01. A direct action which violates the right to life is coded as 01 01. Therefore, the code 01 01 01 01 is a summary execution and 01 01 01 04 is "politically-motivated killing by non-state agent(s)."[38] While this level of detail solves the issue of over simplifying violations, it requires a high degree of knowledge about the different categories. Finding well-educated staff with enough knowledge about human rights may be difficult for some organizations. Clearly, a balance must be struck between detail and simplification in order to create a thorough yet user friendly database.

Conclusion

Even though it is important to standardize the legal terms and vocabulary concerning human rights and their associated violations, we must not reduce human rights violations to little boxes that need to be "ticked." People who have been the victims of human rights or humanitarian law violations do not care how the researchers or academics label their suffering, but they want people to understand their emotions, shock, disbelief, and trauma. Human rights organizations that create databases must not lose sight of this fact. If human rights groups take a *fast food* approach to human rights documentation the group does not do justice to the individual, nor can justice be done for the individual if their story is not accurately reflected and the truth is never told.

Notes

© D. Christopher Decker and Ashgate Publishing Company, 2001. Christopher Decker is the Legal Adviser on Human Rights in Law Enforcement for the Organization for Security and Co-operation in Europe's (OSCE) Mission in Kosovo.

1   In March 1998, "...the Prosecutor confirmed publicly that the territorial and temporal jurisdiction of the tribunal covered any serious violations of international humanitarian law taking place in Kosovo and emphasised that she was empowered to investigate such crimes. The Security Council, in resolution 1160 (1998) of 31 March 1998, requested the Prosecutor to begin gathering information related to violence in Kosovo that may fall under the Tribunal's jurisdiction. The Prosecutor proceeded to request information from States and organisations about violent incidents in Kosovo. The General Assembly, in May 1998, approved a budget request enabling the Prosecutor to recruit a team to undertake preliminary investigations." *Report of the International Tribunal for the Prosecution of Persons Responsible for Serious Violations of International Humanitarian Law Committed in the Territory of the Former Yugoslavia Since 1991*, U.N. Doc. A/53/219 S/1998/737 at para. 118 (1998) *available at* http://www.un.org/icty/ rapportan/rapport5-e.htm#1. Kosovo.
2   There are numerous other alleged war criminals that are being held in Kosovo. Some of those trials are now being conducted in the various District Courts in Kosovo. Additionally, there are secret indictments which may or may not include other alleged war criminals.
3   "No Peace Without Justice"— Report on Serious Violations of International Humanitarian Law in Kosovo in 1998, Introduction (February 1999), available on http://www.radicalparty.org (hereafter "NPWJ report").
4   For more information about ICG *see* http://www.crisisweb.org.
5   INTERNATIONAL CRISIS GROUP HUMANITARIAN LAW DOCUMENTATION PROJECT, KOSOVO. REALITY DEMANDS: DOCUMENTING VIOLATIONS OF INTERNATIONAL HUMANITARIAN LAW IN KOSOVO 1 (Lorna Davidson and Scott Brandon eds. 2000) [hereinafter REALITY DEMANDS].
6   *See id.* at 1.
7   *Id.* at 2.
8   In the case of place names, on first occurrence it will be displayed in Albanian/Serbian and then each subsequent occurrence will be in only Serbian for sake of clarity.
9   Electric outages occurred so frequently that the Project lost about five solid days of work while it tried to purchase a replacement generator from Thessaloniki, Greece or Istanbul, Turkey. Because of the high demand for generators, the area surrounding Kosovo could not keep them in stock. Those generators that were available were exorbitantly priced.
10   The Project took over 4,700 interviews and the interview forms were about 4-5 pages in length.

11 Patrick Ball and Herbert F. Spirer, *Introduction* to MAKING THE CASE: INVESTIGATING LARGE SCALE HUMAN RIGHTS VIOLATIONS USING INFORMATION SYSTEMS AND DATA ANALYSIS 1 (Patrick Ball et al. eds., 2000).

12 *Id.* at 2.

13 *Id.* at 3.

14 Paul van Zyl, *Reality Demands: Truth and Justice After Kosovo*, 39 COLUM. J. TRANSNAT'L L. 283, 288 (2000) (reviewing REALITY DEMANDS: DOCUMENTING VIOLATIONS OF INTERNATIONAL HUMANITARIAN LAW IN KOSOVO 1999 (Lorna Davidson and Scott Brandon eds. (2000)).

15 REALITY DEMANDS, *supra* note 5 at 2.

16 At the end of 1999 many areas of Kosovo resembled a lawless Wild West. The United Nations had been unable to deploy significant amounts of police officers in the major towns to deter criminal activity. This vacuum was not always filled by KFOR and this allowed the KLA a great deal of latitude.

17 The book by Patrick Ball et al. looks at several different documentation projects, primarily focusing on truth commission databases. Nevertheless, this book serves as an excellent source for groups wishing to design human rights databases.

18 Out of the 17 major incidents named in the indictment against Slobodan Milosevic, the Project AORs contained 11 of the incidents. *See* The International Criminal Tribunal for the Former Yugoslavia Indictment against Slobodan Milosevic *et al.* IT-99-37 para. 97-98 (May 24, 1999), *available at* http://www.un.org/icty/indictment/english/mil-ii990524e.htm.

19 This included primarily identification cards, passports and driving licenses.

20 The question concerning the route taken, either in Kosovo or out of Kosovo, was designed to establish the flow of refugees and to ascertain were the checkpoints were.

21 Patrick Ball and Herbert F. Spirer, *Introduction* to MAKING THE CASE: INVESTIGATING LARGE SCALE HUMAN RIGHTS VIOLATIONS USING INFORMATION SYSTEMS AND DATA ANALYSIS 5 (Patrick Ball et al. eds., 2000).

22 Although it is possible to have a "multi-lingual" database, the designers did not utilize this concept. This is possible by using a number set to represent words in multiple language. For example, in a field that requires violations, "01" might represent "killing." Each data processor is supplied with a list of the numbers and the corresponding words in their own language.

23 Patrick Ball and Herbert F. Spirer, *Introduction* to MAKING THE CASE: INVESTIGATING LARGE SCALE HUMAN RIGHTS VIOLATIONS USING INFORMATION SYSTEMS AND DATA ANALYSIS 6 (Patrick Ball et al. eds., 2000).

24 The search engine allows a user to click on a "View Scan" button that will cause the scanned document to be displayed. In addition, digital cameras were used to document such things as evidence of torture, human remains, and destruction of villages. The scanned photographic material or other documents were attached to the end of the electric scan of the interview form. Furthermore, in the general comments field the phrase "Photo/s is/are attached to this statement" to alert the user that there was additional material attached to the record.

25 In the case where more than five incidents occurred a new record was created that had the same alphanumeric reference with the addition of an "a," "b" etc.

26 Patrick Ball and Herbert F. Spirer, *Introduction* to MAKING THE CASE: INVESTIGATING LARGE SCALE HUMAN RIGHTS VIOLATIONS USING INFORMATION SYSTEMS AND DATA ANALYSIS 7 (Patrick Ball et al. eds., 2000).

27 Jamie F. Metzl, *Information Technology and Human Rights*, 18 HUM. RTS. Q. 705 (1996).

28   *Id.* at 707.
29   Metzl, *supra* note, at 725.
30   Patrick Ball, et al., *Information Technology, Information Management, and Human Rights: A Response to Metzl*, 19 HUM. RTS. Q. 836, 840 (1997).
31   *Id.* at 841.
32   Both the OSCE and the American Bar Association Central-Eastern European Law Initiative were also collecting statements and processing them into a database for the ICTY.
33   *Id.* at 851.
34   *Id.* at 852.
35   It should be stressed that the author is not insinuating that any statistics the ICTY releases are invalid. The important issue is that this endeavor by the ICTY could have been so much more complete and precise. Perhaps by design or by mistake the database can only be used for locating witnesses.
36   *See* www.refugeesearch.org.
37   Manuel Guzman, *The Investigation and Documentation of Events as a Methodology in Monitoring Human Rights Violations*, *available at* http://www.huridocs.org/events.htm.
38   *See id.* at table 2.

7 The Intersection of Trade and Human Rights

MALINI MEHRA

This chapter begins with a general introduction to the concerns of citizens' groups and environmental groups, human rights organizations and others with regard to the architecture of the world economic system—particularly in terms of trade agreements. The specific focus is on the World Trade Organization (WTO) and it highlights some of the areas of human rights conflict and compatibility. The analysis then moves on to some of the more important issues of policy formation and policy impact.

The chapter's primary focus is on one of the key institutions governing the international trade regime, the World Trade Organization, and its implications for the enjoyment of human rights world-wide. I work on the issue of international trade and investment with particular reference to environment and development issues. Part of the analysis includes references to the debate on international investment agreements. To this point there have been several failed attempts to negotiate an international investment agreement amongst the Organization for Economic Co-operation and Development (OECD) countries representing the primary industrialized, wealthier nations. The negotiations center on an instrument called the Multilateral Agreement on Investment, or MAI. There are also moves afoot in various other parts of the world to bring together some of the provisions in the failed MAI through bilateral investment agreements and regional investment agreements.

Why the Concerns?

Let me begin with some of the citizens' concerns. Many people are familiar with the scenes of protest and mayhem on the streets of Seattle in 1999 during the ministerial conference of the World Trade Organization. And some may have memories that go further back to the trade conference

75

held in Geneva preceding the Seattle meeting, which also saw riots and protests at the WTO. Citizens' concerns have moved from focusing almost exclusively on the role of the state in respecting, promoting, protecting and fulfilling human rights, to focusing on the supra-national, multilateral bodies and non-state actors such as transnational corporations. We see many campaigns reflective of this new development, for example, on the OECD's MAI that was mentioned above.

The concern on the part of many citizens is due to the tension between the growing power of these multilateral economic agreements and institutions, and the waning national economic sovereignty to which Anthony D'Amato, Noam Chomsky and others have referred. There is a clear political imbalance in the international system and this is something that many developing country organizations, in particular, are pointing to in their own criticisms of international institutions and agreements oriented to trade and investment. We see the balance of power in international bodies and institutions, for example the WTO, tipped in favor of the rich, the G-7 countries and, especially, the G-1 country, the United States. We are also concerned with the effects that cascade down from decisions made at the multilateral level through policies of market opening. These policies have significant impacts on workers, producers, consumers and on the environment and cultures at the very local level.

There is also tremendous concern at the motivation behind these kind of international economic agreements—with many suspecting that they have been created primarily to benefit elite corporate interests. Critics point to the proposed MAI, for example, where firms and other investors were granted unprecedented rights with almost no corresponding responsibilities. There is also concern about the so-called migration of decision-making power, and accountability, from local institutions, be they municipal bodies or provincial governments, or even federal agencies, to these remote multilateral institutions.

The GATT and WTO

The WTO is a relatively recent creation in the history of trade agreements. The WTO was created in 1994, at the end of the last round of trade negotiations, the so-called Uruguay Round which took about seven or eight years to conclude. One of the decisions of the Uruguay Round was to establish an organization to set rules and govern international trade. This organization, the World Trade Organization, would be the successor to the existing arrangement known as GATT, the General Agreement on Tariffs and Trade, which had been agreed to back in 1948.

GATT is a very interesting creation because it was never institutionalized. The reason it wasn't institutionalized had to do with domestic U.S. politics. The U.S. Congress did not want to cede any of its national economic sovereignty to an international body, the originally proposed International Trade Organization. So the GATT was set up as a sort of compromise candidate. GATT's founding statute, the Havana Charter, was agreed to, ironically enough, in Cuba which was one of the original 24 founding member countries. The rationale of the GATT negotiators, the early pioneers, was that they agreed that it was much better to have a rules-based, internationally-accepted world trade system, rather than an unpredictable international system which was determined by the ad-hoc economic interests of the world's most powerful trading nations. So, from the GATT to the WTO, we see a progression from the 24 original member countries to the 135 nations that now comprise the WTO. And you will all, no doubt, be familiar with the controversy about whether China should be allowed to join as member number 136.

The WTO's Three Key Functions

If the GATT creates the framework, what are the functions of the WTO as the implementing institution? The WTO has three key functions: it is a forum for making rules, dealing with disputes, and generally governing the global trade system.

Firstly, the WTO acts as the primary negotiating forum for trade agreements on a global level. There are, however, more than forty regional trade agreements, such as NAFTA, Mercosur, the European Union, and others. But the WTO defines the international trade rules and principles, to which all of these regional trade agreements must conform.

Another innovation of the Uruguay round was that the WTO—unlike its predecessor, the GATT—has now developed a body to settle trade disputes which is binding and has teeth through its various enforcement mechanisms. Some of the rulings of this body, the Dispute Settlement Body or DSB, made by trade tribunals dominated by lawyers and officials, have created much of the concern about this institution. The rulings, for example, that relate to the protection of turtles and dolphins, the safety of additives such as beef growth hormone, and the protection of Caribbean banana growers have been particularly controversial.

Thirdly, the WTO provides some technical assistance and capacity building on trade matters, in particular, to the least developed countries and developing countries. The WTO's primary aim, however, is trade liberalization: defined as the removal of trade barriers wherever they exist. It is important to note, however, particularly in terms of our human rights advocacy, that the Preamble of the Agreement Establishing the WTO, contains a number of social and environmental aims. These aims refer to raising living standards, reaching full employment, and using natural resources in accordance with the principle of sustainable development.

One further note about the historical intentions of the original founders of GATT that is particularly relevant in the context of calls for labor standards in trade agreements—is that the International Trade Organization (the body that the U.S. Congress effectively killed at birth) included worker's rights issues in its statues. In fact, the ITO took on board many of the workers rights conventions which had been agreed to by the International Labor Organization which was founded in 1919. So we have that history to contend with and we must also refer back to it when we consider whether there should be labor rights, and other human rights, included in international economic agreements.

Human Rights Conflict and Compatibility

There are many ways of addressing the issue of the WTO and its conflict or compatibility with human rights. The following analysis looks at it in three ways. The first approach compares the international trade regime with the international human rights regime. The second looks at the issue of policy formation and the entire decision-making process on trade issues at the multilateral and domestic levels. The third part of the analysis examines the issue of policy impact.

The analysis begins with a general comparison of the human rights and trade legal regimes. As an aside, I would like to mention that there has been a considerable amount of work done on comparing the international trade regime and the international environmental regime. There is much we can learn from this analysis which at this point is far ahead of the comparative analysis that has been done on human rights and trade.

But in relation to human rights and trade, the first observation is that both regimes are liberal in outlook and based on positive legal freedoms—such as the right to trade (a fundamental economic right) and freedom from discrimination. However, one of the key differences in underlying principles between the human rights and trade regimes, is the WTO's refusal to discriminate between so-called *like products*. The WTO jargon for this is *process and production methods* (PPMs). In the environmental, as well as the human rights dimension, this refusal to discriminate is absolutely central because the PPM provision means that governments cannot discriminate between goods and services on the basis of *how* they are produced: whether they are produced with child labor, for example, or whether they are produced with chemicals that would not be permitted in the importing country. There is also a considerable push within the WTO to remove subsidies, for example, to remove input subsidies for farmers. But there is not much of an attempt to discriminate between subsidies. Subsidies can be good or bad. Good subsidies are those which enable subsidized inputs to be given to small farmers as an affirmative action measure, bad subsidies are those that perpetuate harmful social or environmental practices such as un-taxed air fuel. But both good and bad subsidies are attacked by the WTO without distinction.

It is important to note, however, that GATT/WTO rules do contain a number of "exceptions" and flexibility clauses. For example, Article XX of GATT says that states may make exceptions to the trade rules if, for example, human, animal, or plant life or health is going to be harmed. Exceptions are also permissible on the basis of public morals, prison labor, balance of payment issues, national defense or exhaustible natural resources. However, these principles, as well as another principle, known as the "special and differential treatment" for the poorer nations, are conspicuous by the very absence of their implementation. And this is one of the main issues raised by developing countries at Seattle. They say, "Great, we've got flexibility built into the WTO. Now you developed countries, especially you the United States, we want to see flexibility for developing countries. For example, in the scheduling of mandatory changes under GATT rules to our laws." Many developing countries lack the resources to change their laws in conformance with trade agreements such as the agreement on Trade-Related Intellectual Property Rights (TRIPs). They say, "give us a longer time frame. Not just the five years or two years which have been given to the least developed countries. Furthermore, we want technical assistance and money to ensure that we are able to conform our national laws and industrial practices with those demanded by the major trading nations." Obviously most of these requests have fallen on deaf ears.

A. *The Core Principles of Human Rights*

International human rights regimes, by contrast, operate using a different set of principles. For example, the principles of non-retrogression, participation, the right to redress, and non-discrimination are core values. Non-retrogression refers to the fact that if nations take positive steps to implement human rights—be they human rights in health, education, or housing—they should strive to continue to advance these gains and not subsequently regress by taking negative steps. The principle of participation is a fundamental one: it holds that people must be able to participate in the decision-making process over any sector that is affecting their lives. Finally, the right to redress in an appropriate form is another fundamental human rights provision. We see this being undermined by the WTO's Dispute Settlement Body which offers no direct access to non-governmental organizations or civil society actors in trade disputes—even to bring points of fact to the attention of the disputants. Access can only be gained at the discretion of the chair of the three-member panel that has been assigned the responsibility of adjudicating any given trade issue. Even this discretionary opportunity is a recent advance established by a panel ruling that enables civil society groups to bring so-called *amicus curiae* (friends of the court) briefs to the attention of the chair.

Finally, the human rights principle of non-discrimination is in conflict with the trade principle of non-discrimination. The human rights principle refers to individuals and groups, the trade principle refers to nations and firms. The principle of non-discrimination is at the core of the WTO and is expressed through the two principles of *Most Favoured Nation* and *National Treatment*. The first prohibits discrimination between states, and the second prohibits discrimination between domestic and foreign firms. Now under human rights law, and in the constitutions of many nations, non-discrimination is often set aside in order to promote greater social justice. For example, through affirmative action programs which discriminate against an ethnically or otherwise dominant group in favor of a weaker group to promote social leveling.

In the context of trade matters, the question becomes one of: "How can we favor domestic producers, consumers and workers in the global economy when we're prevented from doing so on grounds of the non-discrimination rules of the WTO?" This issue takes us back to the MAI where the issue of non-discrimination versus affirmative action came up. The issue was raised by the domestic *Environmental* and *Social Policy* departments of the negotiating countries. They warned that there could be a conflict between existing domestic affirmative action policies and the MAI's provisions granting the same rights to foreign investors as domestic investors had. The U.S. response to this was to exempt its entire federal affirmative action programs, lock, stock and barrel from the MAI.

B. Lack of Democratic Participation in Trade Negotiations

Trade policy formation at the WTO and national level raises problems both internally and externally. There are problems internally as to how the WTO member states come to agree to particular trade rules. But there are also problems externally in terms of domestic policy formation. Both of these processes are entirely opaque. The WTO negotiations are power-driven and all sorts of trade-offs are permissible: even trade-offs that national officials have not mandated or national parliaments made aware. An example of this is what happened in Seattle when the European Trade Commissioner, on his own initiative, agreed to a U.S. proposal to set up a committee on biotechnology at the WTO. Hours after he publicly announced that he was going to be doing this, the weight of European environment ministers and European environmentalists came down on him and there was a public row. They accused him of making an excessive and inappropriate trade-off, saying words to the effect: "Excuse me, you can't do this, because we expressly do not want a committee on biotechnology and this thing is not something to be traded off by you." The Commissioner's response was essentially, "Listen, I have the mandate to do this as the chief European Commission negotiator at the WTO. We can then take the deal back to national parliaments and they can then decide what to do. But I am only doing my job."

This is the crux of the problem. In essence the negotiating process is fundamentally undemocratic. Both parliamentary and citizens' groups need to be engaged in the determination of national trade priorities and policies *before* things reach the negotiation stage. Hopefully this is one of the areas that will change after Seattle.

C. Domination by the Most Powerful Trading Nations

The other problem with the policy formation process is the informal manner in which agreements are made. Decisions taken reflect primarily the voice of the main trading nations and these are not necessarily only the industrialized nations. Some developing countries such as India, Brazil, Malaysia, and South Africa are now powerful economies and can pull their weight when it comes to negotiating with the major powers such as the United States, Canada, European Union, and Japan. The ones who are kept out are the minor or weaker nations such as Namibia, Ecuador, Azerbaijan or Sri Lanka.

Domestic trade policy formation is marked by similar inequalities in terms of who is inside the process and who is kept outside. This is evident at every level: which government departments are involved in the key policy-making process and which departments are excluded. For example, the power departments—commerce and finance—are likely to be there, but you will seldom find the weaker environmental or social policy departments. We also see the representation of major commercial interests in national trade policy and investment decisions. But not those of the poor farmers and other more marginalized groups. Indigenous communities have very little political voice or clout and, while they are often forced to suffer the consequences of trade policies, they do not participate in the decision-making process.

Trade policy-making is very much marked by the dominance of powerful special interests. The TRIPs agreement on intellectual property rights is a case in point. TRIPs was another invention of the GATT's Uruguay Round. Previously, trade policy was all about goods and services, but after the completion of the Uruguay Round it has expanded into all sorts of areas including intellectual property rights. This particular TRIPs agreement was virtually drafted by U.S. and European biotechnology companies. The immediate concern about trade policy formation, however, is twofold. Firstly, there is justifiable concern at the growing importance of the executive arm of governments compared to the diminishing role of national parliaments. And secondly, there is concern at the rapid expansion of trade policy into new areas such as consumer, health, labor and social policy where trade rules are increasingly used to justify the weakening of social protections.

D. The Impact of Trade on Human Rights

The third major category of analyzing trade and human rights looks at the impact of trade policy on human rights. This is a complex area. Critics argue that international trade agreements and investment arrangements are, *prima facie*, having major negative impacts on environment, poverty, health, consumer protection, and workers-rights. But much more empirical study of the actual causal links—direct and indirect—of the impacts of these policies on human rights protection needs to be conducted. It is especially important to distinguish between the impact of international trade liberalization—as opposed to the impact of domestic deregulation which economic strategy has been adopted by most countries in areas such as power, agriculture, commerce, and mining.

It is here where the role of policy assessment is crucial. Assessments should be undertaken *prior to* any new round of negotiations and there should be a backward-looking reflection assessing the impact of previous trade agreements—particularly those reached in the Uruguay Round. This is a very important way of getting parliamentary and civil society groups, including business and trade unions, involved in the whole process. At the WTO level, existing mechanisms also need to be better utilized and enhanced. For example, there is a mechanism at the WTO that every two years member states come up for an appraisal (this is another function of the WTO). This is an appraisal of how they are fulfilling their implementation obligations under WTO rules. This mechanism is called the Trade Policy Review Mechanism. It is time for NGOs to develop a strategy to influence its development and application. One could, for example, suggest an expansion of the criteria of the trade policy review mechanism to include social and environmental criteria, and for the assessment process to be informed by an overarching human rights framework.

Another means of assessing impact is to encourage groups to compile *shadow reports* in the way that some NGOs do at many international UN conferences. For example, NGOs could do a *shadow* country report focusing on the impact of trade agreements on local communities. This kind of *shadow report* would be very valuable when the country in question comes up for its WTO assessment and could contribute to the general democratization of trade policy-making.

The challenge is how we can develop an equitable, international rules-based system that works in favor of social and environmental objectives, and is guided by human rights values and principles, rather than the naked power-based system that seems to exist at present. Is this really too much to ask? Many critics of the WTO argue that *yes, it is just too much to ask, we're not going to see the system change.* There are, however, a number of interesting proposals on institutional reform in the pipeline, and on reform of both the process and the substance of the WTO and related trade issues that NGOs can help push.

An interesting recent development has been the involvement of human rights bodies in the trade policy debate. This is something quite new and happened in part due to activist friends and colleagues in Geneva right before the Seattle ministerial conference of the WTO. They led to a decision taken by the Committee for Economic, Social and Cultural Rights—one of the preeminent UN human rights bodies and the main monitoring body for the International Covenant on Economic, Social and Cultural Rights—to issue a resolution on human rights and trade to the WTO prior to the negotiations in Seattle. The gist of the resolution was: "WTO, please remember that international trade regimes are not exempt from the obligations that bind member states under international human rights law. Please do not do anything in your upcoming current negotiations that will undermine the abilities of WTO member states to fulfill their duties under international human rights conventions." In addition the Committee asked for human rights assessments of existing WTO agreements. This is quite path-breaking stuff.

To conclude, we need a much better informed public debate on the role of bodies such as the WTO. And, perhaps more importantly, a more informed debate on the role of our national elected bodies in setting and assessing the WTO agenda, to ensure that it is informed by public priorities and not controlled only by commercial interests.

8 Protecting the Human Rights Principle in a Globalizing Economy

FRANK J. GARCIA

Introduction

This chapter considers the impact that economic globalization may have on the effectiveness of international human rights law. While globalization of the market economy presents in some respects a unique opportunity for human rights law,[1] such globalization may also threaten the continued effectiveness of human rights law, just as the rise of the market economy itself has been blamed for leading to conditions requiring the formal development of human rights law.[2] Globalization's regulatory framework– international trade law—operates according to a view of human nature, human values, and moral decision-making fundamentally at odds with the underpinnings of international human rights law. If further globalization entails the continued ascendency of this regulatory framework, then the effectiveness of many human rights measures will depend upon the decisions of a regulatory system that, by its nature and operation, cannot properly take into account the core commitment of modern human rights law: that positive human rights are moral entitlements that ground political and legal claims of special force,[3] rights that must be morally and legally prior to society and the state.[4] This is the "human rights principle" to which this Article refers, and it is this principle that is at stake when human rights laws conflict with economic values and trade laws in the new tribunals of globalization, in particular the World Trade Organization's (WTO) dispute settlement mechanism.[5]

This chapter therefore analyzes the effects of market globalization on human rights law as a normative conflict in WTO dispute resolution.[6]

Implicit in this approach is the view that normative conflicts within or between regulatory structures are problems of justice.[7] In other words, the legal and institutional mechanisms created to facilitate and respond to market globalization, and the legal and institutional mechanisms created to define and protect human rights, both involve public order decisions as to the allocation of social benefits and burdens, and the correction of improper gain.[8] The fundamental normative goal of every such public order decision is justice, which is to say that such decisions are to be made in accordance with, and their outcomes must reflect, our basic moral and political principles.[9]

International problems of justice such as the market-globalization-human rights conflict present unique difficulties. They reflect a central feature, if not defect, of the international governance system: the pursuit of global justice is splintered into a myriad of treaties and institutions, in this case into two distinct regimes, one concerned with economic justice (e.g. the WTO) and one with human dignity (e.g. the international human rights system). Therefore, the attainment of comprehensive global justice must include an inquiry into how market globalization affects human rights law, in particular how the regulatory infrastructure of globalization enhances, or interferes with, the contributions of international human rights law. The conflicts engendered by this bifurcation, particularly in view of the preeminence of international trade law,[10] must be addressed in order that we may avoid undoing with the tools of economic justice what we have accomplished with the tools of rights-based justice.

This chapter first discusses the normative conflict underlying globalization/human rights disputes, which reflects the conflict between consequentialist and deontological forms of moral decision-making and justification. This chapter then turns to an analysis of the disposition of globalization/human rights disputes in the WTO, illustrating how the trade-oriented nature of such an institution, coupled with the underlying normative conflict in such disputes, work to disadvantage in that forum certain domestic laws based on human rights claims. Finally, some suggestions are offered as to how WTO doctrine could be amended or interpreted so as to resolve trade-human rights disputes in a manner which respects the human rights principle.

Regulatory Globalization: Utility over Rights

An increasingly globalized economy has brought many new aspects of global economic life into the jurisdiction of trade law and trade institutions, which in turn has facilitated the further globalization of the marketplace. Because of this globalization, however, trade law is now a more complicated business. Institutions created to adjudicate trade disputes are increasingly being asked to resolve non-trade issues and values as well. Trade law now impacts more and more areas of traditional domestic concern, such as environmental protection,[11] labor and employment standards,[12] and cultural identity.[13] The degree to which trade law and institutions are capable of adequately taking into account other non-trade interests and values at the point of conflict, will determine the effect of regulatory globalization on the viability and vigor of human rights law in a global market.

A.   *The Normative Conflict Between International Trade Law and Human Rights Law*

International human rights law and international trade law each have an important role in the implementation of a just global order. Yet the principal normative foundations of each regime are, if not incompatible, then at least in fundamental tension. While economics, which considers resource decision-making, will play a critical role in trade law under *any* theory, other disciplines and models should unquestionably play a role in trade policy analysis involving non-trade values.

1. The Normative Underpinnings of Trade Law

The dominant normative account of trade law is an economic one, which Jeffrey Dunoff has termed the "Efficiency Model." In the Efficiency Model, trade law is *exclusively* concerned with the twin values of economic efficiency and welfare.[14] The goal of trade law is to improve the economic well-being of human beings through the facilitation of efficient exchanges.[15] However, this approach has several important implications for the viability of human rights law within a trade-based regulatory regime.

First, there is a marked tendency for other values besides efficiency and welfare to be viewed as outside the scope of trade law, and even inimical to its purposes.[16] From the viewpoint of Efficiency Model adherents, non-trade values complicate the trade law system with what are at best extraneous concerns such as human rights or environmental protection[17] or at worst simply disguised protectionism.[18] By adopting this stance, Efficiency Model adherents fail to recognize that, while efficiency and welfare are undeniably important values in trade, their pursuit is only a part of an overarching effort to establish a just global order. Because trade institutions adjudicate trade decisions that have serious non-trade effects, non-trade values properly should be considered in trade law decisions.[19]

Were non-trade values to be considered, the economic analysis and methodology that dominate trade institutions will disadvantage such values. Economics adopts a *method* of moral reasoning that is fundamentally at odds with the dominant moral reasoning underlying human rights law. Economic moral reasoning is consequentialist in nature, focusing on outcomes, not on procedures or acts in themselves.[20] Consequentialism is the term for ethical theories that evaluate the rightness or wrongness of an act solely in terms of its consequences.[21] On this view, an act will be judged morally right if its consequences are better than those of any alternative acts.[22] The dominant consequential account of trade law is utilitarianism,[23] which in its classical form determines the morality of an act according to its consequences for the aggregate of individual utility.[24] Modern utilitarianism and the economists who deploy it define utility in terms of preference satisfaction,[25] or more generally as a form of welfarism, in which the sum or average of resulting individual welfare levels determines the correctness of an act, principle or policy.[26]

Thus from a normative perspective, the Efficiency Model asserts explicitly or implicitly the utilitarian argument that free trade is good *because of its consequences*, namely the maximization of aggregate individual welfare from efficiency gains and the operation of comparative advantage.[27] Trade maximizes welfare for many reasons, including lower prices, increased consumer choice, increased employment, enhanced economies of scale, specialization, increased competition and the accelerated diffusion of the fruits of innovation.[28]

Therefore, not surprisingly, arguments in favor of trade liberalization over measures justified by non-trade values will be expressed in utilitarian terms.[29] For example, embargoes based on moral or national security grounds may be attacked on the utilitarian ground that it may be in a nation's best interest to trade with its enemies, because doing so will have more good effects than bad in the economic sense.[30] Trade restrictions justified on environmental grounds may encounter arguments in favor of a utilitarian evaluation of their merits, leading to a preference for market-oriented compromises with trade values.[31] In each case, the relative trade costs and regulatory benefits of a particular law or policy are weighed, and the best policy is determined to be that which, on balance, has the least trade cost or promises the greatest trade benefit, without sufficient regard to the non-trade reasons for the alternative.

2. The Normative Underpinnings of Human Rights Law

In contrast, human rights law is built on a fundamentally different approach to human nature and moral reasoning, which puts it in tension with the normative underpinnings of trade law. The human rights movement has undertaken to establish through human rights law a different aspect of a just global order than that undertaken in trade law, namely the protection of human dignity.[32]

At the core of the concept of human rights is the notion of a transcendental standard of justice by which particular acts of the state can be judged.[33] The dominant contemporary normative justification of human rights law is some variety of Western liberalism.[34] International human rights law is essentially rooted in the liberal commitment to the equal moral worth of each individual, regardless of their utility,[35] and human rights themselves embody the minimum standards of treatment necessary in view of this equal moral worth. Moreover, human rights, the very concept of a right, and the closely associated natural rights tradition,[36] are all linked to a particular strand of liberalism, the non-utilitarian liberalism[37] of Locke[38] and Kant,[39] which provides the normative basis for the rights set out in the various UN instruments.[40]

This model inevitably affects the human rights approach to human nature and moral decision-making, and distinguishes it from a utilitarian economic approach. The *homo economicus* model of human beings presupposed in trade law places little emphasis on the precise end of human activity, assuming it to be individual well-being through the satisfaction of individually determined preferences.[41] In contrast, the human rights view of human nature is obsessed with ends, in particular with the status of the human person as an end in themselves,[42] whose intrinsic dignity and worth are not matters of individual preference or utility, but matters of moral duty and principle.[43]

The normative arguments advanced for the protection of human rights are deontological: they focus on principles about how people are to be treated, regardless of the consequences.[44] Deontological moral reasoning determines an act's rightness by the nature of the act itself, specifically whether it is in accord with a specified moral principle, regardless of the act's consequences. In this sense, rights are things that are valued in themselves, and not for their consequences.[45] For example, the widely-recognized international prohibition against torture[46] is justified on the ground that torture is wrong as a direct violation of human dignity, *despite* its utility, *despite* the fact that it might lead to information of value to the state, or deter conduct that threatens the state.[47] This is in direct contrast to the consequential form of moral reasoning that predominates in trade and in economics generally, and that could theoretically determine torture, slavery and other human rights violations to be economically advantageous or justifiable, and hence appropriate.

The deontological nature of human rights principles also has important implications for situations in which competing claims or values are at stake. Human dignity and moral worth, which are at the core of human rights, are expressed in absolute terms: human beings have a dignity and worth that should not be compromised by competing consequential justifications. Hence human rights claims "ordinarily trump utility, social policy, and other moral or political grounds for action."[48] A human rights-based claim should therefore take priority over counterclaims based in utility, and other consequentialist appeals.[49] Where human rights claims are in conflict with other sorts of claims, human rights theory dictates that human rights claims receive a very high, if not trumping, value in such disputes.

3. *International Trade Law and Human Rights: Normative Approaches in Conflict*

What we find, then, when we examine international trade law and international human rights law, are two attempts to identify and implement the obligations that a broadly liberal theory of justice place on us in international relationships. We find the international trade law system attempting to establish a liberal view of the *Right Order* with regard to economic well-being, along utilitarian lines. We find the international human rights system attempting to establish a liberal view of the *Right Order* with regard to human dignity and worth, along deontological lines. And we find that these two powerful mechanisms for global justice are brought into conflict through the regulation of globalization through economic law and institutions.

At the practical level, the conflict between trade law and human rights law is not, at first glance, an obvious one. Short of a trade treaty providing directly for trade in the products of prison or slave labor,[50] it is hard to imagine a direct conflict between trade law and core human rights, for example, rights involving life, liberty and the security of one's person.[51] Moreover, if one considers human rights more broadly to include property rights and the rule of law,[52] it would appear that in many cases trade law is in fact working in favor of human rights, as for example when investment and intellectual property protection and increased transparency are negotiated as part of a trade agreement.

Rather, one is more likely to encounter a conflict between international trade law and measures taken at the *national* level *to protect* human rights, usually by imposing some form of economic sanction on a state violating human rights. When instituted between parties of a trade-liberalizing treaty such as the GATT, such measures may constitute unlawful trade restrictions. Given the ascendancy of international economic law and its institutions, a challenge of this restriction will likely be brought in a trade forum, such as the WTO dispute settlement process. But here, in a utilitarian-oriented international trade institution, the normative conflict outlined above will result in the deontologically—justified human rights measure being challenged along utilitarian lines.

At the meta-ethical level, there is reason for concern that in the contest suggested above, it is the human rights law that will lose. The deontological morality underlying human rights law has traditionally been recognized as difficult to reconcile with the utilitarian and other consequentialist forms of moral reasoning predominating in trade law.[53] The deontological nature of human rights renders it difficult for human rights law to operate successfully within a consequentialist system like trade law, because in the hypothetical conflict identified above, the trade institution will follow its own normative approach, which commits it to sacrificing human rights protection when doing so would yield a greater aggregate satisfaction of human preferences. Utilitarian theory in fact *presupposes* that determinations of human worth will involve the trading-off of one life against another.[54] To a pure act-utilitarian,[55] the fact that a particular trade policy or trade decision undercuts protection of a human right is of no consequence in itself,[56] and rule-utilitarianism is not an improvement in this respect.[57] Even if human rights are justified on rule-utilitarian grounds as useful for increasing utility, there is always the possibility that human rights as a utilitarian-based set of rules will be cast off if the utility calculus changes.[58] This must be so because utilitarianism is committed to ignoring natural human rights, which people hold simply by virtue of their status as persons.[59]

In contrast, human rights law refuses such tradeoffs. Because human rights are privileged over other competing claims, such claims, which might overcome human rights in a utilitarian context, are trumped. Human rights by their very nature and justification are not subject to compromise in the pursuit of good consequences, but it is precisely such compromises that international economic law excels in. For this reason,[60] a utilitarian approach to trade cannot adequately incorporate human rights concerns based on deontologically justified rights.[61] Consequentialist "trade-off" approaches to trade and human rights conflicts are in their very method of analysis biased against human rights and place human rights at risk because they are unwilling to accord human rights claims the privilege that the human rights principle requires.[62] Hausman and McPherson point out that strictly deontological approaches to rights are disturbing to contemporary economists,[63] precisely because such approaches view rights as absolutely inviolable, essentially foreclosing the analysis that economists engage in when evaluating a policy or course of conduct. Yet this absolute quality that economists find disturbing about rights is what human rights advocates find essential.

B.   Trade-based Decisions on Trade/Human Rights Conflicts: Doctrinal Approaches to Normative Conflicts

The theoretical risk posed to human rights law from the vying approaches to moral decision-making adopted by trade law and human rights law is borne out at the doctrinal level in the WTO dispute settlement system, which resolves conflicts between trade and non-trade values. Returning to the hypothetical first posed above–a domestic trade-restrictive measure adopted at the national level against an egregious rights-violating state–this chapter now turns to the trade law analysis of such a measure. Concrete examples of such measures might include a national-level decision to suspend GATT-obligated MFN treatment as a response to particular human rights violations,[64] the imposition by a sub-federal unit of a government procurement ban as a response to human rights violations,[65] or the imposition of a trade ban on the products of indentured child labor, either unilaterally[66] or perhaps in response to a future ILO convention prohibiting such practices.[67] The common denominator in all of these cases is a domestic trade sanction against foreign states violating human rights, as a mechanism to both punish the state and to encourage compliance with international human rights law.

1. Human Rights Trade Sanctions in the WTO

In any of these cases, the target state would challenge such action in a WTO dispute settlement proceeding, assuming all states-parties are WTO Member States. The most likely basis for such a challenge would be that the measure violates the most-favored-nation and national treatment rules contained in GATT Articles I and III. The challenged measure would be determined a *prima facie* Article I violation because the like products from other WTO Member States, which are not targets, are not subject to the trade restriction.[68] The measure is also likely to be determined a *prima facie* Article III violation because domestic like-products are also not subject to the same trade restriction.[69] Therefore, the sanctioning state must find a GATT-authorized exception applicable in such cases, or the measure will be found to nullify or impair the target state's expected trade benefits, resulting in WTO-authorized sanctions against the sanctioning state itself if it fails to amend or withdraw the measure.

As the GATT treaty stands today, there is no single, clearly-applicable exception for such a human rights-oriented measure. There are, however, several exceptions that might apply if interpreted with a human rights slant. One possible avenue is that the sanctioning state would seek the shelter of the national security exception in Article XXI, which permits a state to unilaterally enact trade-restrictive measures "necessary for the protection of its essential security interests" during a time of "emergency in international relations."[70] However, this is a controversial provision that has not been interpreted to extend to human rights.[71]

A more likely candidate is Article XX, whose exceptions are intended to permit GATT violations, including Articles I and III violations, in pursuit of several categories of non-trade policy goals.[72] Three Article XX exceptions in particular may be relevant in connection with human rights measures: Article XX(a) permits measures "*necessary* to protect public morals."[73] Article XX(b) permits measures "*necessary* to protect human, animal or plant life or health."[74] Finally, Article XX(e) permits measures "relating to the products of prison labour."[75] The availability of each of these exceptions is subject to difficult interpretive questions.

While the prison labor exception presents the clearest case of a human rights-based exception, it is least likely to serve in this case because it is so clearly drafted to refer to a single category of products, those produced by prison labor.[76] The public morality exception should apply in at least a subset of human rights-related claims,[77] but its broader applicability turns on whether the provision can be interpreted to encompass a wide range of human rights concerns beyond traditional "public morals" issues.[78] Interpreting Article XX(b) to include human rights violations as threats to "human . . . life or health," would run counter to existing, albeit limited, GATT jurisprudence on this issue.[79] Finally, availability of both the public morals and human life and health exceptions depends upon whether Articles XX(a) and XX(b) would be interpreted as available for "outward-oriented" measures designed to influence the human rights policies of another jurisdiction,[80] which existing GATT jurisprudence calls into question.[81]

If these interpretive issues could be resolved so as to bring human rights-based domestic measures within the ambit of either Article XX (a) or (b), then adjudication of the GATT claim would ultimately rest on the application of the "necessity" test required by the language of both articles.[82] As the test is applied, the WTO panel would rule that the disputed measure was not in fact necessary, and therefore a GATT violation, if it were to find that another less trade-restrictive measure was "reasonably available."[83] In so conditioning the availability of these Article XX exceptions, and therefore any human rights-favorable resolution of this conflict, on the necessity test, the GATT is employing a "trade-off" device, which allows it to compare the trade burden of a given measure against its intended non-trade regulatory benefit.[84]

2. Trade-off Mechanisms in Trade Linkage Disputes

As a preliminary matter, it should be noted that trade-off devices have as a defining feature of the willingness to juxtapose, and in many cases to commensurate between, trade values on the one hand and non-trade values on the other. Such an approach is consistent with the consequentialist approach taken by most economists and economically-minded analysts to trade matters.[85] It has in fact been said that utilitarianism is preeminently "a theory about trade-offs."[86] It should not be surprising to find such a market-oriented measure in a trade-based dispute settlement mechanism.[87]

In contrast, the very notion of trade-off devices runs counter to the deontological approach to human rights. Normatively, human rights rest on the *incommensurability* of rights, which is alien to utilitarian theories.[88] In human rights terms, one cannot morally trade any amount of human rights impairment in exchange for a greater amount of trade welfare benefit, even if the latter is seen as enhancing or embodying other human rights. While it is foreseeable that a trade-based forum may be legally required to engage in some sort of balancing analysis, weighing the trade costs of protection against the human rights costs of acquiescence, such an analysis might be objected to by human rights advocates at the outset as simply inadequate in view of the absolute moral obligation to enforce human rights regardless of the consequences.[89] On this view, the preeminent mechanism for resolving policy disputes in trade institutions by its very nature defeats the fundamental tenet of human rights law.

In thus failing to distinguish a subset of values the tradeoff of which is not permitted, some may view any trade analysis as already skewed in favor of trade values over human rights values. However, it may nevertheless be inevitable that a trade-off type of analysis will be carried out in the event of regulatory conflicts, at least under the current international governance regime. Some form of balancing is often involved in policy formation: one compares two options in terms of their mutual effects on identified values, and one decides. In particular, where the dispute is not directly between trade law and human rights law, but trade law and domestic measures enacted to *enforce* human rights, it is conceivable that balancing be used in determining the appropriate or most effective *means* towards achieving the human rights goals when there is a trade cost.

Any such approach, however, and in particular the trade-off device actually employed, must be carefully examined and carefully utilized in policy decisions where rights are involved, or the very nature and principle of rights can be violated at the outset. Therefore, it becomes important to evaluate each trade-off device in terms of the degree to which it discriminates against human rights. Trachtman concludes that from a trade perspective certain measures are to be preferred over others, citing in particular the necessity test.[90] It is not surprising, therefore, that from a human rights perspective, a different set of preferences emerges, in fact the opposite one.

3. The WTO Necessity Test as a Trade-off Device

Notwithstanding the argument that some sort of balancing is required in policy-formulation where competing values are at stake, the necessity test is clearly objectionable in human-rights terms as a trade-off device on the ground that it is biased in favor of trade values.[91] In other words, the test evaluates measures favorably precisely insofar as their impact on trade is the least possible, despite the fact that more trade-impacting measures might be more effective in realizing the non-trade value. Not only does this trade-off mechanism fail to recognize the high priority that rights must hold in any policy determination, but the necessity test in fact turns this on its head, and privileges trade values over all other competing values.[92]

To a limited extent the "reasonably available" qualification invites some consideration of the effectiveness of the disputed measure in accomplishing its non-trade regulatory purpose, because any less trade-restrictive measure which forms the basis for invalidation of the chosen measure must be "reasonably available" in view of the state's non-trade regulatory objectives. The extent of such consideration, however, depends entirely on the interpretation of such language, and the application of the qualification, by the GATT panel. In particular, the language clearly does not require specific consideration of the *effectiveness* of alternative measures in achieving their non-trade goals, in the way that similar language in the Sanitary and Phytosanitary Agreement does refer to the level of protection achievable by the alternative measure.[93]

Therefore, it would be consistent with the language of the necessity test as currently interpreted for a GATT panel to find that a measure significantly less effective in achieving the non-trade purpose would nonetheless be identified by the panel as "reasonably available," and therefore serve as the basis for invalidating the chosen measure. Since such a measure was in fact *not* chosen by the sanctioning state, this language would have the effect of substituting the trade forum's opinion of the rationality of alternatives for the opinion of the legislating forum.[94] If one considers that domestic legislatures may, in principle and at least in certain cases, produce legislative outcomes "on the merits," then it is clear that the language of Article XX(a) and (b) invites the questionable substitution by a panel of trade experts, with a built-in bias favoring trade values, of a less effective human rights measure in the place of a more effective, democratically-selected, human rights measure on the basis of the measure's effects on trade.[95]

Protecting Human Rights in the Institutions of the Global Market: Doctrinal Solutions for Normative Conflicts

The resolution of globalization/human rights conflicts in a manner that enhances the effectiveness of human rights law is going to require a mechanism for the recognition within international trade law of the priority which at least certain fundamental human rights must enjoy. In other words, there must be some mechanism for a constitutional level of deference within international trade law toward at least certain elements of international human rights law, such as the core rights involving life, freedom, security and bodily integrity, and the recognition within international trade law of rights-enforcement techniques such as trade sanctions, which make such rights effective, and which cannot be balanced or traded off in international economic law dispute resolution decisions. Where some sort of trade-off is inevitable, there must be clear recognition of the priority that human rights claims must have in any value conflict.

A. *Preempting Conflicts Among Different Sets of Rules*

At the global level, resolution of the trade/human rights conflict is complicated by the defects, from a constitutional viewpoint, of international governance.[96] It is a fundamental feature of the landscape of global social policy in the late 20th century that no one institution has the effective jurisdiction to create and adjudicate norms in all aspects of global social concern.[97] Instead, we find separate treaty regimes and separate institutions, built and justified according to conflicting normative principles, yet both ultimately reflecting critical aspects of a liberal vision for global social life.

As a result, it is likely that norms affecting both human rights and trade will continue to be negotiated in the context of a treaty or treaty-making conference predominantly oriented towards one or the other of these areas of social concern. And it is likely that disputes involving both human rights and trade law will, absent modification of the existing governance mechanism, continue to be resolved in dispute resolution fora that will be constrained by treaty law and institutional paradigm to give priority to one set of concerns over another. Therefore, a natural first solution to consider is whether to create a mechanism to either expand the scope of the WTO to include human rights norms themselves, thus bridging the regulatory chasm, or concede the institutional disjunction and limit the jurisdiction of trade institutions over human rights measures.

1. Include Human Rights Rules in Trade Agreements

It has been suggested that one approach would be the incorporation of certain human rights norms into the WTO agreements.[98] Modifying the WTO to include human rights is more attractive than adding trade issues to the scope of existing human rights treaties and institutions, since the WTO has an effective enforcement system and significant international prestige. Moreover, the GATT treaty does recognize to a certain extent certain important social policy concerns based in values other than trade.[99] Stirling suggests adding to that foundation by interpreting Article XX(e) as a broad human rights exception,[100] modifying the WTO agreements to add a core list of recognized human rights,[101] and creating a specialized human rights body within the structural framework of the WTO, with authority to hear human rights related complaints and to impose trade sanctions.[102]

This approach has the benefit of reversing the current trend of institutional specialization that complicates the trade-human rights and other trade linkage issues. However, there does not appear to be the requisite degree of political support that such a sweeping overhaul would require. In fact, the trend seems in the opposite direction, as the majority of the world's trading nations have decided that the WTO is not the appropriate institution to articulate human rights norms, leaving that to other specialized agencies such as the ILO.[103]

2. Limiting Trade Jurisdiction over Human Rights Measures

Alternatively, the jurisdiction of the WTO could be limited such that the legitimacy of any human rights-related trade actions would not be adjudicated in the WTO.[104] The broadest across-the-board restriction on the WTO's jurisdiction over human rights measures would be a general exception added to either the GATT, the WTO Charter or the WTO Dispute Settlement Understanding, excluding from WTO review national measures taken in response to violations of human rights.[105] An alternative approach, more limited in scope, would defer only to measures taken pursuant to human rights treaties involving products that themselves embody or are the fruits of human rights violations, such as pornography and the products of indentured child labor; or taken pursuant to any human rights treaties drafted to expressly provide for the use of economic sanctions in response to human rights violations.[106]

This approach could be implemented through inclusion of a pure hierarchy of norms provision, ensuring that in the event of a conflict between a trade measure and a measure taken pursuant to an obligation under such an enumerated treaty, the obligations of that treaty should prevail. A "pure" hierarchy of norms provision does not incorporate a trade-off mechanism requiring panel review, in contrast to a hierarchy of norms provision, such as NAFTA's for example, which imposes a reviewable necessity test on measures taken pursuant to the listed environmental treaties.[107] Otherwise, human rights-based measures would not really be excluded from WTO review, but still be subject to adjudication according to the chosen of trade-off mechanism.[108] Alternatively, an exception for human rights measures could be added to the GATT, but drafted along the lines of the national security exception in Article XXI, vesting in the sanctioning state some form of unilateral discretion in the face of human rights violations, rather than existing Article XX exceptions, which incorporate some form of trade-off mechanism presupposing panel review. In either case, the WTO would be required to recognize the legitimacy of sanctions imposed within the constraints of such a treaty, and such measures would not have to undergo the necessity test as applied through the Article XX exceptions.[109]

There are several benefits to adopting either of these variants. First, this approach would represent the decision by the international community at the *political* or legislative level[110] that trade-related human rights measures are appropriate despite their potentially adverse trade effects. Second, either amendment eliminates the interpretive problems attendant to including human rights measures within the scope of existing exceptions.[111] Third, in its Article XXI-like form, such an exception would grant the broadest possible scope for state action, including both economic measures taken pursuant to a human rights treaty authorizing sanction, and economic measures taken unilaterally by a state in response to violations of rights that, while they are the subject of binding international custom or treaty law, are not expressly contained within instruments authorizing economic sanctions. In its narrower, treaty-based form, such an amendment would still grant a very high level of deference to at least treaty-based human rights measures.

In granting to human rights measures an automatic exclusion from review according to trade values and trade principles, such a general exception would be quite congenial to the philosophic approach of the human rights movement, which seeks recognition of the priority of human rights claims.[112] However, the very breadth of such an approach, coupled with its preference for human rights over trade values, would make such an amendment difficult to enact in the face of concerted opposition from WTO Member States committed to a higher priority for trade values. Moreover, an Article XXI approach, or a pure hierarchy of norms, would be unpopular for its very non-justiciability, already a concern with the existing Article XXI exception. This non-justiciability would be resisted on formal grounds, in view of the strong preference in the WTO for rule-based adjudicative dispute resolution, and by Member States reluctant to open themselves to such broad un-reviewable use of economic sanctions. Finally, such an approach would raise quite legitimate concerns over the invitation to protectionist abuse that such a blanket exception would invite.[113]

B. Rights-deferential Trade-off Mechanisms Where Conflicts Must Arise

Absent the implementation of a preclusive approach such as those discussed above, one must then face the existing problem of how to adjudicate trade disputes involving human rights, where measures based on human rights norms are at issue within a trade forum that is treaty-bound to consider only trade-based factors. The remainder of this section will focus on ways to avoid or minimize such conflicts as they might arise in trade dispute settlement fora, attempting to reconcile trade and human rights claims in a way that more accurately reflects the preeminent status that human rights claims must be afforded in policy disputes. This may be accomplished by altering the text of trade obligations or the interpretation of present WTO language.

1. Amending the GATT to Apply a Different Trade-off Mechanism

To the extent that trade-human rights conflicts are going to be adjudicated within trade institutions, it becomes critical to revise the trade-off mechanisms that will be applied in trade dispute resolution mechanisms to better take into account human rights law and principles, while permitting the trade panel to identify and rule against disguised protectionism.

The national treatment rule is not inherently inimical to human rights, because it merely requires a level of consistency between foreign and domestic treatment of goods or producers with regard to any legislation, including one addressing human rights violations.[114] If domestic and foreign products are banned equally, then there is no national treatment violation, and the inquiry should stop there. But current WTO language, in focusing on the physical product, disallows measures that are aimed at rights-oppressive practices, which in many cases are not connected to "production," let alone the product.[115]   Therefore, national treatment analysis should be modified to focus on the sanctioned conduct and not on the products that are the targets of the sanctions.[116] Under this analysis, the key issue would be if the conduct that forms the basis of the sanction is also prohibited domestically.[117]

Alternatively, the current necessity test imposed by Articles XX(a) and (b) should be modified to require only "rationality." If there is a rational, means-end relationship between the sanction and the targeted conduct, the inquiry should stop there.[118] A trade sanction imposed against a vital export of the abusive country, with conditions for its removal clearly tied to changes in human rights practices, should satisfy such a test.

If employing a "rationality" test poses too much of a threat of disguised discrimination, a more trade-deferential form of trade-off device such as proportionality would be a compromise. The proportionality test requires that the trade cost be proportionate with reference to the non-trade benefits.[119] This test might still be applied in a way that favors trade values, in that the trade cost of rights-protective measures might appear disproportionate to trade policy experts disinclined to recognize the priority of the human rights principle. Nevertheless, a proportionality standard is flexible enough to protect human rights measures if the forum recognizes the priority of human rights to a sufficient degree that the resulting trade burden would be considered appropriate. But this depends entirely on the trade forum's characterization of the importance of the value being protected by the legislation in conflict.

2. Modifying the Necessity Test through Judicial Interpretation

The political factors attendant to WTO amendment and the strong, if not overwhelming, pro-trade bias of the institution, may preclude any sort of amendment substituting a potentially more human-rights deferential trade-off mechanism, leaving the necessity test in place. If some sort of necessity test must perforce be utilized, its interpretation should be modified to grant increased deference to human rights values. One approach would be to simply introduce such modifications into the jurisprudence of Article XX through a decision by the WTO Appellate Body. Although this is less formally protective than an explicit amendment of the language, it is procedurally more readily attainable.[120] A logical place to consider an interpretive amendment would be in the application of the existing "reasonably available" qualification.   A rights-protective interpretation would stipulate that, in order for the existence of a less trade restrictive alternative to invalidate a human rights measure, it must be shown that the less restrictive alternative is *equally effective* in terms of its impact on the human rights abuse in question. So interpreted, the WTO necessity test would resemble the necessity test embodied in the NAFTA's hierarchy of norms provision.[121]

Alternatively, a somewhat less rights-protective approach would conform the necessity test in Article XX to the one established in the WTO Sanitary and Phytosanitary (SPS) Agreement. The SPS Agreement requires that a less-restrictive measure be both "significantly" less restrictive, and eligible to disqualify the challenged measure only if it meets the "appropriate" level of protection.[122] This is clearly not as deferential as the NAFTA test, since an "appropriate" level may be somewhat lower than the "equally effective" level NAFTA requires. However, it is still an improvement over the necessity test as currently interpreted.

Conclusion

Conflicts between international human rights and the regulatory infrastructure of globalization must be analyzed as justice questions. In practice this means paying attention to the decision-making process employed in such conflicts, in that it reflects a process of moral reasoning about issues of justice, and is not simply an exercise in identifying trade-liberalizing and trade-restrictive practices. This Article has argued that such an examination reveals a normative conflict underlying the trade/human rights doctrinal conflict, which in trade fora threatens the effectiveness of human rights. Unless the WTO approach to trade/human rights conflicts is modified as suggested, globalization could mean the triumph of utilitarian approaches to values over deontological ones, and therefore the triumph of trade over human rights. This is not a victory for free trade, but a defeat for our efforts to establish a just global order.

Notes

© Frank J. Garcia and Ashgate Publishing Company 2001. Frank J. Garcia is an associate professor of international and comparative law as the Boston College Law School. This paper is an abridged, revised and updated adaptation of an earlier article published in the Brooklyn Journal of International Law at 25 BROOK. J. INT'L L. 51 (1999), and appears here with the permission of that journal. The author would like to acknowledge the substantial contribution of his research assistant Benjamin James Stevenson in preparing this adaptation.

1   Globalization has the potential to promote broad, if not universal, international consensus on the basic principles of Western liberalism: free markets, democratic government, and human rights. *See* Alex Y. Seita, *Globalization and the Convergence of Values*, 30 CORNELL INT'L L.J. 429, 431 (1997). Moreover, globalization can contribute directly to the enjoyment of economic rights, due to the relationship between

economic activity and the human freedom and dignity we express in our decisions as producers and consumers. Indirectly, globalization may enhance the effectiveness of human rights law by contributing to the attainment of the economic preconditions for socioeconomic rights through the significant increases in global welfare, which trade theory predicts should follow such globalization. Furthermore, globalization can contribute to the enforcement of human rights, through the effects that increased contact between the citizens of oppressive regimes and the citizens and products of rights-protective regimes may have on the continuing viability of oppressive regimes. Finally, participation in the market itself may increase domestic pressure for increased political and social rights.

2   "Modern markets also created a whole new range of threats to human dignity and thus were one of the principal sources of the need and demand for human rights." JACK DONNELLY, UNIVERSAL HUMAN RIGHTS IN THEORY AND PRACTICE 64 (1989). It may be, for example, that the globalization of markets erodes the social and normative preconditions for human rights protection, as well as for the market itself. Hausman and McPherson point out that core trade and economic values such as economic efficiency depend upon ethical values that paradoxically may be undermined by market economies. *See* Daniel M. Hausman and Michael S. McPherson, *Taking Ethics Seriously: Economics and Contemporary Moral Philosophy,* 31 J. ECON. LITERATURE 671 (1993). Hausman and McPherson list honesty, trust, and goodwill as three values critical to the efficient function of markets, which may in fact be undermined by appeals to rational self-interest in the economies, at least in certain forms. *See id.* at 673.

3   *See* DONNELLY, *supra* note 2, at 9.

4   *See id.* at 70.

5   Understanding on Rules and Procedures Governing the Settlement of Disputes, Dec. 15, 1993, Final Act Embodying the Results of the Uruguay Round of Multilateral Trade Negotiations, 33 I.L.M. 112 (1994) [hereinafter DSU]. *See generally* Ernst-Ulrich Petersmann, *The Dispute Settlement System of the World Trade Organization and the Evolution of the GATT Dispute Settlement System Since 1948,* 31 COMMON MKT. L. REV. 1157 (1994) (reviewing the structure and function of the WTO dispute settlement process).

6   Globalization has a recognized normative aspect. *See* Alex Y. Seita, *Globalization and the Convergence of Values, supra* n. 1 (stating "globalization is an important source of common economic and political values for humanity"); Jost Delbrück, *Globalization of Law, Politics, and Markets—Implications for Domestic Law—A European Perspective,* 1 IND. J. GLOBAL LEGAL STUD. 9, 11 (1993) (noting the term globalization itself is often used as a normative term, in that it presupposes a value judgment "that the common good is to be served by measures that are to be subsumed under the notion of globalization"). In particular, the conflicts that globalization can engender between trade law and other bodies of law, such as environmental law and labor law are inescapably normative. *See* Philip M. Nichols, *Trade Without Values,* 90 Nw. U. L. REV. 658, 672-73, 680 (1996). On the applicability of normative theory to international relations, *see* CHARLES R. BEITZ, POLITICAL THEORY AND INTERNATIONAL RELATIONS 5 (1979); STANLEY HOFFMANN, DUTIES BEYOND BORDERS: ON THE LIMITS AND POSSIBILITIES OF ETHICAL INTERNATIONAL POLITICS 1 (1981); Anthony D'Amato, *International Law and Rawls' Theory of Justice,* 5 DENV. J. INT'L L. AND POL'Y 525, 525 (1975); Alfred P. Rubin, *Political Theory and International Relations,* 47 U. CHI. L. REV. 403 (1980) (reviewing BEITZ 1979).

7   I outline the arguments in favor of this view in an earlier essay, which is itself drawn from a larger work in progress on the problem of justice in contemporary international economic law. Frank J. Garcia, *Trade and Justice: Linking the Trade Linkage Debates*, 19 U. PA. J. INT'L ECON. L. 391, 395-406 (1998).

8   This is Aristotle's classic subdivision of Plato's general concept of justice as Right Order into its main constituent parts, which distinction continues in influence to the present day. *See* ARISTOTLE, NICHOMACHEAN ETHICS, bk. V., chs. 2, 4, *in* INTRODUCTION TO ARISTOTLE 400, 404-07 (Richard McKeon ed., 1947); Alan Ryan, *Introduction, in* JUSTICE 1, 9 (Alan Ryan ed., 1993) (citing the continuing influence of this categorization).

9   *See* Garcia, *supra* note 7, at 395-96.

10   *See, e.g.,* Joel P. Trachtman, *The International Economic Law Revolution*, 17 U. PA. J. INT'L ECON. L. 33, 35-36 (1996).

11   *See, e.g.,* World Trade Organization Appellate Body Report on United States—Import Prohibition of Certain Shrimp and Shrimp Products, WT/DS58/AB/R, *available in* 1998 WL 720123 [hereinafter Shrimp Case]; Robert Howse, *The Turtles Panel: Another Environmental Disaster in Geneva*, 32 J. WORLD TRADE 73 (1998).

12   *See* World Trade Organization, *Singapore Ministerial Declaration*, WTO Doc. WT/MIN(96)/DEC/W, Dec. 13, 1996, 36 I.L.M. 218 (1996) [hereinafter *Singapore Declaration*] (reviewing WTO position on trade and international labor standards); Virginia Leary, *Workers' Rights and International Trade: The Social Clause (GATT, ILO, NAFTA, U.S. Laws)*, *in* 2 FAIR TRADE AND HARMONIZATION: PREREQUISITES FOR FAIR TRADE? 175 (Jagdish Bhagwati and Robert E. Hudec eds., 1996).

13   *See* World Trade Organization Appellate Body Report on Canada-Certain Measures Concerning Periodicals, WT/DS31/AB/R, *available in* 1997 WL 398913; W. Ming Shao, *Is There No Business Like Show Business?   Free Trade and Cultural Protectionism*, 20 Yale J. INT'L. 105, 105 (1995)

14   *See* Jeffrey L. Dunoff, *Rethinking International Trade*, 19 U. PA. J. INT'L ECON. L. 347, 349-50 (1998). *See also* G. Richard Shell, *Trade Legalism and International Relations Theory*, 44 DUKE L.J. 829, 877-85 (1995) (discussing what Shell calls the "Efficient Market Model" of trade law).

15   *See, e.g.,* DAVID RICARDO, PRINCIPLES OF POLITICAL ECONOMY AND TAXATION 93 (3d ed. 1996).
     Under a system of perfectly free commerce, each country naturally devotes its capital and labor to such employments as are most beneficial to each.   This pursuit of individual advantage is admirably connected with the universal good of the whole.   By stimulating industry, by rewarding ingenuity, and by using most efficaciously the peculiar powers bestowed by nature, it distributes labor most effectively and most economically: while by increasing the general mass of productions, it diffuses general benefit and binds together, by common ties of interest and intercourse, the universal society of nations throughout the civilized world.
     Id.; JOHN H. JACKSON, THE WORLD TRADING SYSTEM: LAW AND POLICY OF INTERNATIONAL ECONOMIC RELATIONS 8-9 (2d ed. 1989) (arguing that efficiency-based increases in general welfare are the preeminent goal of trade law).

16   *See* Nichols, *supra* note 6, at 700 ("That the trade regime gives primacy to trade is evidenced throughout the history of GATT dispute settlement, as well as in the writings of officials and scholars closely allied with the General Agreement and the nascent World Trade Organization").

17   *See* Steve Charnovitz, *The World Trade Organization and Social Issues*, 28 J. WORLD TRADE 17, 23 (1994) [hereinafter Charnovitz, *Social Issues*] (citing objections by

GATT and WTO members to efforts in 1991 and 1994 to begin work on labor and environment issues on the basis that such issues were not trade issues); Robert E. Hudec, *GATT Legal Restraints on the Use of Trade Measures Against Foreign Environmental Practices, in* 2 FAIR TRADE AND HARMONIZATION: PREREQUISITES FOR FAIR TRADE?, 95, 108 (arguing that GATT has a good reason to be skeptical of linkage claims).

18 *See* Charnovitz, *Social Issues, supra* note 17, at 32 (quoting then-GATT Director General, Peter Sutherland: "[s]implistic demands for drastic trade remedies against so-called eco-dumping or social dumping sometimes bear a striking similarity to more conventional forms of protectionist rhetoric . . . .").

19 *See* Robert Howse and Michael J. Trebilcock, *The Fair Trade-Free Trade Debate: Trade, Labor and the Environment, in* ECONOMIC DIMENSIONS IN INTERNATIONAL LAW (Jagdeep S. Bhandari and Alan O. Sykes eds., 1997) (observing that "[a] visceral distrust of any or all demands for trade restrictions has impeded a careful analysis of the kinds of normative claims at issue and has allowed fair traders to characterize free traders as moral philistines").

20 As Hausman and McPherson put it, "[t]he standard definition of a social optimum compares social alternatives exclusively in terms of the goodness of their outcomes (rather than the rightness of their procedures), and identifies the goodness of outcomes with satisfaction of individual preferences." Hausman and McPherson, *supra* note 2 at 687.

21 For a good introduction to consequentialism in general, *see* G.E.M. Anscombe, *Modern Moral Philosophy*, 33 PHIL. 1 (1958); Germain Grisez, *Against Consequentialism*, 23 AM. J. JURIS. 21 (1978).

22 *See* ALAN DONAGAN, THE THEORY OF MORALITY 52 (1977).

23 *See* RAJ BHALA, INTERNATIONAL TRADE LAW 36 (1996) (discussing how the economic foundation of trade law furnishes utilitarian justifications for free trade regime); Robert W. McGee, *The Fatal Flaw in NAFTA, GATT and All Other Trade Agreements,* 14 NW. J. INT'L L. AND BUS. 549, 549 (1994) (noting that the "vast majority" of trade scholarship analyzes trade from a utilitarian perspective).

24 Forms of utilitarian ethics can be distinguished according to whether they focus on the justification of acts, which is classical or act-utilitarianism, or the justification of rules that in turn justify or constrain acts, which is rule-utilitarianism.

25 *See* R.G. Frey, *Introduction: Utilitarianisms and Persons, in* UTILITY AND RIGHTS 3, 5 (R. G. Frey ed., 1984) ("In recent years, however, numerous writers have moved away from a mental-state view of utility and value, on the ground that it is too confining to restrict utility to a concern with states of mind, to an interest-satisfaction view, in which 'interests' is a generic term covering a multiplicity of desires or preferences. Thus, construed as I have done here, preference-utilitarianism is classical utilitarianism with an expanded value theory"); Hausman and McPherson, *supra* note 2, at 705 ("[N]o prominent theorist now defends a hedonistic conception of utility. All of the other specifically utilitarian theorists . . . join economists in taking utility not as an object of reference, but as an index of preference satisfaction").

26 Put in economic terms, utilitarianism takes morality as the maximizing of some function of the welfare of individual members of society. *See* Hausman and McPherson, *supra* note 2, at 689.

27 *See supra* notes 14-15 and works cited therein.

28 *See, e.g.,* JACKSON, *supra* note 15, at 10-13; McGee, *supra* note 23, at 552-54.

29 This begs the question of which methodology to use in resolving these conflicts. But what is unfortunate is that in trade institutions the utilitarian approach has presumptive

validity to the exclusion of others. Debunking this presumption, let alone replacing it with another approach is difficult to say the least. Compare this to what Richard Rorty has said about the conflict between analytic and therapeutic philosophy: "The trouble with arguments against the use of a familiar and time-honored [analytic] vocabulary is that they are expected to be phrased in that very vocabulary. They are expected to show that central elements in that vocabulary are 'inconsistent in their own terms' or that they 'deconstruct themselves.' But that can never be shown." RICHARD RORTY, CONTINGENCY, IRONY, AND SOLIDARITY 8 (1989).

30   *See* McGee, *supra* note 23.

31   Richard B. Stewart, *International Trade and Environment: Lessons From the Federal Experience,* 49 WASH. AND LEE L. REV. 1329, 1332, 1371 (1992).

32   "Human rights represent a social choice of a particular moral vision of human potentiality, which rests on a particular substantive account of the minimum requirements of a life of dignity." DONNELLY, *supra* note 2, at 17.

33   Joy Gordon, *The Concept of Human Rights: The History and Meaning of its Politicization,* 23 BROOK. J. INT'L L. 689, at 694 (1998).

34   Despite this foundation, human rights advocates generally claim some form of universalism for human rights. Henkin and others claim a form of positivist universalism on the grounds that human rights instruments have been ratified by the vast majority of the states of the world. *See, e.g.,* LOUIS HENKIN, THE AGE OF RIGHTS ix (1990); Pieter van Dijk, *A Common Standard of Achievement: About Universal Validity and Uniform Interpretation of International Human Rights Norms,* 2 NETH. HUM. RTS. Q. 105, 109-10 (1995). Others claim a normative universalism for some or all human rights, either on philosophical or empirical grounds. *See* Fernando Tesón, *International Human Rights and Cultural Relativism,* 25 VA. J. INT'L L. 869, 873 (1985) (arguing that the liberal theory of justice underlying human rights is demonstrably correct across cultural lines); Christopher C. Joyner and John C. Dettling, *Bridging the Cultural Chasm: Cultural Relativism and the Future of International Law,* 20 CAL. W. INT'L L.J. 275, 297 (1990) (positing that universalism is assertable where it can be empirically shown that cultural practice does *not* in fact vary with respect to a given principle, such as the prohibition against arbitrary killing and violence).

35   *See* DONNELLY, *supra* note 2, at 68 (following Dworkin).

36   *See* JOHN FINNIS, NATURAL LAW AND NATURAL RIGHTS 198 (1980) ("Almost everything in this book is about human rights ('human rights' being a contemporary idiom for 'natural rights': I use the terms synonymously)"); *but see* S. Prakash Sinha, *Freeing Human Rights From Natural Rights,* 70 ARCHIV FÜR RECHTS – UND SOZIALPHILOSOPHIE 342, 343 (1984) (disputing necessity or adequacy of natural rights as basis for human rights).

37   Millsian utilitarianism, though it is a liberal theory, is a problematic theory for human rights because it is consequentialist in nature. While such a theory can illuminate the moral importance of the consequences of an act for human dignity, the theory is an inadequate justification for human rights in that it countenances consequential approaches to rights questions themselves. *See infra* notes 53-63 and accompanying text.

38   For an overview of Locke's contribution and the Enlightenment roots of contemporary international human rights law generally, *see* Gordon, *supra* note 33, at 711-20.

39   On the Kantian basis for international human rights, *see* Fernando Tesón, *The Kantian Theory of International Law,* 92 COLUM. L. REV. 53, 60-70 (1992).

40   *See* H. J. McCloskey, *Respect for Human Moral Rights Versus Maximizing Good, in* UTILITY AND RIGHTS 121, 121 (R. G. Frey ed., 1984).

41 Instead, the inquiry concerning *homo economicus* focuses on the range of means available towards attainment of this end, and the effects of particular choices on the conditions for the satisfaction of preferences.

42 *See* Tesón, *supra* note 39, at 64 (observing that the Kantian view of international law is based on our duty to treat human beings as ends in themselves, which requires that the state incorporate respect for human rights); Upendra Baxi, *Voices of Suffering and the Future of Human Rights,* 8 TRANSNAT'L L. AND CONTEMP. PROBS. 125, 166 (stating that "[t]he diverse bodies of human rights found their highest summation with the Declaration on the Right to Development, insisting that the individual is a *subject* of development, not its *object*") (footnotes omitted) (emphasis added).

43 Frey notes that while the preservation of human life can be advocated on utilitarian grounds, there is no absolute bar to a change in circumstances such that killing could subsequently be justifiable on the same utilitarian calculus, thus demonstrating the unfitness of utilitarian theory as a grounds for human worth and dignity. *See* Frey, *supra* note 25, at 8-9.

44 *See* Tesón, *supra* note 39, at 71 ("Kant's international ethics follow from the categorical imperative. Just as individuals may not use human beings as mere means to an end, so foreigners, and specially foreign governments, may not use the persons that form another state . . . ."). The deontological approach is reflected in the nature of human rights themselves and in the language of human rights instruments. For example, the Universal Declaration of Human Rights states these rights are based on the "inherent" dignity of the human person. *See* Universal Declaration of Human Rights, G.A. Res. 217A, U.N. GAOR, 3d Sess., pt. I, 183d plen. mtg., U.N. Doc. A/810 (1948) [hereinafter UDHR]. Our constitutional tradition also echoes the sense that these rights are inalienable, that is, they cannot be separated from the human person. Regarding the U.S. approach to human rights as constitutional rights, see HENKIN, *supra* note 34, at 83-108.

45 *See* Hausman and McPherson, *supra* note 2, at 694.

46 *See* UDHR, *supra* note 44, art. 5; Convention Against Torture and Other Cruel Inhuman or Degrading Treatment or Punishment, Dec. 10, 1984, 23 I.L.M. 1027 (entered into force June 26, 1987) [hereinafter Convention Against Torture]; Filártiga v. Peña-Irala, 630 F.2d 876, 884 (2d Cir. 1980) (noting that torture is prohibited by "law of nations").

47 *See* Convention Against Torture, *supra* note 46, art. 2.2 ("No exceptional *circumstances* whatsoever, whether a state of war or a threat of war, internal political instability or any other public emergency, may be invoked as a *justification* of torture") (emphasis added).

48 DONNELLY, *supra* note 2, at 10.

49 As Donnelly puts it, "[a]s the highest moral rights, [human rights] regulate the fundamental structures and practices of political life, and in ordinary circumstances they take priority over other moral, legal and political claims." *Id.* at 1.

50 Unfortunately, this is not as far fetched as it sounds—history reveals that such international economic arrangements are quite possible, and theory suggests they are fully justifiable on an Efficiency Model of trade, however reprehensible they are on other terms. *See* Nichols, *supra* note 6, at 703 (referring to trade in human beings).

51 In fact, the GATT contains a provision explicitly permitting bans on trade in the products of prison labor, thus arguably reducing an incentive for the exploitation of prisoners. *See infra* notes 75-76 and accompanying text. Of course, here there is a strong economic rationale as well, in that it is difficult for firms employing free, compensated labor to compete with the products of unpaid prisoners.

52 *See* UDHR, *supra* note 44, arts. 6-8, 17; *see generally* Ernst-Ulrich Petersman, *Constitutionalism and International Organizations*, 17 NW. J. INT'L L. AND BUS. 398 (1996-97).

53 *See* Frey, *supra* note 25, at 10 (stating that "[classical utilitarianism] is, without refinement, inimical to some claim that there are incommensurable values (such as human life)"). While preference-satisfaction utilitarianism ameliorates some of the unpleasant effects of classical utilitarianism, it is subject to the same basic criticisms. *Id.* at 13.

54 *Id.* at 8.

55 *See supra* note 24.

56 *See* Frey, *supra* note 25 at 11.

57 Though consequentialist arguments can be framed for rights, such as rule-utilitarian arguments, there remains a core content to rights that is not exhausted by their usefulness. *See* Hausman and McPherson, *supra* note 2, at 695-96. Moreover, the criticisms that apply in this regard to act utilitarianism also apply to more sophisticated forms of rule-utilitarianism. *See* McCloskey, *supra* note 40, at 124; Frey, *supra* note 25, at 4.

58 *See* Frey, *supra* note 25, at 11 ("[F]ar from providing a persuasive case over the wrongness of killing, classical utilitarianism . . . seems perpetually to place persons and their vital interests at risk, a risk that will be realized if the contingencies fall out one way rather than another"); *see also* McCloskey, *supra* note 73, at 124 (incorporation of a rights-principle into a rule-utilitarian system, while normatively more attractive, does not insulate it from criticism). There is reason to fear that the human rights principle reaches that cast-off point precisely when enforcement would interfere with the powerful economic benefits at stake in trade decisions, when human rights are at their most vulnerable.

59 *See* McCloskey, *supra* note 40, at 121.

60 Other reasons include the concern that utility theory is inadequate to measure gains and losses. *See* McGee, *supra* note 23, at 555, as well as the libertarian argument that there is no public interest or public good, only individuals. *Id.* at 559.

61 *See* Frey, *supra* note 25, at 11. Since utilitarian reasoning can justify trade-offs . . . whenever contingencies so dictate, and since there are no person-relative principles that bar utilitarian sacrifice of persons and their vital interests within the unconstrained theory, there seems no way to deflect the risk to persons. And constraints that might deflect the risk, for example, *that a life is of inherent worth irrespective of its pleasure or capacity for pleasure, that life is an incommensurable value and so beyond the compass of utilitarian trade-offs, that this or that person-relative principle could secure persons and their vital interests from such trade-offs*, do not obviously form part of the classical theory. *Id.* (emphasis added). The same basic criticism holds true for preference-satisfaction forms of utilitarianism. *Id.* at 15.

62 *Id.* at 17 (questioning whether any consequential theory can adequately account for the wrongness of fundamental rights violations such as killing).

63 Historically, arguments for capitalism were often rights-based, in that they lauded capitalism less for its efficiency-enhancing capability than for the protection of individual freedom offered by the separation of economic and political power. *See* Hausman and McPherson, *supra* note 2, at 693. However, with respect to modern economics, rights-oriented moral theories are more difficult to link to traditional forms of economic analysis. *Id.* at 672.

64 For example, consider the much-debated Helms-Burton legislation, Title I of which is aimed at trade in goods. For a recent overview of the arguments concerning the legality

of the Helms-Burton legislation under WTO law, including citations to the extensive literature on the matter, see John A. Spanogle, Jr., *Can Helms-Burton Be Challenged Under WTO?*, 27 STETSON L. REV. 1313, 1313 and n.1 (1998). For a review of the history of U.S. sanctions against Cuba, see Andreas F. Lowenfeld, *The Cuban Liberty and Democratic Solidarity (Libertad) Act*, 90 AM. J. INT'L L. 419 (1996). For an interesting analysis of the Helms-Burton legislation and its furor from an international relations perspective, see David P. Fidler, *LIBERTAD v. Liberalism: An Analysis of the Helms-Burton Act from Within Liberal International Relations Theory*, 4 IND. J. GLOBAL LEGAL STUD. 297 (1997).

65 The Massachusetts government procurement statute sanctioning Myanmar (formerly Burma) was recently declared unconstitutional as an impermissible infringement on the federal government's power to regulate foreign affairs. *See* National Foreign Trade Council v. Baker, 26 F. Supp. 2d 287, 1998 U.S. Dist. LEXIS 17789 (D. Mass. 1998). Massachusetts plans a similar law against Indonesia. *See* David R. Schmahmann et al., *Off the Precipice: Massachusetts Expands Its Foreign Policy Expedition from Burma to Indonesia*, 30 VAND. J. TRANSNAT'L L. 1021 (1997). On the matter of federal and sub-federal relations in trade law generally, *see* Matthew Schaefer, *Searching for Pareto Gains in the Relationship Between Free Trade and Federalism: Revisiting the NAFTA, Eyeing the FTAA*, 23 CAN.-U.S. L.J. 441 (1997).

66 The United States enacted such a ban in 1997, forbidding the importation of products "mined, produced or manufactured by forced or indentured child labor." Treasury, Postal Service, and General Government Appropriations Act of 1998, § 634, Pub. L. No. 105-61, 111 Stat. 1272, 1316 (1997).

67 The United States, among others, has called for such a convention. *See* President William Jefferson Clinton, State of the Union Address (Jan. 19, 1999).

68 *See* Philip M. Nichols, *GATT Doctrine*, 36 VA. J. INT'L L. 379, 437 and nn. 333-335, panel proceedings cited therein and accompanying text (discussing elaboration and application of most-favored-nation test).

69 *See id.* at 436 n. 327, 332, the panel proceedings cited therein and accompanying text (discussing elaboration and application of national treatment test). In certain cases, the product may be so closely linked to the human rights violation that the same products are prohibited domestically. This may be the case, for example, with trade involving body parts or organs of prisoners. In such cases, there may be no underlying national treatment violation.

70 *See* General Agreement on Tariffs and Trade-Multilateral Trade Negotiations (The Uruguay Round): Final Act Embodying the Results of the Uruguay Round of Trade Negotiations, Apr. 15, 1994, art. XXI(b)(iii), 33 I.L.M. 1125 (1994) (GATT 1947 was incorporated into the WTO as GATT 1994 in Annex IA to the WTO Agreement) [hereinafter GATT].

71 *See* Raj K. Bhala, *Fighting Bad Guys with International Trade Law*, 31 U.C. DAVIS L. REV. 1, 6-20 (1997) (critically assessing Article XXI); Spanogle, *supra* note 64, at 1328-35 (reviewing problems raised by invoking Article XXI exception).

72 As a preliminary matter, it should be noted that the availability of any of the Article XX exceptions is limited by the *chapeau* test prohibiting that measures otherwise justifiable under that article be applied so as to be "a means of arbitrary or unjustifiable discrimination . . . or a disguised restriction on international trade." GATT, *supra* note 70, art. XX; *see also* Shrimp Case, *supra* note 10 (interpreting and applying the *chapeau* test).

73 GATT, *supra*, note 70, art. XX(a) (emphasis added) (highlighting the "necessity" test). *See infra* notes 83-84 and accompanying text. *See generally* Steve Charnovitz, *The*

Moral Exception in Trade Policy, 38 VA. J. INT'L L. 689 (1998) [hereinafter Charnovitz, *Moral Exception*] (discussing the legislative history and policy issues of this provision).

74 GATT, *supra* note 70, art. XX(b) (emphasis added) (highlighting the "necessity" test); *infra* notes 83-84 and accompanying text. Much has been written about the Article XX(b) exception in connection with trade/environment linkage problems. *See, e.g.,* DANIEL C. ESTY, GREENING THE GATT (1994); Steve Charnovitz, *Free Trade, Fair Trade Green Trade: Defogging the Debate*, 27 CORNELL INT'L L.J. 459 (1994) [hereinafter Charnovitz, *Green Trade*] (reviewing the history of trade and environmental issues).

75 GATT, *supra* note 70, art. XX(e). *See* Christopher S. Armstrong, *American Import Controls and Morality in International Trade: An Analysis of Section 307 of the Tariff Act of 1930*, 8 N.Y.U. J. INT'L L. AND POL. 19 (1975) (reviewing legislative history and policy issues relating to this exception).

76 *See* GATT, *supra* note 70, art. XX(e); *but see* Patricia Stirling, *The Use of Trade Sanctions as an Enforcement Mechanism for Basic Human Rights: A Proposal for Addition to the World Trade Organization*, 11 AM. U. J. INT'L L. AND POL'Y 1, 33-39 (1996) (arguing it would be a "logical extension" of Article XX(e) to apply it to a broad range of human rights violations).

77 *See* Charnovitz, *Moral Exception*, *supra* note 73, at 729-30 (suggesting claims involving slavery, trade in weapons, narcotics, liquor and pornographic materials, religion, and compulsory labor).

78 *Id.* at 742-43 (suggesting that international human rights law be used to interpret the vague scope of the exception). See also Salman Ball, *International Free Trade Agreements and Human Rights: Reinterpreting Article XX of the GATT*, 10 Minn. J. Global Trade 62, 76-79 (2000)(reviewing arguments for including workers' rights within Article XX(a)); Robert Howse, *The WTO and the Protection of Workers' Rights*, 3 J. Small and Emerging Bus. L. 131, 142-144 (1999) (arguing for an evolutionary interpretation of "public morals" to encompass labor practices).

79 This author is not aware of any GATT panel in which the issue is directly raised. However, the approach taken by the panel in the Thai Cigarettes case, for example, would suggest that the provision only exempts measures aimed at products that *themselves* pose a threat to human life or health, such as cigarettes. Thailand—Restrictions on Importation of and Internal Taxes on Cigarettes, Nov. 7, 1990, GATT B.I.S.D. (37th Supp.) at 200 (1991) [hereinafter Thai Cigarettes case]. This is consistent with the approach taken by the first Tuna panel regarding the "process/product" distinction in Article III violations, in which a measure aimed at the *process* by which a product was made would not be eligible for consideration under more favorable GATT provisions involving measures aimed at the product itself. GATT Dispute Panel Report on United States Restrictions on Imports of Tuna, 33 I.L.M. 1594 (1991) [hereinafter Tuna I]; see generally Bal, *supra* note 78, at 79-87; Howse, *supra* note 78 at 144 (reviewing applicability of this exception to human rights claims).

80 The exception for the products of prison labor does not raise this issue, as by its terms it is drafted to permit importing states to take into account the prison labor practices of other jurisdictions in deciding whether to permit or block the importation of certain products.

81 *See* GATT Dispute Panel Report on United States Restrictions on Imports of Tuna, 33 I.L.M. 839, ¶ 5.16 (1994) [hereinafter Tuna II]; Charnovitz, *Green Trade*, *supra* note 74, at 718-24 (discussing the distinction between "inward" and "outward" oriented

measures, and disfavor towards outward-oriented measures expressed in the Tuna cases).

82   *See supra* notes 73-74 and accompanying text. The exception for the products of prison labor does not impose a "necessity" test, requiring merely that the measure in question be one *"relating* to the products of prison labour," thereby incorporating the more lenient "rationality" test. *See infra* note 118 and accompanying text.

83   *See* Thai Cigarettes case, *supra* note 79, ¶ 75 (stating that the measure is not "necessary" if there exists a less trade-restrictive alternative a state could "reasonably be expected to employ" in pursuit of its non-trade objectives); Tuna I, *supra* note 79, ¶ 5.18; Tuna II, *supra* note 80, ¶ 3.72.

84   Joel Trachtman, in his pioneering study of trade-off devices, identifies as potential trade-off devices national treatment rules, simple means-end rationality tests, necessity/least trade restrictive alternative tests, proportionality, balancing, and cost-benefit analysis. Joel P. Trachtman, *Trade and . . . Problems, Cost-Benefit Analysis and Subsidiarity,* 9 EUR. J. INT'L L. 32, 32 (1998).

85   Trachtman accepts as a general proposition that trade-offs must be made between trade values and other social values. *See id.*; *accord* Hausman and McPherson, *supra* note 2, at 696 (discussing Nozick).

86   Frey, *supra* note 25, at 16.

87   Indeed, Delbrück notes a preference for market-oriented strategies and mechanisms for globalization problems, where "the globalization of trade as a means of maximizing economic welfare for the greatest number constitutes the policy goal." Delbrück, *supra* note 6, at 19.

88   *See id.*

89   *See* Hausman and McPherson, *supra* note 2, at 696 (child torture example).

90   *See* Trachtman, *supra* note 84, at 81-82.

91   *See* Nichols, *supra* note 6, at 699-700.

92   Thomas J. Schoenbaum has argued that the current GATT/WTO interpretation of the Article XX(b) necessity test turns the provision "on its head" in a literal sense, in that "necessary" refers syntactically to the need for protection of life and health, and not to the trade effects of the measure, and is thus wrong on textual grounds. Thomas J. Schoenbaum, *International Trade and Protection of the Environment: the Continuing Search for Reconciliation,* 91 AM. J. INT'L L. 268, 276 (1997).

93   "[A] measure is *not* more trade-restrictive than required unless there is another measure, reasonably available taking into account technical and economic feasibility, *that achieves the appropriate level of sanitary or phytosanitary protection* and is significantly less restrictive to trade." Agreement on the Application of Sanitary and Phytosanitary Measures, Dec. 15, 1993, Final Act Embodying the Results of the Uruguay Round of Multilateral Trade Negotiations, 33 I.L.M. 9, art. 5 n. 3 (1994) (emphasis added). *See infra* note 124 and accompanying text.

94   Also, if the test is interpreted, as it has been, to require justification not of the entire regulatory scheme but of each specific trade restrictive component, then the burden is much more difficult to meet. Trachtman in fact concedes that the alternative would be much more favorable to non-trade values. Trachtman, *supra* note 84, at 69.

95   *Accord* Schoenbaum, *supra* note 92, at 277 ("this interpretation of 'necessity' constitutes too great an infringement on the sovereign powers of states to take decisions (one hopes) by democratic means so as to solve problems and satisfy their constituents"). Trachtman concedes that in this approach the characterization of the measure to be evaluated introduces "a certain degree of outcome-determinative

discretion." Trachtman, *supra* note 84, at 69. This discretion is, of course, in the hands of trade policy experts.

96 In fact, national measures are more likely to be used in absence of international government. *See* Charnovitz, *Social Issues, supra* note 17, at 19.

97 For an excellent discussion of the problems that this institutional fragmentation creates in the trade/environment area, see Jeffrey L. Dunoff, *Institutional Misfits: The GATT, the ICJ and Trade-Environment Disputes*, 15 MICH. J. INT'L L. 1043 (1994).

98 *See* Stirling, *supra* note 76, at 33.

99 However, the adequacy of the measures adopted can be questioned, as can the extent to which such concerns are recognized. Moreover, the underlying normative source of the conflict is not recognized explicitly, principally because the GATT adopts a trade values-based regulatory system. *See* Charnovitz, *Social Issues, supra* note 17, at 23-24.

100 It seems Article XX(a) or (b) could also be interpreted to the same effect.

101 *See* Stirling, *supra* note 76, at 39-40.

102 *Id.* at 40-45.

103 *See Singapore Declaration, supra* note 12.

104 This is the approach Philip Nichols advocates for linkage issues in general. *See* Nichols, *supra* note 6, at 709-12.

105 *Cf.* Kevin C. Kennedy, *Reforming U.S. Trade Policy to Protect the Global Environment: A Multilateral Approach*, 18 HARV. ENVTL. L. REV. 185, 204 (1994) (arguing that amending GATT to draft new environmental exception is the best approach to the trade/environment linkage problems).

106 This might resemble the practice under certain environmental treaties to provide for trade-restrictive measures to be taken with regard to delineated products that harm the environment. *See* Protocol on Substances that Deplete the Ozone Layer, Sept. 16, 1987, 26 I.L.M. 1550, art. 4 (entered into force Jan. 1, 1989)[hereinafter Montreal Protocol]; Convention on International Trade in Endangered Species of Wild Fauna and Flora, Mar. 3, 1973, arts. III-V, VIII 12 I.L.M. 1085 (entered into force July 1, 1975) [hereinafter Wild Fauna Convention] (both providing for the total ban of unlawful trade in covered substances, even with non-parties to the agreement). Of course, in the case of these treaties, the restrictions apply to products that themselves produce the harm.

107 Article 104 of NAFTA states that, where there is an inconsistency between NAFTA obligations and the obligations imposed by certain listed treaties, including the Montreal Protocol, *supra* note 106, and the Wild Fauna Convention, *supra* note 106, the obligations under the listed treaties shall prevail to the extent of the inconsistency, provided that the Party has chosen the least inconsistent means of complying with the conflicting obligation, where the party in fact has a choice among "equally effective and reasonably available" means of compliance. North American Free Trade Agreement, Dec. 1992, Can.-Mex.-U.S., 32 I.L.M. 605 (1993).

108 Nichols seems to blur this point, in that the operation of his exemption would still require an investigation by a dispute settlement panel into the measure's purpose. *See* Nichols, *supra* note 6, at 709-12 (positing implementation of human rights measures through modification or interpretation of the DSU).

109 The GATT already recognizes this principle in its exception for economic sanctions implemented in response to a U.N. Security Council Resolution. GATT, *supra* note 70, art. XXI(c). Particularly when one considers that such a measure would still be subject to multilateral review and constraint within its own system, such an exclusion may not be too broad for advocates of the trade system.

110 On the distinction between legislative and adjudicatory approaches to the problem, *see* Nichols, *supra* note 6, at 691-99.

111 *See supra* notes 76-82 and accompanying text.

112 Moreover, the conflict at the norm-creation stage remains less constraining, in that states are free to reach negotiated compromises between different sets of values in the creation of a treaty, in a way that treaty-based dispute settlement mechanisms are not.

113 Such an exception could still be conditioned on the *chapeau* test for arbitrary discrimination or disguised restrictions on trade, and thus would not be a blanket invitation to protectionist legislation. Adding a *chapeau*-style test would change the nature of the exception from a limitation of jurisdiction to an amendment altering the nature of the trade-off device. It may also be possible to determine a rule or metric for distinguishing "authentic" from "protectionist" invocations of such a human rights exception, as Jeffrey Atik has proposed regarding linkage issues generally. *See* Jeffrey Atik, *Identifying Anti-democratic Outcomes*, 19 U. PA. J. INT'L ECON. L. 229 (1998).

114 Interestingly enough, however, Trachtman characterizes national treatment as in fact biased in favor of non-trade values and is critical on this basis. *See* Trachtman, *supra* note 84, at 72. However, from the perspective of human rights, one would expect that any trade-off mechanism employed *should* be biased in favor of human rights.

115 In the child labor example, however, there is a link between the embargoed product and the suspect process. Nevertheless, the product/process distinction, if carried forward into WTO jurisprudence, would be fatal to measures addressing human rights violations that arise in the production of certain products. *See* Tuna I, *supra* note 79; Tuna II, *supra* note 80.

116 The panel report in Tuna I may not be an insurmountable obstacle in this regard, in that it has been much-criticized and, in any event, was not adopted. *See* Tuna I, *supra* note 79; Charnovitz, *Green Trade*, *supra* note 74, at 723.

117 This approach would be consistent with an early draft of the predecessor to Article XX in the Draft ITO Charter, as noted by the panel in Tuna I: "exception (b) read: 'For the purpose of protecting human, animal or plant life or health, *if corresponding domestic safeguards under similar conditions exist in the importing country*'" (emphasis added). Tuna I, *supra* note 79, ¶ 5.26.

118 This would bring the language of Article XX(b) into line with the existing language of Article XX(e), which merely imposes a rationality test. *See supra* note 82 and accompanying text.

119 Trachtman, *supra* note 84, at 81.

120 The effectiveness of these approaches would, of course, depend on the precedential effect of WTO appellate body rulings. To the extent that the emerging doctrine of *stare decisis* in WTO decisions continues to evolve, such approaches may be equally as effective as formal amendments, and more readily attainable. *See* Raj K. Bhala, *The Myth About Stare Decisis and International Trade Law*, 14 AM. U. J. INT'L L. AND POL. (1999); Raj K. Bhala, *The Precedent Setters: De .Facto Stare Decisis in WTO Adjudication*, 9 J. TRANSNAT'L L. AND POL'Y (1999); Rutsel Silvestre J. Martha, *Precedent in World Trade Law*, 64 NETH. INT'L L. REV. 346 (1997).

121 *See supra* note 107.

122 *See supra* note 93 and accompanying text.

9 Trade Rights Conditionalities and Human Rights

MARIANNE MØLLMANN

This chapter explores the legality under international law of labor rights conditionalities attached to trade relations between developed and developing countries. In the analysis this chapter assumes that a linkage between trade and labor rights in the form of trade conditionalities is effective in raising labor rights standards internationally. Indeed, this has been shown in studies covering such diverse areas as Central America and Asia. The focus here is on whether the linkage between trade and international labor rights standards in general is desirable or indeed legal under international law.

In order to do this, a series of related questions are addressed. First, the analysis asks whether it is possible to legislate for trade and human rights independently. The conclusion is that in the current context of accelerated globalization the premises used for a separate treatment of trade and human rights has outlived any relevance it may have had, and that the linkage not only is possible, but necessary.

The chapter then discusses whether the legality of labor rights conditionalities depends on the nature of the trade relation to which they are attached: i.e., "normal" or preferential treatment. Both possibilities are examined and it is argued that human rights standards enforced through conditionalities may take primacy over trade concerns in both types of cases.

The next issue is whether the motivation behind trade conditionalities is important. The conclusion reached is that though this is particularly the case under international trade law, the sincerity of the stated motivation is important in all cases.

The discussion then addresses the often-voiced criticism that labor rights conditionalities are the expression of developed country priorities. Notwithstanding that local definitions of minimum age levels, limits on working hours, and decent standards of working conditions depend on levels of development, we shall see that labor rights *are* human rights, and that their status as universal transcends concerns with levels of development.

Finally, a framework for the determination of the legality of labor rights motivated trade conditionalities is extracted from the previous sections.

The Tension between Labor Rights, Trade, and Human Rights

The rights conferred on workers in any given country—labor rights—have an impact on that country's ability to compete internationally and these rights are, therefore, intrinsically related to trade and trade policy. Many countries—developing and developed alike—maintain that labor rights regulation is adequately dealt with at the International Labor Organization (ILO), and that the world trading system per definition must concentrate on "trade issues" only. This logic is inherently flawed. As a recent report requested by the United Nations Sub-Commission on the Promotion and Protection of Human Rights (UN Sub-Commission) concludes: "[T]he status of labor rights is significantly implicated in any discussion of policy and practice relating to international trade, investment, and finance."[1]

A. Moving Beyond the Cold War Framework

The current resistance to linking trade regulation to human and labor rights standards as evidenced in the debate at the WTO, must be seen in the context in which the international human rights discourse has developed. The Cold War created the framework for a division between civil and political rights on the one hand and economic, social, and cultural rights on the other, consequently sidelining labor rights as a socialist concern. With the collapse of the Iron Curtain, the "living alternative" to Western capitalism "not only disappeared but was thoroughly discredited," and "democracy and free market economies came to be almost universally (if mistakenly) discussed as if they were interchangeable and inseparable."[2] At the same time, emerging economies in former colonies or elsewhere were struggling for national independence and economic prosperity. In these countries—particularly in South America—the 1960s and 1970s saw the emergence of import-substitution policies that became "linked to the promotion of more or less official trade union organizations."[3] As these policies failed to create sustainable growth, and as many developing countries were forced by World Bank and International Monetary Fund (IMF) conditionalities to dismantle, *inter alia*, any regulation that could be seen as a barrier to investment, trade unionism became synonymous with a negative impact on economic growth.[4] In this climate of rights hostility in the economic discourse, the idea of a "right to development" emerged in international human rights debate, and the discussion of trade and human rights became dependent upon the definition of development as a concept.

B. *The "Trickle Down" and Human Rights Arguments*

Increased trade is currently proposed as a major agent for development in the discourse both of the Bretton Woods institutions and of the rest of the UN system.[5] The World Bank, the World Trade Organization (WTO), and the IMF assert that wealth created in a free trade system will trickle down, and that a stronger enforcement of human rights standards automatically will follow.[6] This view is built upon a concept of development measured in terms of growth in gross domestic product (GDP).

The other approach to development is represented by UN human rights institutions such as the UN Sub-Commission. This body has lately shown increased concern with the adverse impact "free trade" can have on the protection of human rights, in particular economic, social, and cultural rights. This discourse is based on an insistence that morally motivated minimum standards are integral to sustainable development, and that development, in fact, is a fundamental human right.

There are obvious difficulties with both the purely economic, and the purely human rights based approach to development, though empirical data most conclusively disproves the former. Commentators have pointed out the extreme declines in real wages in both sub-Saharan Africa and Latin America in the 1980s and the 1990s, as the regions became both more open and interdependent in terms of trade. Likewise, South East Asia showed strong economic growth and reasonable wealth distribution during times of government regulation of investments. Empirical evidence would thus seem to support the conclusion that the current international reality is too complex for separate treatment of trade and human rights.

C. *Confusing Economic Means with Human Rights Ends*

Indeed, a joint treatment seems theoretically inevitable. Firstly, it is worth relaying the comments made in a recent UN Sub-Commission report: "The principal problem with the [... "separating trade, development, and human rights" ...] approach [...] is that it subordinates the international human rights instruments [including the provisions of the UN Charter] to the charters of the agencies [such as the World Bank and the IMF], when, as a matter of law, the reverse should be the case."[7] In other words, the fulfillment of human rights is the end, GDP growth through international lending, trade interdependence, and development only the means to reach it. Though the world trading system set up through the Uruguay Round Agreements is less directly subordinated to the UN Charter, the case can be made that most WTO participants are also UN members, and thus subject to UN authority on Charter (and through that, human rights) issues.

Furthermore, international trade-related standard setting is often put forward as a necessary precondition for world peace. At the same time, the UN Charter explicitly acknowledges that without human rights protection there will be no world peace—even if this means international supervision of issues formerly considered exclusively under domestic sovereignty. One could say that in a world where nations argue that military intervention for human rights reasons is *not* a breach of the UN Charter,[8] it is hard to argue that trade related regulation including the protection of previously agreed upon human rights standards *is*.

D. The WTO, ILO, and the "Split Forum" Argument

Moreover, the most commonly used argument for exclusion of human rights standards in WTO-rules is not one of sovereignty, but one of proper choice of forum for regulation and enforcement of standards. The WTO is put forward as the proper forum for enforcing trade law, as defined in the Final Act of the Uruguay Round, whereas the ILO is seen as the proper enforcer of labor rights. One suspects the ILO may not have been put forward as the perfect forum for labor rights standard enforcement, had it actually had the power to enforce. Leaving that aside, the argument for a "split forum" is logically flawed.

Firstly, it is argued that joint regulation creates barriers to trade, and that these barriers obstruct economic growth and therefore impede social justice and human rights adherence. This argument is based on the classical economic theory of comparative advantage, which prescribes the removal of state-imposed controls on the activities of market agents. This economic deregulatory process is thought to promote global efficiency in resource use, expand economic freedom, and lead to economic growth with in turn, it is submitted, will generate more resourceful, freer and therefore more conscientious consumers. However, "the rhetorical use of terms such as freedom and regulation in the debate on international trade suggests a pre-existing 'natural' state of the economic system which is disturbed by artificially imposed regulations [...an assumption which] is both historically inaccurate and descriptively false."[9] "[Even e]conomic theory acknowledges that markets fail in their allocative role [and that] there is a role for state intervention to correct market failure."[10] Thus, the desirability of state intervention (or in the case of human rights: international supervision) in markets is not a question of political and moral absolutes but of judgment. The signatories to the Agreement Establishing the World Trade Organization have already acknowledged this in the document's first paragraph:

The parties to this agreement [recognize] that their relations in the field of trade and economic endeavour should be conducted with a view to raising standards of living, ensuring full employment and a large and steadily growing volume of real income and effective demand, and expanding the production of and trade in goods and services, while allowing for the optimal use of the world's resources in accordance with the objective of sustainable development, seeking both to protect and preserve the environment and to enhance the means for doing so in a manner consistent with their respective needs and concerns at different levels of economic development.[11]

The WTO's "End Run" of Labor, Environmental, and Human Rights Standards

The WTO Agreement's Preamble thus clarifies that the deregulation stipulated in the rest of the Uruguay Round texts does not trump social and environmental considerations. Consequently, social concerns such as labor rights and environmental protection must be addressed—and given primacy—in the WTO trading system in order to give proper effect to its governing document. By calling for the regulation of labor rights through the ILO—an institution with no enforcement powers—whilst mandating enforceable economic deregulation through the WTO, the contracting parties are essentially nullifying the purpose of the WTO as set out in its constituting document.

Unfortunately, the WTO preambular language is malleable enough that it has been used as an excuse for lowering labor rights standards, rather than as a call to regulate for them within the trading system. Developing countries, in particular, invoke their lack of economic development as justification for lower levels of human rights standards adherence, labeling developed countries' wish to regulate for labor rights standards within the WTO system "a disguise for protectionism."

From a human rights law perspective, this argument is doomed because the nature of international human rights obligations is such that their fulfillment cannot be postponed because of a lack of economic resources. Higgins has succinctly noted that if one "[defines] a right by reference to the ability of the party upon whom the obligation lies—the state—to provide it immediately ... then there is no right."[12] From a trade law perspective, the "protectionist" argument is doomed because it presupposes that, without labor rights standards protection, the WTO system would be the pinnacle of free trade, and—as such—"neutral." We have already seen that free trade in general is not neutral. With regard to the WTO in particular, it is worth noting that the system is quite protectionist when it comes to intellectual property rights, patents, copyrights, and other monopolies. More importantly, by defining "development" and "growth" in purely macro-economic terms (GDP growth), the WTO ensures that labor rights standards only enter the equation as a production cost that may or may not be passed on to the consumers. This significantly narrows the scope of the debate on the appropriate forum for international labor rights regulation, by claiming on the one hand that the issue is irrelevant, arguing that the WTO is for trade concerns only or on the other that it is already adequately addressed through the belief that economic development defined as GDP growth will automatically lead to human rights adherence. Nothing on the purpose of the WTO warrants such an interpretation.

In summary, we have seen that both the inclusion and the exclusion of human and labor rights standards in trade and investment regulation is the result of a politically charged choice—that neither of the above positions *is* "neutral." We have also seen that the resistance to a linkage is based on a historically explicable but currently unjustifiable discourse dichotomy. We have noted that the world trading system cannot meaningfully define itself as outside an international order based on the maintenance of world peace through a rules-based system, and that a development-based argument against inclusion of human and labor rights standards in multilateral trade agreements fails at least a preliminary examination on both the empirical and the legal level. Finally, we have noted that social concerns necessarily must be given primacy over economic deregulation at the WTO, if the organization is to give effect to its governing document.[13]

Human Rights Trade Conditionalities and Sovereignty

An important element in the determination of the legality of human rights motivated trade conditionalities is the nature of the trade relation to which the conditionalities are attached. These can be divided into two sub-groups: "normal" trade relations—"unless you do X, we will not trade with you at all"—and preferential trade relations—"if you do X, we will reward you with extra concessions."

In order to decide whether the trade relation underlying the conditionalities is a pertinent concern for our analysis, we must look at the conceptual basis for inter-State relations in general, and for international trade in particular.

A. *"Relative" Sovereignty*

Scholars have shown that the notion of sovereignty, mentioned by the "sovereign equality" clause of the UN Charter as basis for all interchange between UN members,[14] in the current context of international interdependence necessarily must be understood as "relative sovereignty." This is so, because "if a State was to be allowed to disregard ... international law, in view of its claim to [absolute sovereignty], there would no longer be any reliable basis for the inter-State relations required by the fact of the interdependence of the several sovereign States."[15] Consequently, for the sake of international stability, states "transfer" part of their legislative sovereignty to international organizations such as—for example—the UN and the WTO. The resulting vacuum is filled by the organizations exercising their own legislative power.

This "transfer" of legislative power is relevant, insofar as labor rights conditionalities are an expression of inter-State exchange, and that they thus exist in the sphere governed by international legislation and organizations. This, indeed, is the most basic underlying premise for the study of international law altogether. We thus assume that the conditionalities could be subject to both international trade law and international human rights (labor rights) law. We are furthermore concerned with whether either regime treats the conditionalities differently depending on the trade relation to which they are attached.

B. *"Normal" and Preferential Trade Relations*

International trade law would seem to make a distinction between "normal" and preferential trade relations. Whilst the WTO Agreement's Preamble recognizes the different "needs" and "concerns" of developing countries, the articles governing the exchange of goods explicitly apply to—indeed, prescribe—homogenous treatment of all products regardless of origin. Preferential trade treatment over and above the "normal" trade status required by the Uruguay Round Agreement texts is governed by a special agreement, the *Enabling Clause*.[16] The text of this agreement makes it clear that any preferential treatment in the context of the world trade system is entirely at the discretion of the bestowing country and thus not subject to other substantial WTO-derived obligations.

Human rights conditionalities on trade are not the fulfillment of a human rights obligation, but rather a way of enforcing another country's perceived obligations. In this, there is no difference between conditionalities attached to "normal" and preferential treatment: in both cases, the enforcement is by a (relatively) sovereign state against an equally (relatively) sovereign state.

We thus maintain that the nature of the trade relations to which the conditionalities are attached makes a difference for their treatment under international trade law, but not necessarily under international human rights law.

Conditionalities and Motivation

Labor rights conditionalities are, on the face of it, motivated by concern with labor rights standards. This concern may spring from humanitarianism—i.e. protection of foreign workers and concepts of morality—or from protectionism—i.e. protection of domestic workers against social dumping. We will now look at whether the legality of the conditionalities depends upon the underlying motivation.

The motivation behind any act matters in almost all legal contexts. Thus, basic principles of public international law such as "good faith" and *opinio juris* are based upon the assumption that a distinction can be made between an act that was carried out willingly and an act that was carried out grudgingly and—moreover—that this distinction matters. In domestic criminal law, most systems distinguish between acts based on the "intent" behind the act, and many have built a proportionate punitive system upon this distinction.

A relevant question in this context is therefore if "motivation" matters in international human rights law, in trade law, and—ultimately—if it matters with regard to the legality of human rights related conditionalities.

Human rights standards are often formulated to project disinterest with regard to the motivation of the potential violator. Thus the 1984 Convention Against Torture (CAT) and the 1948 Convention on the Prevention and Punishment of the Crime of Genocide (Genocide Convention) make clear that there is no excuse for torturing, or for committing genocide, not even that the order (motivation) came from someone else. Similarly, the 1979 Convention on the Elimination of All Forms of Discrimination Against Women (CEDAW) and the 1965 International Convention on the Elimination of All Forms of Racial Discrimination (CERD) forbid action that have discriminatory "intention" *and* actions that have discriminatory "effect." This apparent indifference with the motivation behind potential violations emphasizes the primacy of the rights invoked: they must not be infringed under any circumstances. However, a closer look shows that motivation is quite central to human rights law.

First, the underlying motivation may be an intrinsic part of the definition of the right and its violation, as with the definition of "torture," for example. Second, the motivation behind a statutory or regulatory limitation of a right determines whether such a limitation constitutes an infringement or a legal narrowing of the scope of the right. The right to freedom of expression and the right to manifest one's religion, for example, may be limited by concerns for public morals and for other reasons. Several rights may be limited for reasons of national security; a notion contained in the state-of-emergency clauses of most human rights conventions.

Third, human rights monitoring bodies often examine a country's motivation for not fulfilling even non-derogable rights in order to determine the extent of the infringement. Thus, the non-fulfillment of some rights has from time to time been excused by lack of resources, and the international community has accepted this explanation as legitimate. That is, non-fulfillment is seen as less of a breach of obligation if the *motivation* for fulfillment exists, thought the *resources* do not. This latter concept is incorporated into the labor rights conditionalities connected to preferential treatment of imports from developing countries under the U.S. Generalized System of Preferences Program, which prohibits the U.S. President from bestowing benefits on a country that "has not taken steps or is not taking steps" to fulfill international rights standards. In other words, the intent— "taking steps"—is as valid for the determination of benefits as the *de facto* protection of the rights involved.

Here we are, however, not concerned with the motivation behind the fulfillment (or not) of labor rights obligations, but rather with the motivation behind their enforcement through trade mechanisms. Seen from this perspective, the motivation behind the conditionalities matters insofar as it is an indication of the bestowing country's intention to transfer part of its legislative sovereignty to the international sphere. If invoking internationally recognized rights standards, this intention may be assumed, thus subjecting the domestic measure to scrutiny according to the principles of international human rights law.

This, indeed, is the position of Philip Alston, who has argued that all action purporting to be based on concern with human rights must adhere to, at least, four of the major assumptions underlying the international human rights regime. One manner of testing the legality of labor rights conditionalities would thus be to apply Alston's four-step test:[17]

Are they based on internationally agreed upon standards (i.e. are they based on conventional human rights definition, or—alternatively—have the norms invoked been defined by custom)?

Are they applied only to States that are bound by them (i.e. are they based on conventional obligations, or are the norms invoked part of international customary law)?

Is normative consistency sought (i.e. are the standards applied in a manner consistent with the internationally defined norms)?; *and*

Are the sanction mechanisms based on clear criteria, and do they follow fair and consistent procedures (i.e. do they apply equally to all States, and is it possible for the target States to predict what actions will be sanctioned)?

Human Rights Motivation and International Trade Law

If the intention is *not* humanitarian, it is necessarily commercial. We now turn our attention to *whether*, and in that case *how*, the motivation behind human rights conditionalities matters under international trade law.

In the world trading system, motivation seems to matter more in the *exception* to the rule that in the application of the rule itself. Thus, we find that the three GATT Articles concerned with "equal" treatment—Articles I, III, and XI—are more or less unconditional. Article I stipulates that most-favored nation (MFN) status must be accorded "immediately and unconditionally" to "any products" from "any contracting party." Article III(2) prohibits even a discriminatory *effect* on imported products of the application of internal laws and regulations, and Article XI only permits *temporary* exceptions to the removal of quotas if motivated by basic survival needs (food shortage). In other words, the motivation behind domestic measures that affect trade is relatively irrelevant to the obligations undertaken under the GATT. Indeed, a literal reading of Article III(2) would be that a measure could have discriminatory *intent* and still be GATT-legal, as long as it does not have discriminatory *effect*.

The justification of measures that constitute exceptions to these basic GATT principles is, nevertheless, based on the motivation behind the measures. GATT Article XX permits exceptions motivated by protective necessity. Indeed, in order for the exception to be GATT-legal, it must not only be motivated by protective necessity, it must be motivated *solely* by protective necessity, as the *chapeau* of Article XX prohibits "disguised restriction on international trade," that is: protectionist intent. In fact, most WTO disputes invoking Article XX exceptions turn on a determination of the defending country's discriminatory intent.

Further, the *Enabling Clause*, which exempts preferential trade programs from requirements of reciprocity, includes a notion of motivation, as the preferential treatment given to developing countries must be "designed" to further trade with the countries involved.

Under international trade law, the legality of labor rights motivated trade conditionalities thus very much depends on the underlying motivation. It is important to stress that the GATT does not leave room for conditionalities devoid of any human rights or other "non-discriminatory" protectionist motivation. Thus, if trade conditionalities *de jure* or *de facto* are seen to have a restrictive effect on international trade without the justification of "protective necessity" which may come with the invocation of international human rights standards enforcement, they are *prima facie* illegal under international trade law.

As we have seen, trade conditionalities imposed on "normal" trade relations will most likely be scrutinized in a trade context. The most direct manner to invoke labor rights standards under the GATT is by defining product and processing methods (PPMs) as relevant for the definition of "like product" under Article III(2). Thus, a country could place bans or extra tariffs on products manufactured by children, applying the rationale that a football made by a five-year-old is inherently different from a football made by a 25-year-old. This was the reasoning invoked by the U.S. in the (in)famous cases, where it was argued that tuna fished in the manner harmful to dolphins is inherently different from tuna fished in a manner that takes precautions not to harm dolphin populations. The claim was rejected, with the GATT and later WTO panels arguing that GATT Article III(2) only applies to regulations affecting "products as such" and not the circumstances of their production.[18]

A more indirect manner to invoke human and labor rights standards under GATT has been labeled the "level playing field" argument. This argument goes, that from an exclusively economic standpoint, WTO Member States necessarily face policy choices in order to fulfill their obligations under Articles I, III, and XI, since all Articles are comprehensive, prohibiting *any* discriminating or restricting direct or indirect measures. However, from an international perspective, government inaction (lack of legislation) is as much a subsidy as is direct funding: a company that does not have to pay, for example, a minimum salary will—all things being equal—be economically better off than a company that does. So there is an inherent question often left unanswered in free trade theory: what is the "natural," "neutral" or non-subsidizing level of domestic or international regulation?

With regard to human rights, it would seem logical to define the "non-subsidizing" level of regulation as that delimited by already multilaterally negotiated human and labor rights standards, such as those contained in the 1966 International Covenant on Civil and Political Rights (ICCPR), the 1966 International Covenant on Economic Social and Cultural Rights (ICESCR), and the 182 ILO Conventions on work-related human rights standards. First, the majority of WTO members have already ratified the most central of these treaties.[19] Second, by arguing that the ILO is the proper forum for enforcement of labor rights, the WTO Member States have accepted the ILO Conventions as the authoritative instruments for labor rights definition.

Consequently, from a legal perspective, a scenario in which one Member State brings a case before a WTO panel charging another Member State with illegal subsidizing of its local industry through weak labor rights regulation or enforcement is conceivable. Unfortunately, in light of the existing WTO jurisprudence, the opposite is more likely to happen. Let's therefore look at what defense the GATT offers for a country charged with the erection of barriers to trade through insistence on human and labor rights standards in normal trade relations.

The purpose of GATT Article XX is to allow for exceptions from the general obligations of the GATT Agreement. Article XX allows for the adoption or enforcement of unilateral measures deemed necessary for, *inter alia* public morals, the protection of human, animal, or plant life, the regulation of products of prison labor; and conservation of scarce natural resources. The exception is tempered by the *chapeau* of the Article, which cautions that the protective measures must not be "applied in a manner which would constitute a means of arbitrary or unjustifiable discrimination against countries where the same conditions prevail, or disguised restriction on international trade."

Until now, Article XX has never been invoked successfully.[20] In particular, the interpretation of the requirement that the measures be "necessary" has caused a hurdle. Successive WTO Panels have equaled "necessary" with "least trade restrictive" which is a dubious interpretation at the very least, since the "least trade restrictive" criteria is a notion borrowed from the WTO Agreement on Technical Barriers to Trade which does not form part of GATT obligations in general or GATT Article XX obligations in particular.

If challenged, the defense of trade conditionalities based on human or labor rights concerns would necessarily be based on Article XX(a) or (b)— concern with public moral and human life and health respectively—and would be subject to interpretation as to their "necessity." We shall, however, also look at WTO Panel reasoning concerning Article XX (g)— the conservation of exhaustible natural resources—because the arguments have turned largely on the legality of measures meant to influence policy choices abroad.

We shall deal with the requirements derived from the word "necessity" first.

In both *Tuna-Dolphin* cases, the panels arrived at a definition of "necessary" that was considerably stricter than that favored by other international tribunals. The European Court of Human Rights has, for example, on several occasions reiterated that "necessary" does not mean "indispensable." Moreover, the GATT and WTO Panels' sidelining "necessary" with "no existing alternative" was contrasted by a significantly less absolutist reading by the E.U.—who was the challenging State in the cases. The E.U. argued that if a "reasonable government" faced with the dilemma at hand—here, how to enforce a domestic ban on tuna fished by methods unsafe to dolphins—could implement the regulation at dispute and invoked Article XX(b) in good faith, the regulation passes this first hurdle.

In the case of human rights conditionalities, the invoking government could very well argue that it is "necessary" for it to impose conditions as to human rights standards enforcement, in order to protect human life and public morals domestically, because lack of such enforcement abroad would make domestic enforcement meaningless. The "reasonableness" and "good faith" of this argument could, for example, be deduced from the invoking government's own human rights record and from the consistency with which it enforces the conditionalities.

We now turn to the argument against unilateral actions with extrajurisdictional effect—an inherent element to human rights trade conditionalities. GATT Panel interpretations have maintained that a legal distinction must be made between "extraterritorial" and extrajurisdictional" enforcement. The Panels point out that multilateral rule making is to be preferred over unilateral acts, an opinion hard to contest. However, it is also hard to argue with the fact that multilateral rule making can be painstakingly slow, and that, meanwhile, the "free rider problem" needs attending to. This latter concern is particularly pertinent in a trade context, where a "free rider" may benefit from other countries implementing environmental and human rights standards whilst dodging the costs, and thus—all things being equal—producing products that may be more price-competitive than more socially conscious products.

In fact, Article XX(e), exempting prison labor products from normal GATT rules, is already both extraterritorial and extrajurisdictional, a notion that has yet to be contested by WTO Member States. There is therefore no reason why the application of Article XX(a) cannot also be extrajurisdictional as well as extraterritorial.

Having established that unilateral human rights related conditionalities could be seen to be "necessary" under Article XX(b)—and by extension Article XX(a)—and having concluded that their extrajurisdictional application need not be illegal, the question remains whether the insistence on work-related human rights standards are pertinent to the protection of "human life and health" or "public morals." To this question we now turn.

Generally speaking, "human rights and health" are moreover objective notions—either human life and health are threatened or they are not—whereas "public morals" require a moreover contextual and subjective interpretation. Both the objective and the subjective are inherent to the concept of human rights. The basic idea of human rights is that they are rights "held simply by the virtue of being a human person [and that] they are part and parcel of the integrity and dignity of the human being."[21] This definition clearly related the notion of human rights to "human life" (integrity) and "health" (dignity). At the same time, whilst the concepts are universal and inherent to all human beings, the manifestation of "dignity" and "integrity" may vary according to the culture. As such, they are intrinsically related to value choices, and thus to "public morals." In other words, human rights are conceptually connected to both human life, health, and morals, as a careful reading of the International Bill of Rights will show: the rights can meaningfully be divided into those that protect the individual's life (right to life, prohibition of torture, due process safeguards, etc.), those that protect the individual's mental and physical health (right to the highest obtainable standard of health, freedom from slavery, freedom of expression, etc.), and those that protect the individual's morals (freedom of religion, right to privacy, etc.).

We now turn to a more focused analysis of whether human (labor) rights standards would fall under Article XX(a) and (b) exceptions.

With regard to Article XX(a), "public morals" in the context of international human rights law is generally used as a qualification of the absoluteness of another right. Thus, "public morals" modifies, for example, the right to freedom of expression, in the ICCPR, the European Convention on Human Rights (ECHR), and the American Convention on Human Rights (ACHR).

The European jurisprudence on this topic is relevant, because the temperance of the rights to freedom of expression by reverence to public morals is phrased the same way as the temperance of GATT obligations: the measures invoked must be "necessary" to protect public morals. Through the European jurisprudence it becomes clear that the central question in this regard is not *what* morals we are talking about, but rather *whose* morals: the majority of the legal discussion on the topic is concerned not with what "public morals" are, but with what is necessary to protect them, and who is to be the judge. This has led to interpretations of the word "necessary" and its relation to public morals and domestic sovereignty, all concepts highly relevant to the application of Article XX(a) and (b) to unilateral human right motivated conditionalities. The European

Court of Human Rights has, *inter alia*, argued that "necessary" should be interpreted as lying somewhere in between "strictly required by the exigencies of the situation" and "desirable," and that national authorities should made at least the initial assessment of the "pressing social need" or "necessity" of the implemented measures. This is comparable to a reading of Article XX(a) where the country invoking exceptions to other GATT provisions on public moral grounds is the primary judge of the "morals," but where this "margin of appreciation" is tempered by the *chapeau* of the Article: the measure must not be unduly discriminatory or serve as disguised protectionism. We thus return to the requirement of "good faith" and "reasonableness" of judgment.

With regard to Article XX(b), only the strictest reading of the clause would interpret internationally recognized human rights standards as *not* necessary for the protection of human life and health. And—as the Appellate Body in the WTO Beef Hormone Case concludes—"merely characterizing a treaty provision as an 'exception' does not by itself justify a 'stricter' or 'narrower' interpretation of that provision [...]."[22] Even so, requirements for working conditions that respect and promote worker health and safety fall within even the narrowest definition of measures "necessary" for the protection of human health, and provisions to end slavery, forced labor, and child labor, can easily be seen as "necessary" to protect human life.

In conclusion, both Article XX(a) and (b) should provide an adequate defense for human and labor rights conditionalities. In the context of human rights conditionalities, a good measuring tool for the sincerity of the country invoking both exceptions might be the status of human rights convention ratifications of that country, including any reservations it made, the domestic status of the standards invoked, the uniformity with which the standards are required of other states, and the general discourse of that country with regard to the human rights in question.

Arguably, the most central notions in the world trading system as contained in the rules of the Uruguay Round Agreement Texts are multilateralism and reciprocity. It is thus submitted that the world trading system has banned *random* unilateral action. As we have seen, WTO Members who wish to avail themselves of the unilateral trade actions as a policy tool must justify their actions either under GATT Article XX, or negotiate—multilaterally—an exception to the general WTO rules. Such a negotiated exception is contained in the so-called *Enabling Clause*, which allows WTO Members to "accord differential and more favorable treatment to developing countries, without according such treatment to other contracting parties." The *Enabling Clause* specifically allows programs for preferential treatment of developing countries, if these 1) are designed to facilitate trade of developing countries, 2) do not constitute an impediment to the reduction of trade barriers, and 3) employ a dynamic definition of developing countries that take into account the changes in status of these countries over time.

Until now, we have used the concepts "labor rights" and "human rights" interchangeably. We have, however, seen that the historical "dead" policy-choices such as import-substitution and East-block-style communism, and the concept of human rights, narrowly understood, to market economies. We have also seen that a logical definition of the "natural level" of subsidies should be guided by international human rights and labor rights conventions, and that—from a trade perspective—the determination of "public moral" as a legitimate exception to trade rules is closely related to notions of human rights.

It is now legitimate to ask if the distinction between labor rights and human rights matters in the determination of our ultimate question—the legality of labor rights conditionalities. If we answer this question in the affirmative, we must go on to determine *how* the distinction matters, and *what* rights fall under each heading.

As already touched upon earlier in this chapter, labor rights are often seen as domestic concerns, as obligations dependent upon the level of development of any given country, or—at best—as part of the more "programmatic" and "idealistic" set of internationally recognized rights. This is in sharp contrast to "human rights" that at least in political discourse have become a legitimate concern of the international community. We can thus say that it matters, on a general level, if a particular labor right is a human right, because human rights in this perspective are seen as both more directly justiciable, and to a great extent as legitimately subject to international supervision than labor rights. To answer our question we must, however, be more specific than that.

Inherent to human rights is a notion of universality. This notion withstands criticism that "rights are relative, contingent on culture and religion," both in a purely legal positivist analysis and from an international relations perspective. Countries that generally proclaim cultural relativity such as, for example, China, condemn certain human rights abuses, such as torture, as universally reproachable. Universality of rights is thus not an impossibility under international law, even in the mind of the most persistent objectors.

From an international relations perspective, the process of pronouncing certain rights "culturally relative" is interesting. International Criminal Court Judge Rosalyn Higgins has argued that cultural relativity "is a point advanced mostly by states, and by liberal scholars anxious not to impose the Western view of things on others [but] rarely ... by the oppressed, who are only too anxious to benefit from perceived universal standards."[23]   In Higgins' opinion—and I would tend to agree—the universality of human rights is proved by the contention that "individuals everywhere want the same essential things: to have sufficient food and shelter; to be able to speak freely; to practise their own religion [etc.]."[24]

Other scholars have successfully shown how universality of rights—that is, a common core of values—is best defined by focusing on the impact the fulfillment of one right has on other rights. Any right that can be seen to set the framework for a more equitable fulfillment of another is "closer to the core," as it were.   For example, notwithstanding notions of universality and indivisibility of rights, the right to self-determination through political participation in a democracy is "more universal" than, say, the right to secondary education, because it empowers the individual to participate in the decision-making process with regard to the prioritization of rights. As such, the right to self-determination relates directly to the notion of "human dignity" that underlies the concept of human rights, *and* it allows for culturally specific definitions of "dignity."

The parting assumption here is that societies consist of numerous groups with very different interests, that the voice most often heard is the voice of the elite, that cultural diversity may lead to different prioritization of rights, and that the more "universal" rights are the ones that transcend this cultural diversity. It follows, that the only really legitimate condition of international (inter-cultural) trade is respect for rights that transcend cultural differences as well, i.e. rights that are subject to existing international consensus. In other words: universal human rights.

The next step in the determination of the legality of labor rights related trade conditionalities is therefore to establish what labor rights have reached the status of human rights. For the purposes of this chapter, we shall concern ourselves solely with the rights most commonly invoked in trade conditionalities, namely freedom from forced labor, minimum age for the employment of children, acceptable conditions of work in terms of minimum wage and occupational health and safety, right to freedom of association, right to collective bargaining, and freedom from discrimination on the basis of race or gender.

A preliminary answer to this question can be found by examining the UN Bill of Rights, in particular the two binding documents thereof: the 1966 International Covenant on Civil and Political Rights (ICCPR), and the 1966 International Covenant on Economic, Social, and Cultural Rights (ICESCR). Both conventions contain rights relating to work. The ICCPR prohibits discrimination, slavery and forced labor, and secures the right to freedom of association, including the right to form and join labor unions. The ICESCR guarantees the right to work, the right to fair working conditions, including a fair salary, non-discrimination at the work-place, safe working conditions, equal opportunity, and holiday, and the right to freedom of association and collective bargaining, including the explicit right to strike.

It has often been submitted in human rights discussions that the rights contained in the ICCPR *per* definition have a stronger standing under international law than the rights contained in the ICESCR, because the former are "negative" obligations, to be implemented immediately, whereas the latter are "positive" obligations of programmatic nature. Notwithstanding the fact that many rights contained in the ICCPR may involve extensive and costly structural reforms (a functioning judiciary does not come cheaply), and although there are obvious substantive differences in obligations undertaken under the two Covenants, it is worth reiterating that they all are, in fact, obligations, and that the two sets of rights are interdependent from a theoretical and empirical viewpoint. Indeed, after the signing of the 1993 Vienna Declaration and Programme of Action by a broad cross-section of nations—including the most persistent objector to the concept of economic, social, and cultural rights as "human rights," the United States—it is hard to argue that the rights contained in the ICESCR have an inherently lesser status than the ones contained in the ICCPR.

Besides the UN Bill of Rights, the 182 Conventions adopted by the ILO provide the most commonly recognized conventional basis for definition of labor rights. The ILO Governing Body has identified seven of these Conventions, representing five labor rights concepts, as defining fundamental human rights standards: Conventions 98 (Rights to Organize and Collective Bargaining), 87 (Right to Freedom of Association and Protection of the Right to Organize), 29 (Forced Labor), 105 (Abolition of Forced Labor), 111 (Discrimination), 100 (Equal Remuneration), and 138 (Minimum Age).

We thus find that there is conventional basis for considering many labor rights "internationally recognized human rights." This, of course, does not take away from the fact that some work-related rights have a separate status as internationally recognized rights insofar as they might be considered part of international customary law.

We now have all the elements for the construction of a framework for the determination of the legality of labor rights trade conditionalities under international law. The proposed framework is derived entirely from the above discussion and conclusions, and is illustrated by a flowchart on page 133.

First, we are satisfied that trade cannot meaningfully be regulated independently of human rights concerns. As a generic proposition, linking human rights to trade—through, for example, conditionalities—is thus legal.

Second, we have seen that in the current context of international interdependence, the concept of "absolute sovereignty" has eroded, so that all nations involved in the international society of nation states can be assumed to have transferred some degree of legislative sovereignty to the international sphere. As human rights conditionalities on trade relations happen in the interchange between two or more nations on at least two levels—the commercial and the human rights related—the nations employed such measures can be assumed to have accepted the partial sovereignty of the international legal regimes related to these two topics: international trade law and international human rights law. This settles what areas of law—within the larger area of public international law—are relevant to the determination of the legality of human rights trade conditionalities.

Third, we have concluded that international human rights law does not justify conditionalities motivated solely by commercial concerns, and not tolerated under international trade law. The first test for determination of legality of the "human rights" conditionalities is whether they are indeed motivated by the fulfillment of international human rights standards. To determine this, we must look at the stated objective of the conditionalities, and at the status under international human rights law of the rights invoked. If the motivations behind the conditionalities are seen to be purely commercial, they are *prima facie* illegal (flowchart, at A).

If the conditionalities *are* motivated by human rights concerns, or if they—as is mostly the case—have sprung from a mixed motivation, we must determine whether they are attached to "normal" or preferential treatment. As we have seen, international trade law is concerned mostly with "normal" trade relations, and thus with any conditions attached to these. International human rights law, on the other hand, is concerned with the fulfillment of internationally agreed upon human rights standards in a manner consistent with principles of public international law, regardless of the context.

Though international law is sensitive to the different levels of development of nominally "equal" states, preferential trade treatment is still considered more a "concession" than an "obligation." This, however, does not exempt preferential conditionalities from scrutiny under international human rights law, as they pretend to invoke internationally agreed upon standards. A test for the legality of the conditionalities under the international human rights law regime could be Philip Alston's four-point test. We recall that the test requires the conditionalities to be based on internationally agreed upon standards that apply to the State on which they are "imposed." Some labor rights—such as the prohibition of forced labor—have been accepted as customary norms under international law, and are thus binding on all States regardless of their conventional obligations. Others—such as the abolition of child labor—have yet to crystallize as customary norms, and the legality of any conditionality invoking these standards will therefore depend on the existence of a conventional agreement between the invoking and the receiving State. Alston's test also requires the imposing State to employ well-defined and clear criteria for the imposition of sanctions, and for these sanctions to be employed in a normatively consistent manner. If this is not the case, again the conditionalities fail to meet international standards of legality (flowchart, at B).

We now turn to the legality under international trade law of conditionalities attached to "normal" trade relations.

We have seen that human rights standards could (perhaps should) be a relevant concern in the definition of "like products" under GATT Article III (2), but that this is unlikely to happen in the current context, and that a defense of labor rights conditionalities on "normal" trade relations most probably would fall under GATT Article XX(a) and/or (b). In this connection, we have submitted that human rights concerns are "necessary" for the protection of public morals, human life, and health, in accordance with a criterion of "reasonableness" employed in "good faith." The real test of human rights conditionalities under GATT Article XX should therefore be whether they intentionally discriminate against foreign products (do they satisfy the Article XX *chapeau*).

A test of the sincerity of the human rights motivations underlying the conditionalities could be the status of human rights convention ratifications in the country invoking them, as well as its domestic application of the norm it wishes to impose on another country. If the conditionalities are judged unjustifiably discriminatory—e.g. much stricter norm adherence is required of foreign products than of domestic products—the conditionalities are illegal under international trade law (flowchart, at D).

Finally, a justified invocation of Article XX presumes some degree of human rights motivation behind the conditionalities attached to the "normal" trade relations. They must, therefore, also pass some test of legality under the international human rights law regime, for example the Alston test, as above (flowchart, at B and C).

The short answer to the question of whether labor rights conditionalities on trade relations are legal is therefore: it depends. As with most other international intervention, if they are invoked in relatively good faith with relatively clean motivations they cannot be faulted. Moreover— as already mentioned in the beginning of this chapter—I believe that trade conditionalities are one of the most effective manners of enforcing human rights law.

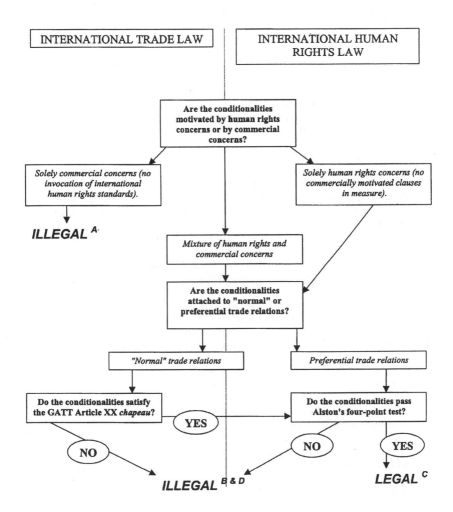

Notes

© Marianne Møllman and Ashgate Publishing Company 2001. Marianne Møllmann is the Executive Director of the Network in Solidarity with the People of Guatemala (NISGUA), a Washington-based grassroots organization working for justice and human rights in Guatemala.

1   J. Oloka-Onyango and D. Udagama, Human rights as the primary objective of international trade, investment, and finance policy and practice, UN Doc. E/CN4/Sub.2/1999/11, 17 June 1999, para. 23.

2   David Montgomory, *Labor Rights and Human Rights, A Historical Perspective, in* (LANCE COMPA AND STEPHEN DIAMOND EDS.) HUMAN RIGHTS, LABOR RIGHTS, AND INTERNATIONAL TRADE, 16, University of Pennsylvania Press, 1996.

3   *Id.*, at 14.

4   John Weeks, *Wages, Employment and Worker's Rights in Latin America, 1970-98*, 138 INTERNATIONAL LABOUR REVIEW 151, 1999, at 163.

5   For general UN discourse *see* Boutros Boutros-Ghali, *An Agenda for Development, Report by the Secretary-General* UN Doc. A/48/935, May 6 1994, para 41: "Economic growth is the engine of development as a whole [...]"); for Bretton Woods discourse *see* Articles of Agreement of the World Bank as amended on February 16 1986, Article 1.i: "The purposes of the Bank are to assist in the [...] development of territories of members by facilitating the investment of capital for productive purposes [etc...]."

6   For a representation of this view, *see* KYM ANDERSON, THE ENTWINING OF TRADE POLICY WITH ENVIRONMENTAL AND LABOUR STANDARDS, Centre for Economic Policy Research, 1995.

7   Oloka-Onyango and Udagama, *supra* n. 5, at para. 33.

8   *See* UN Security Council Resolution 688 (1991), *April 3, 1991, S.C.O.R., 46th Year, Resolutions and Decisions, p. 31* (Authorizing military action against Iraq for protection of *inter alia* the human rights of all Iraqi citizens).

9   Bhaskar Vira, *Environmental Regulation and Economic Deregulation*, in (GERAINT PARRY ET AL, EDS.) THE LEGAL AND MORAL ASPECTS OF INTERNATIONAL TRADE 150, 154, Routledge 1998.

10   *Id.*

11   1994 Agreement Establishing the World Trade Organization, Preamble, para. 1.

12   Rosalyn Higgins, *Problems and Process: International Law and How We Use It*, 99, Clarendon, 1994.

13   Whether social concerns should be given primacy at the WTO itself or by vesting the ILO or another labor rights motivated institution with enforcement powers is beyond the scope of this chapter.

14   1948 UN Charter, Article 2(1): "The Organisation is based on the principle of sovereign equality of all its members."

15   Ignaz Seidl-Hohenveldern, *International Economic Law*, 1 Martinus Nijhoff, 1992 (2nd ed), at 22.

16   Agreement Relating to the Framework for Conduct of International Trade, Differential and More Favourable Treatment, Reciprocity and Fuller Participation of Developing Countries, Nov. 28, 1979 [hereinafter Enabling Clause].

17   Philip Alston, *Labor Rights Provisions in U.S. Trade Law*, in (LANCE COMPA AND STEPHEN DIAMOND, EDS) HUMAN RIGHTS, LABOR RIGHTS, AND INTERNATIONAL TRADE, 73, Univ. of Pennsylvania Press, 1996.

18   This is not necessarily the better interpretation. We shall, however, for the purposes of this chapter, accept it as the status of international trade law at the moment of writing.

19   As of November 1999, of 134 WTO members, 104 had ratified or acceded to the ICESCR, and 105 to the ICCPR. 112 had ratified ILO Convention No. 105 (Abolition of Forced Labor), 110 ILO Convention No. 98 (Right to Organizing and Collective Bargaining), and 100 ILO Convention No. 87 (Freedom of Association and Protection of the Right to Organize).

20   This chapter was edited before the WTO Panel ruling on the case of Canada vs. the EU regarding measures affecting asbestos and products containing asbestos (DS135/R) and (DS135/R/Add.1).

21   Higgins, *supra* n. 12, at 96.

22   European Union—Measures Concerning Meat and Meat Products, WT/DS26/AB/R, Report of the Appellate Body, Jan 16, 1998, para. 104.

23   Higgins, *supra* n. 12, at 96.

24   *Id*, at 97.

10 Trade, Environment and Human Rights: The Paradigm Case of Industrial Aquaculture and the Exploitation of Traditional Communities

DAVID BARNHIZER*

The intersection of trade, environment and human rights reflects the collision of powerful and competing forces. The strategic question for human rights activists is how those colliding forces can be brought into at least a rough balance in which the power of the market is used to advance our humanity rather than weaken it. There is little question that uncontrolled market dynamics have caused serious problems in the spheres of human rights abuse and environmental protection. Lofty rhetoric about the benefits of economic development too often masks the unfair allocation of the costs and benefits of development. A former official of the World Bank once admitted during a seminar on cost-benefit analysis in which I participated that in many of the Bank's projects the benefits went to the more well off people in developing countries while the costs were disproportionately borne by the already disadvantaged.[1]

Globalization and Industrial Shrimp Aquaculture

This chapter explores the collision of competing systems and values in the specific context of the human rights consequences of large-scale industrial shrimp aquaculture—a form of lucrative international commodity trade that has exploded in scale over the past twenty years and is consuming the coastlines of many developing countries. In addition to undermining the coastal ecosystems, industrial aquaculture is ruining the lives and harming the livelihoods of many traditional users of coastal resources.

While aquaculture has been practiced for many centuries, industrial scale shrimp aquaculture is of very recent origin—in most instances starting up no more than two decades ago. Shrimp aquaculture offers a paradigm case of the inherent conflict between the processes of a globalized economy and the rights and interests of local people. Shrimp aquaculture is one of the points at which the demands of a market economy, the dominance of capital, the need (or desire) for export-driven foreign exchange earnings and the rhetoric of globalization clash most intensely with the dynamics and fundamental values of more traditional user economies and smaller scale fishing and agriculture activities.

Industrial shrimp aquaculture was created in tropical developing countries as a high value cash crop to feed restaurants and supermarkets in the United States, Europe and Japan. Shrimp is a key part of the menu and an important determinant of the profitability of restaurants. It also sustains the seafood sections of supermarkets in the developed countries of the North, representing billions of U.S. dollars in annual sales. The result of the profit to investors that results from the high demand for shrimp from the restaurants and supermarkets has been uncontrolled growth of extensive aquaculture farms on the coasts in many tropical developing countries. The typical pattern is that domestic and foreign investors with few or no ties to local communities exploit the areas and undermine the base of natural productivity on which the traditional residents depend. This has destroyed the livelihoods and rights of many traditional users of the coasts and smaller communities whose members have had no voice in the development.

The harms produced by large-scale shrimp aquaculture are in part an effect of the sheer scale of operations on fragile coasts and ecosystems that were never designed to sustain such heavy burdens. In Thailand and other shrimp producing countries, miles of shrimp ponds have been placed end-to-end and side-to-side in ways that alter the coastlines and block traditional users' access to coastal resources. Before the extensive aquaculture farms came into place the coasts were typically filled with mangrove forests that served the needs of local users. Now the ponds change and deplete the ecosystem, pollute the waters, destroy the mangrove forests and their productive capacity, reduce the quality of fishing, introduce salt into freshwater supplies, and harm local agriculture.[2] They also lead to fences, guard towers, human rights violations, and land-grabs by the shrimp farming industry.

But equally significant with the issue of excessive scale of operations in fragile ecosystems has been the overall irrationality and lack of effective government planning and monitoring that has characterized the expansion of shrimp aquaculture. Its advocates among international and bilateral development institutions have seen aquaculture as a key element of an economic revolution that would bring jobs and opportunity to poorer developing countries. In most instances the intentions of the international institutions were benign. They only saw shrimp aquaculture as a means to improve the economic development of poorer countries. But the international development institutions, as has far too often been the case, chose to remain ignorant about the full range of effects created by their development projects and about who gained and lost in the process.

But many officials in national governments as well as individuals who invested in shrimp aquaculture had no benign social concerns. They have seen only the opportunity for quick profits through the exploitation of coastal areas that previously had been seen as too difficult or expensive to develop. Until the aggressive expansion of shrimp aquaculture the remote coastal areas had been left alone by investors and government officials because they perceived no sufficiently profitable way they could use the areas. Shrimp aquaculture changed this perspective. The problem is that the coasts were already being used as a productive commons system by existing residents of the areas that have now been invaded by the shrimp farms.

The first step taken by many of the shrimp producers was to gain user rights to those coastal areas from friendly governments that were already close to the new investors. Very often government officials took an equity share in the shrimp operations. This created a financial incentive for government officials to grant user or ownership rights to the new shrimp producers and investors at the expense of the local communities and traditional users. Given these developments and incentives, producers were allowed to operate in a poorly regulated context with virtually no oversight or protection of traditional users and local communities. This has caused unnecessary harm to communities and environments in many nations where the industrial shrimp producers have located their farms. Along with these disruptions have been numerous instances of human rights violations.

Human Rights Violations

A recent report from Bangladesh shows the intensity of the conflict in many countries. A news report described how people desiring to develop shrimp farms in a contested area resorted to arson and murder to drive out the residents. The report from *The Daily Star*, dated October 4, 2000, stated that: "About 50 makeshift houses were torched at Kaliganj-Lebukhali under Baniapara thana here Monday by miscreants, allegedly led by OC [Officer in Charge] of a local police station. More then 60 people including women and children were hurt during the incident. The miscreants also hurled hand made bombs at the villagers. Villagers, who tried to resist, suffered serious burns while about 350 families living in the makeshift houses on the khas land [land leased from the government] fled fearing attack." The motive behind the attack was to grab the khas land for shrimp culture, sources said.[3]

I recently traveled to Bangladesh and spent part of the trip visiting a memorial dedicated to a Bangladeshi woman, Korunamoyee Sardar, who had been a leading protester against the encroachment of shrimp farms into the area where she lived. She was murdered and beheaded, and her head impaled on a tree limb in an effort by powerful interests to intimidate others who might oppose their desires. But her martyrdom only symbolizes the widespread cancer that shrimp aquaculture has brought to numerous developing countries. Our investigation in Bangladesh revealed that local police ignore violations, that they assist the "Shrimp Lords" in intimidating and filing false charges against local villagers; that murders, rapes and beatings by thugs working for the Shrimp Lords are common, and that the police and judicial system look the other way.

In Thailand many local authorities fear to enforce aquaculture laws against many producers because of the threat of violent reaction. The fears are not hypothetical. It was recently reported that, "Siripote Cheechang, a member of the tambon Pa Khlok Administrative Organization who led local people against mangrove forest encroachment, was severely injured when hit twice by a car. Police believe the incident was attempted murder plotted by some forest encroachers."[4] Even more recently some shrimp farmers in Thailand appear to have moved from attempted murder to murder. Jurin Ratchapol, an activist leading the effort against illegal shrimp farming was shot to death. The report in *The Bangkok Post* reports that: "His family said he had received death threats from workers at the Watchara prawn farm who wanted him to stop his conservation activities. Jurin's 41-year-old widow, Ladda, said his murder could not force her to give up the fight against over-exploitation of natural resources. Like other local villagers, the Ratchapols earn their living from small-scale fishing and gathering of forest products."[5]

Globalization and its Impact on the Less Powerful

Globalization has become a code word for the massive and penetrating expansion of market-based economic activity throughout the world. Thomas Friedman has described globalization as involving "the inexorable integration of markets, nation-states and technologies to a degree never witnessed before—in a way that is enabling individuals, corporations and nation-states to reach around the world farther, faster, deeper and cheaper than ever before, and in a way that is also producing a powerful backlash from those brutalized or left behind by this new system."[6]

The phenomenon of globalization has resulted in sharp increases in the volume and value of internationally traded products, and the expansion of regional trade and economic alliances such as the European Union, NAFTA, GATT and the World Trade Organization (WTO), ASEAN, and Latin America's Mercosur. More arrangements of this type are on the way. As this transformation and realignment of world economic activity and supporting institutions has occurred there has been a shift toward greater privatization of economic power and the creation of various versions of free-market capitalism. An important result has been the dilution of formal governmental power over business enterprises, especially those enterprises with a global reach.[7] Accompanying and supporting this change has also been the enormously increased scale and rate of mobility of private capital flows. A 1999 World Bank report related that developing countries received $155 billion in net direct foreign investment in 1998. This was more than 16 times the amount of net direct foreign investment seen in 1990. Net capital flows from government development assistance programs declined from slightly above $50 billion to slightly below $50 billion during the same period.[8]

Human Rights, Land Use, and Market-Driven Globalization

Private property, or at least the legal right to claim exclusive long-term user rights for land and coastal areas, represents a fundamental challenge to traditional cultures. The problem is that private property is inherently exclusionary. To a market-oriented entrepreneur the resulting ability to have a monopoly right to extract the value from land is a desirable good. But to a person dependent on being able to harvest food and other products from a commons area and to protect against the effects of pollution of land, water and local fisheries, intensive development of private use rights can destroy an area's culture, community and economy that has been developed over generations in a careful balance with nature. The clash between the different systems can be managed only with great care. This requires effective regulation, laws and institutions and they simply do not exist in any meaningful combination.

The UN Food and Agriculture Organization's *Code of Conduct for Responsible Fisheries* provides a benchmark and frame of reference that *in theory* include protecting the environment, respecting the rights of local communities, and contributing to improvements in social justice while still managing to build sound economic activity.[9] The reality of what exists in the field and how national governments and producers have failed to take responsible steps to implement the *Code of Conduct* has proved to be different. At present there are frequent proclamations of good intentions by the shrimp industry, by national governments, and international financial institutions but with virtually no serious follow through to implement actions to protect the lands and rights of local communities. The harmful impacts continue to occur at the same time that governments and industry issue public relations statements proclaiming their commitment to "sustainable" aquaculture that protects communities and traditional users. But those proclamations are public relations oriented window dressing, not reality.

The challenge of achieving responsible shrimp aquaculture that limits or avoids severe impacts on traditional communities and cultures, protects against environmental and ecosystem degradation, and does not countenance human rights violations can not be overstated. It is a fundamental political, economic and cultural clash between the *haves* and *have-nots*. One approach could be to responsibly implement the FAO's *Code of Conduct for Responsible Fisheries*. It is dedicated on paper to ensuring the improvement of the quality of life for poorer communities. It recognizes the importance of efforts to create investment models that ensure participation of local people in ways that result in enhanced training and the ability to share in the benefits of economic development. But this has not been done. One of the reasons is that many of the countries that produce farmed shrimp have rigidly stratified social systems in which there is no space or desire on the part of the most powerful to facilitate the upward mobility of "lower" classes.

The Clash Over Land and Water Rights

It should not be surprising that many of the violations of local peoples' traditions and rights involve disputes over the preservation and use of land and water. Shrimp aquaculture has intruded into mangrove ecosystems and other resource systems on which many people have traditionally depended for their livelihood. Much of the conflict over shrimp aquaculture comes down to the protection, allocation, and management of land and water rights. Land and water rights are points of severe disagreement and tension in the siting of shrimp aquaculture. In many shrimp producing nations the coastal zones that are the primary sites of shrimp farms are commons areas freely used by residents for many generations. These areas are often owned by the State with the government having the authority to grant concessions or even sell the land and use rights to private owners. The desire to protect the traditional users of land and coastal zones that were not privately owned lies at the core of the *Code of Conduct for Responsible Fisheries*. Yet the *CCRF* contemplates a shift to private land rights as an important part of the expansion of shrimp aquaculture.

A significant part of community and environmental opposition to the growth of shrimp aquaculture has stemmed from the widespread devastation of mangrove forests. Most shrimp producers and government development and finance ministries have tended to view mangroves and other wetlands ecosystems as nothing more than trees, salt flats and seasonal lagoons that are unproductive areas that are obstacles to "real" economic development. Those who live in or near the mangroves and similar "commons" systems see them very differently. To those people such areas are the critical element in a highly productive ecosystem on which their livelihoods and culture depend.

Globalization and its emphasis on the market economy demand private property rights recognized by law. In a private market economy a person seeking to establish a shrimp aquaculture farm or needing additional capital for expansion or improved operations needs to acquire rights to the necessary land. For those raised on the sanctity of western market economics this fact seems inevitable and even desirable. But for more community-oriented and smaller-scale systems the approach is destructive.

Acquiring land and user rights will often be a matter of buying the land outright, or acquiring land through a lease or government concession. No rational private sector economic actor will invest significant private funds in a venture over which it lacks long-term control. Any rational shrimp farmer would be a fool to make long-term investments in a shrimp farm operation in a situation where the farmer lacks clear title to the land or holds only a short-term concession from the government. Even if the concession is renewable every five or ten years investors can't take the chance and make the kind of infrastructure investments required to become a fully responsible shrimp producer. Without long-term ownership or use rights a farmer will not make capital investments in the operation beyond what is reasonably necessary to maximize short-term returns.

Corruption of a Legal System as a Human Rights Violation

Human rights traditionally made a distinction between state and private action. The lines are becoming increasingly blurred as a great deal of "public" power is mirrored in the global scale and enormous power of the private sector to such a degree that it is appropriate to consider the more powerful corporate actors as wielding a form of quasi-state power in relation to which it is necessary to apply human rights responsibilities to those quasi-state actors. In any event, law is one of the fundamental areas through which state power is exercised and for which states should be held accountable for serious deviancy or failure to use state power to act appropriately or to protect citizens from abuses.

A serious issue of what constitutes a cognizable violation of human rights involves the corruption of a nation's legal system. When fair treatment can not be consistently guaranteed, the Rule of Law does not really exist—regardless of form. There are, of course, issues when a legal system performs badly for everyone across the board. At some point matters are below the human rights "radar." But when a legal system is controlled by corrupt interests for their own purposes without recourse for those harmed by its decisions, there has been a violation of human rights. Jorge Varela's description of the inadequacy of the Honduran legal system, its refusal to enforce numerous existing laws against shrimp producers who violate laws with impunity, and the lack of any prosecutions following the murders of fishermen near shrimp farms offers a powerful example. Similarly, the lack of any real penalties in Ecuador for violations by shrimp farmers engaged in illegal activity, the presence of corruption and threats addressed to regulatory officials, and the inability to convince judges to act against violators repeats the pattern found in Honduras, Bangladesh, India and elsewhere.

In a system where corruption is present the best farmers might well find their concession not renewed because someone else wants to take over their high quality shrimp farm. Investors in Bangladesh and India have told me that there is a danger in their countries of such behavior when powerful local figures decide to take over their operations, particularly for smaller-scale farmers with virtually no resort to the legal system.

Legal systems in many of the nations where shrimp aquaculture has grown most rapidly are either generally ineffective or skewed toward the interests of those with power and capital. Most nations are ill-equipped to create the complex, expensive and integrated management systems that would be required to satisfy the demands of market economy entrepreneurs and simultaneously protect the needs of existing communities or "commons-based" economies and cultures while preserving the quality and productive capacity of natural resources and ecosystems. Almost without exception, exclusionary private land rights are threats to more traditional and dispersed local communities of the kind found in the coastal zones most favored by shrimp farmers. The more intensive economies of scale that characterize export-driven industrial shrimp farming deplete or harm natural resources that are essential for the health of the local economies.

Examples of Human Rights Violations in Honduras, India and Ecuador

A. Honduras

In the past 15 years Honduras has seen extensive mangrove cutting and incursions into coastal wetlands in the Gulf of Fonseca region due to the explosive expansion of shrimp farms. Local people have found themselves cut off from access to the Gulf of Fonseca or required to make lengthy detours. Local environmental and community organizers report that there has been significant violence between coastal fisher people and the shrimp companies. Community activists have been shot at on several occasions. The actual situation may be even more serious.

On the human rights front, at least two fishermen are alleged to have been murdered by interests aligned with the producers. Other reports collected by environmentalists indicate that "ten people have died in the Honduran Fonseca Gulf as a result of the conflict between CODDEFFAGOLF members and the shrimp industry organized under the Association of National Aquaculturists of Honduras (ANDAH). The most recent tragic deaths are those of the fishermen Israel Ortiz Avila (30) and Marin Seledonio Peralta Alvarado (27) assassinated October 4, 1997 in "La Iguana" ecological reserve. Israel Ortiz was found with 7 bullet wounds and Marin Seledonio with three bullet wounds, both from an AK-47 caliber gun. Both fishermen's bodies contained bullet wounds in the left leg as well as burn marks, as if they had been tortured."[10]

There has been some dialogue between NGOs and the industry and government but the solutions have been partial at best. There has been significant pollution runoff from farms. Enforcement and compliance remain a significant problem. There has also been a significant amount of wetlands preserved by aggressive NGO actions. NGOs have been engaged in efforts to conduct a "carrying capacity" study of the Gulf of Fonseca, with the participation of the Honduran government. The Honduran government declared a moratorium on the expansion of shrimp farms in the Fonseca area and on the cutting of mangroves, but that moratorium wasn't enforced.

The Shrimp Sentinel's report on Honduras observes: "In August 1996, after strong urging from CODDEFFAGOLF, the Honduran government decreed a one-year moratorium on new licenses for shrimp farms. Yet despite this moratorium, some 60 new shrimp farms [were] established in violation of the restrictions. After several days of sit-ins and high-level meetings with federal officials, the government promised to increase enforcement measures and agreed to extend the existing moratorium through June 1998. Decree No. 105-97 declared a moratorium on the installation of new shrimp farms or the expansion of existing ones in the Gulf of Fonseca. The decree also called for environmental impact studies to recommend all the measures necessary to conserve mangrove forests and coastal wetlands, assure the sustainability of the shrimp agro-industry, and diminish the negative impact of the giant shrimp farms in local communities. Yet according to a CODDEFFAGOLF publication of March/April 1998, in the six months since the passage of Decree No. 105-97, no studies have yet been undertaken and the expansion of shrimp farming is growing uncontrollably."[11]

Although serious efforts have been made by both Honduran and international NGOs to work with the Honduran government and ANDAH to develop a wetlands preserve, the promises seem to always founder on the rock of continuing shrimp farm development and no real government enforcement. Recently the NGOs with which I work received a report that a critical Ramsar wetlands preserve has been invaded by shrimp farmers who built illegal farms in the area. A Ramsar representative for Central America met with the Honduran Environment Minister to protest the illegal activity. There is no question the illegal farming is in fact occurring, but the Honduran government has taken no action against the shrimp farmer who has violated both Honduran law and the Ramsar Convention. This is not surprising. A recent report concluded that: "The [Honduran] government... refuses to look to the long-term and fund reforestation projects or the three large bioreserve projects it gave to the National Institute for Environment and Development (INADES) to manage. It frequently runs "scare" articles in the national tabloids on "ecoterrorism" to divide the environmental movement. Its new cabinet level environmental ministry is underfunded and rarely consulted."[12]

The rhetoric of sustainable development will remain empty so long as governments in developing countries face the enormous pressures of servicing public and private debt obligations owed to foreign governments and banks. One analysis concludes that: "The core problem is the crippling level of Honduras' debt—the highest in Central America. At the end of 1997 it stood at USD4.46 billion—roughly 85 per cent of GDP. Annual servicing of this totals USD564 million, equivalent to 22.7 per cent of exports. In post-Mitch Honduras, the government consequently finds itself in the unenviable position as having to pay USD1.55 million per day to repay loans, much of which were used on projects which have since been washed away."[13] Even if the motives of the Honduran government (or any other) were pure, the debt-service obligation almost compels governments to look the other way when foreign and domestic investors offer some hope of increasing economic development and hard currency earnings from foreign trade.

Most shrimp producing countries are in a roughly similar position. They can't service existing debt obligations and desperately need revenue from foreign trade exports to keep afloat. Responsible aquaculture development and its requirements of planning, increased governmental oversight, monitoring, scientific research, siting, environmental control and treatment, infrastructure financing, extension services, and enforcement costs a significant amount of additional money. Producer countries and producers face what is called a Hobson's Choice in which if they push hard to actually achieve sustainable shrimp aquaculture in the sense defined by the CCRF then the purposes for which governments have sought to facilitate the development of their shrimp industry and the returns that led investors to invest in shrimp aquaculture tend to disappear.

B. India

Land rights and siting issues are at the center of the controversy over shrimp aquaculture in India. A December 1996 decision by the Indian Supreme Court imposed a buffer zone on the proximity of shrimp farms to the coastal area due to the pollution from the farms that harmed surrounding villages and water supplies. The December 1996 decision of the Supreme Court of India was a landmark ruling against the shrimp industry. This ruling has of course been challenged by industry in court and in legislative amendments with the support of many parts of the Indian government. It has been a source of constant maneuvering and tension since its issuance.

The Supreme Court decision required that industrial shrimp aquaculture farms operating within the Coastal Regulation Zone cease all operations. The Court defined the Coastal Regulation Zone (CRZ) as including "coastal stretches of seas, bays, estuaries, creeks, rivers and backwaters which are influenced by tidal action ... up to 500 metres from the High Tide Line." (*The Coastal Regulation Zone Notification in India*). The Court also ruled that the industry was required to compensate local farmers displaced by the shrimp farms and pay its workers compensation plus six years wages. The Supreme Court's ruling had little impact on the practices of the Indian shrimp aquaculture industry. A petition to review the judgment was submitted to the Court by the shrimp industry and review was granted. A stay order was issued.[14]

In any event, the Supreme Court's ruling appears to have had little impact on the shrimp industry. A report observes: "Three years ago, India's Supreme Court ordered the closure of large shrimp farms within

500 meters of the high tide mark (New Scientist 21, December 1996, p. 8). It ruled that they were encouraging the penetration of salt into coastal water supplies and rice paddies, as well as polluting the lands with pesticides. But despite the move, the lucrative business continues to grow. The death and destruction in Orissa may prompt a reappraisal."[15]

India is a particularly problematic situation, about as far from being sustainable in relation to the CCRF as can be imagined. There are significant conflicts between the industry and local communities. The Indian government has misrepresented key facts regarding shrimp farming and local conflicts. A great deal of violence has occurred with local police allegedly playing a significant role on the side of the shrimp industry. A still embargoed study by Human Rights Watch conducted in 1996 and 1997 documented serious humans rights abuses in India related to the aquaculture industry.

The industry is diverse, complex, undercapitalized, and virtually impossible to regulate with any semblance of sustainability. Severe credit and debt problems beset India's shrimp farmers who are heavily obligated to feed and supply companies that advance the farmers materials on credit. There is a high level of water pollution and many abandoned farms. Shrimp disease outbreaks have seriously damaged the industry's productivity. Significant conflicts exist within the Indian legal system between opponents of shrimp aquaculture and the producers and government trade and development ministries who consider aquaculture an important part of India's economic activity.

Mangrove forests have been cut extensively. One recent report assigns part of the blame for the many deaths in Orissa to mangrove cutting linked to shrimp farms. "This coastline was once covered by mangrove forests," says Tom Spencer of the Cambridge Coastal Research Unit at Cambridge University. "In the past, the mangroves would have dissipated the incoming wave energy." Mangroves grow on tidal coasts between the high and low-water marks. They trap sediment in their roots, which gives the seabed a shallow shape. This absorbs the energy of waves and tidal surges, protecting the land behind. The trees themselves also form a barrier against wind. In the past 40 years, India has lost more than half of its mangrove forests. "The mangroves in Orissa have been mostly destroyed, says Spencer. This has left it wide open to attack by the wind and waves of the cyclones that regularly lash the coast of eastern India and neighboring Bangladesh."[16]

As in many countries, one of the main problems in most irresponsible shrimp aquaculture is the short-term chase after a quick profit. In commenting on India, one report observes: "A major reason that the shrimp aquaculture industry has been so difficult to control and curb in India is it is so lucrative. Shrimp farming is a fast way to make a lot of money for the shrimp farm owner. The industry has been subsidized in India through tax breaks, favorable loans, and free land. All of these benefits are supposed to be in exchange for the income that the industry brings in by exporting virtually all of its crop to markets in Europe, Japan, and the United States. Many reports, including the NEERI report that the industry contests, have been compiled that show that the costs of the industry, social and environmental, outweigh its income potential for the state."[17]   One newspaper reports, "[i]n their rush to garner profits, the governments have also become party to violations of national land and environmental laws."[18]

Salinization of drinking water has also been a frequent result of the incursion of irresponsibly sited and managed shrimp farms. In Andhra Pradesh it is reported that "[b]ecause the cultivation of shrimp requires brackish water, seawater is typically pumped from the ocean to mix with fresh water in the shrimp ponds along the coast. In time, the salts from the seawater seep into the soil and eventually into aquifers and drinking water tables. The result is often that the villages' drinking water supply becomes so saline that it is no longer potable. In some cases, not only has the water supply been ruined for drinking, but also for bathing. Skin rashes from unhealthy water are another common problem in these communities...."[19]

Another problem is the impact of shrimp farming on other agriculture, particularly rice farming. How this works is illustrated by an example from an area well-known for rice production. "[T]he same salty seepage that ruins the drinking water tables is responsible for destroying neighboring rice paddies. ... [N]ot only has the shrimp aquaculture industry taken lands that were once used for rice paddies (which produces a food crop that the villagers themselves can eat, unlike the cash crop of shrimp which is exclusively for export), but it also makes infertile the remaining fields that are available for rice production."[20] But for some shrimp farmers there is even a benefit and profit from their neighbor's distress and loss of productive capacity through saline pollution. The benefit is that: "Poor landowners with [a] dwindling rice crop often have little choice but to sell their fields at bargain prices to aquaculture owners.   Thus, the more polluting the shrimp farm is, the easier it is for it to acquire more land and do more environmental and social damage."[21]

C. Ecuador

There are continual failures in Ecuador to enforce laws against illegal cutting and illegal expansion of existing shrimp farms. There are several causes of this failure to enforce the laws, according to Yolanda Kakabadse: "One of the main obstacles to protecting the environment from shrimp farms... is an overworked judicial system that gives no priority to preserving mangrove ecosystems."[22] She concludes that, "[I]llegal shrimp farms have only been given minimal fines, if that. Since shrimp farming is so lucrative, the fines do not stop the illegal cutting of the mangroves.[23] While awareness about the importance of maintaining mangroves is growing, judges need to understand why communities are filing suits against illegal shrimp farmers and not put these cases at the bottom of the pile," she says.[24]

When the first Taura disease epidemic struck the shrimp industry in the early 1990s many producers abandoned ponds in the Guayas area and moved to the undeveloped Esmeraldas region in the northern part of the country. Particularly in the area of Esmeraldas Province there has been frequent illegal expansion of shrimp farms into local communities whose current economic activity is based on fishing, clam digging, and harvesting shrimp naturally occurring in the ecosystem. These activities depend on the continued existence and health of the mangrove ecosystems that are the targets of shrimp aquaculture.

There is a significant social distinction in Ecuador between the mostly black coastal residents of Esmeraldas Province and the shrimp farmers who are primarily of Hispanic descent. According to Olsen and Coello, the shrimp farms have driven thousands of families from their homes and sources of livelihood.[25] They conclude that the lowered quality of water from the shrimp farms and the depleted mangroves have degraded the fauna in the ocean as well as the cultural fabric of surrounding coastal communities. Many coastal dwellers expressed concern for their future and that of their children.[26] This has produced a serious controversy between local communities that have traditionally used the coastal areas for their livelihoods and the producers. The tension this represents reflects a fundamental element of the conflict over shrimp aquaculture and the demand that if it be done, it must be done in ways that meaningfully integrate local people into the development with strategies that make them empowered participants rather than temporary sources of cheap labor.

This controversy has been intensified because for the past two years the government of Ecuador has been proposing legislation that authorizes the sale or long-term leasing of coastal lands to producers to ensure shrimp producers can use the land to acquire loans. Part of the resistance is related to who wins and who loses as shrimp aquaculture spreads into an area. While the CCRF focuses on the need to make local people partners in economic development, the likelihood is that at best local residents become hourly wage earners. This outcome is almost automatic as the scale of aquaculture operations increase.

The irony for environmental activists seeking to protect the ecosystem against irresponsible shrimp aquaculture is that the added costs that result from being what is considered environmentally "sustainable" virtually guarantees the benefits of aquaculture will go to those with money in a private sector economy engaged in business activity whose aim is to produce products for export trade. The competitive scale required to engage meaningfully in international trade erects market barriers for smaller units of economic activity. Those barriers cannot be overcome without significant capital. The shrimp industry in Ecuador, for example, falls under the Fisheries Law, which requires that all commercial operations be integrated to include all aspects of farming and shipping. This channels a great deal of the economic benefits of shrimp farming, processing, and exporting to wealthy Ecuadorians or to foreign investors who can afford the required capital inputs.[27]

Enforcement remains a serious problem. Nancy Celi Icaza, the Ecuadorian Undersecretary of Fisheries in 1997 and a past and present official with the National Chamber of Aquaculture, stated in connection with citizen complaints about illegal shrimp farming activities that: "There has not been a correct process in following these complaints about illegal activity ... to the government. Many of these complaints have 'rested in peace,' after they have been received, that is true."[28] Undersecretary Celi agreed that: "To really enforce that regulation, we will be submitting a request for a new law... to the Congress increasing the sanctions for the mangrove cutting. At present, if you read [the existing law] carefully it will not make anyone scared. There is a lot of very nice text in it [the present law] but the sanctions are very weak and will not scare anyone. We hope the new law will be approved very easily and the sanctions will be very, very strong so we will be able to discourage people who are doing this [illegal mangrove cutting]."[29]

Effective enforcement requires monitoring, investigation, and realistic sanctions that are actually imposed. Ecuador again has the right idea, but there is inadequate implementation. Nancy Celi describes the creation of "units of surveillance and control [Unidades de Control y Vigilancia (UCVs)] ... [with] officers from the Undersecretariat [of Fisheries] ... participating in this unit of control. And it is working fine. But what happens is that the follow up is not working well."[30] She goes on to say, "I hope that will be fixed with this agreement and with increased sanctions."[31] The UCVs are comprised of representatives from the forestry department, fisheries, and navy who are charged with regulating and policing the estuaries. The UCV program represents an effort to cooperate between those key government agencies. The UCV program does not create a new institution but combines the work that had previously been distributed among the institutions. The head of each UCV "Ranger Corp" is the port captain for the province.

Ecuador has attempted to decentralize much of the planning and monitoring activities related to shrimp farming. On paper this appears sound, but I was told in confidence by highly placed governmental regulators that corruption and influence pervades the system to the extent that enforcement is ineffective. There is a substantial degree of corruption that occurs through combinations of bribes and threats. Producers have also learned how to pit one regulatory agency against another in order to exploit conflicting legal definitions as to which governmental institution has jurisdiction over mangroves depending on high water line. One regulator said he would like to enforce the laws but that he and others would receive telephone calls from very powerful people who told them to back off. He said if the regulators did try to enforce the laws against illegal activity they would be placing their careers, the well-being of their families, and even their lives in jeopardy. Ecuador also has a significant problem with enforcement in which the policing authority over shrimp aquaculture is in the hands of local Port Captains who may be under the influence of the larger shrimp farmers.

Conclusion

Crimes against humanity and large-scale human rights violations such as in Rwanda, Cambodia and the former Yugoslavia possess such a high-profile that their intensity makes it seem as we are looking into a bright spotlight that both illuminates and blinds. The murders of thousands of people, the victimization of women and children, systematic torture and similar heinous crimes cry out for the spotlight that must be shown on such horrible violations of our humanity. This must not stop and in fact must become even more a focus.

But the need to focus on those terrible violations blinds us an entire other form of quieter and less visible human rights violations, even to the extent that they are never seen or do not seem very important. The trade and human rights consequences for local communities trying to protect their communities and ways of life from the aggressive ravages of market investors and the operation of the export-driven global economy represents an almost invisible violation of the human rights of millions of people in developing countries. As has been the case in Honduras, Ecuador, India, Bangladesh, Indonesia, Thailand and many other countries where shrimp aquaculture has expanded rapidly to feed the machinery of export trade, many local people have seen their ways of life destroyed, their economic system undermined, their access to essential resources cut off. They have had no voice in what has been done to them. This is an invisible type of human rights violation that is unacceptable in a democratic system.

Notes

© David Barnhizer and Ashgate Publishing Company, 2001. David Barnhizer is Professor of Law at the Cleveland State University and Senior Advisor to the International Program of the Natural Resources Defense Council in Washington, DC.

1   "Yale Cost Benefit Analysis Notes: October 10-13, 1999," on file with author.
2   *See*, e.g., Naylor, R., R. J. Goldburg, H. Mooney, M. Beveridge, J. Clay, C. Folke, N. Kautsky, J. Lubchenco, J. Primavera, and M. Williams. 1998. "Nature's Subsidies to Shrimp and Salmon Farming," *Science*, October 30, 282:5390.
3   "50 houses torched, by miscreants in Satkira," *The Daily Star*, dated October 4, 2000.
4   See, "Suspect in bid to murder green activist denied bail," *Bangkok Post*, Page 2, Oct. 7, 2000.
5   Achattaya Chueniran, "Jurin's family vow to carry on his work: Murder will not end conservation battle," *Bangkok Post*, February 2, 2001.
6   Thomas Friedman, *The Lexus and the Olive Tree*, at 8.
7   *See*, e.g., the discussion of the shift toward private power in Daniel Yergin and Joseph Stanislaw, *The Commanding Heights: The Battle Between Government and the Marketplace That is Remaking the Modern World* (1998).
8   *See*, 1999 WORLD DEVELOPMENT REPORT (World Bank 1999).
9   *See* the UN FAO's website at, http://www.fao.org/fi/default.asp. Last visited April 30, 2001.
10 "Honduras National Report," *Shrimp Sentinel*, www.earthsummitwatch.org/shrimp
11 "Honduras National Report," *Shrimp Sentinel Online*.
12 Jeff Boyer; Aaron Pell, "Mitch in Honduras: A disaster waiting to happen," 9/1/99 NACLA Rep. on Americas 36, 1999 WL 24592577, *NACLA Report on the Americas, North American Congress on Latin America*, Sep/Oct 1999, Wednesday, September 1, 1999, Volume 33, Issue 2; ISSN: 1071-4839.
13 "Debt: squaring the circle," *HONDURAS: REVIEW 1999*, 12/20/99 Am. Rev. World *Info.* 1, 1999 WL 31210890, *Americas Review World of Information*, Monday, December 20, 1999.
14 "India National Report, Letter from MPEDA," August 14, 1998, *Shrimp Sentinel Online, supra* n. 10.
15 "INDIA, An Unnatural Disaster, Clearing India's Mangrove: Forests Has Left the Coast Defenseless," *New Scientist*, November 6, 1999.
16 *Id.*
17 "India National Report," *Shrimp Sentinel Online, supra* n. 10.
18 "Aquafarming: the money factor," *The Hindu*, June 15, 1997.
19 "India National Report," *Shrimp Sentinel Online, supra* n. 10.
20 "India National Report," *id.*
21 "India National Report," *id.*
22 Danielle Knight, "ENVIRONMENT-ECUADOR: Mangroves Need Protection from Shrimps," July 28, 1999, *InterPress Service*.
23 Danielle Knight, "Mangroves Need Protection from Shrimps," *id.*
24 Danielle Knight, "Mangroves Need Protection from Shrimps," *id.*

25 Stephen Olsen, Segundo Coello, "Managing Shrimp Mariculture Development," *Eight Years in Ecuador*, ed. Donald Robadue, 1994: 76.
26 Olsen, Coello, 85.
27 Olsen, Coello, 75.
28 "Presentation of Nancy Celi Icaza, Undersecretary of Fisheries, Ecuador, to the April 1997 session of the Shrimp Tribunal: Ecuador National Report," *Shrimp Sentinel Online, supra* n. 10.
29 Presentation of Nancy Celi Icaza, *id.*
30 Presentation of Nancy Celi Icaza, *id.*
31 Presentation of Nancy Celi Icaza, *id.*

11 The Human Rights Consequences of Inequitable Trade and Development Expansion: The Abuse of Law and Community Rights in the Gulf of Fonseca, Honduras

JORGE VARELA MÁRQUEZ

Honduras is an example of the way in which laws are ignored and violated and human rights broken in order to satisfy the demands of a major industry created to serve the interests of the globalized economy. The human rights problems in this case center on the shrimp farming industry. The human rights consequences of inequitable trade and development caused by the explosive growth of the shrimp farming industry in Honduras are increased when the large-scale shrimp producers are allowed to expand into coastal wetlands on which thousands of local people have long-depended for their livelihoods. In Honduras, in 1973, the shrimp industry established itself on 80 hectares which is equal to 200 acres. In 1989 the shrimp industry reached 5,500 hectares of shrimp farms on the coastal wetlands. By 1995 the expansion reached 12,000 hectares and by 1998, 16,000 hectares.

The Gulf of Fonseca borders the Pacific Ocean through an area shared by El Salvador, Honduras and Nicaragua. The Gulf forms a marine area of more than 3,200 square kilometers, with a coastal length of 261 kilometers. Of this coastline, 29 kilometers are in El Salvador, 47 in Nicaragua and 185 kilometers in Honduras. The population that relies directly or indirectly on the resources of the Gulf of Fonseca is more than a million people.

The Importance of Coastal Resources for Local Communities

The coastal-marine resources, including rich mangrove forests and seasonal salt flats and lagoons, have sustained a growing population for many years. The seasonal lagoons are called that because in the rainy season they turn into beautiful lagoons that play an important role in the hydrologic balance of the coastal and estuarine waters. They serve as habitats and breeding sites for a wide biological diversity that plays an important role in the coastal marine environment and provides food and a source of income to local communities. During the dry season, while these productive ecosystems continue their important role in the area's hydrology, they become dry during the day and are called *playones*. These dried lagoons have traditionally been used to sustain the salt industry, but since 1973 the shrimp farming industry, supported by international financial institutions (IFIs) and the U.S. Agency for International Development, has converted many of the *playones* and seasonal lagoons into barren shrimp farms.

In 1987, 47,000 hectares of mangrove forest ecosystems existed in the Honduran coastal zone. Mangrove forests are comprised of a variety of species of trees or shrubs that have adapted to a salty environment such as is found in estuaries where salt and fresh water mix through tidal action. Periodically irrigated by the tides, mangroves are viviparous species and can reach heights of more than 15 meters. They have leaf coverage the entire year and help against global warming. Along the coasts and estuaries there were also more than 24,000 hectares of seasonal lagoons generally located adjacent to mangroves. Until 1987 there were found in Honduras' coastal zone 70 species of resident and migratory birds; 50 commercial fish species; 22 mammalian and reptilian species and various mollusks and crustacean species. All of them interacted with the five different mangrove species then found in the Gulf of Fonseca area.

It is important to understand the significance of the Gulf of Fonseca for those who live nearby. Coastal wetlands made up of mangrove forests, lagoons and estuaries contain a wide array of biological resources that satisfies the needs for food, income, shelter and economic well-being for thousands of fishermen and farmers. At the edge of estuaries and within the mangrove forests and lagoons can be found firewood, timber, fish, crustaceans, mollusks, reptiles and others. This suggests a great amount of traditional economic activity, and harvesting for sustenance is carried out near and inside the mangrove forest as it has been done for decades.

The Gulf of Fonseca is the area where shrimp aquaculture has been stimulated most strongly in Honduras and supported by institutions such as the World Bank. This has caused much harm to local communities and to the coastal marine environment on which many people depend for their livelihoods. A result has been increased poverty for many of the people living in the area. At the same time the national elite and international investors have been enriched at the expense of many local people.

International financial organizations, international aid agencies that seek to stimulate economic development, and organizations concerned with issues of food security tend to work with the national elites of developing countries to enrich them. They also tend to support the production of cheap food for export and the generation of high incomes for investors from the developed countries. The problem is that the trade and development institutions such as the World Bank, InterAmerican Development Bank (IDB) and U.S. AID (Agency for International Development) very seldom consider the problems of communities' loss of their local culture and quality of life, of the population migration that results when an area is altered, and the serious environmental degradation their projects cause. This failure to consider the human and cultural consequences of their activities in the context of the rapid expansion of large-scale shrimp aquaculture projects has had significant impacts on Honduras as well as many other nations.

The rapid and uncontrolled expansion of the shrimp aquaculture industry on coastal wetlands throughout much of the world has been stimulated by financial institutions concerned with the food security of developing countries in the South. However, the tragic lack of planning for the development of the shrimp aquaculture industry has caused serious consequences for countries' environments and local communities. Many of the mangrove forests of the world are disappearing quickly as are other critical coastal wetlands, mainly because of the uncontrolled and explosive growth of industrial shrimp aquaculture. The efforts of local people and fisherpeople who are dependent on access to the areas being destroyed by industrial aquaculture and have attempted to resist and protest the expansion of this industry have generated murders and injuries among fishermen or other inhabitants of the coastal zone.

Human Rights Abuses

The abuse of law and communities' rights in the area of the Gulf of Fonseca, Honduras, is also manifested by a series of murders that have been committed between October 1992 and May 10, 1998. Over that time at the estuaries near shrimp farms operated by companies such as Granjas Marinas San Bernardo, Promasur, Acuacultura Fonseca, Cumar, Crisur, and Sea Farm, eleven fishermen have been found dead by shooting or by machete. Those murders were reported to the corresponding authorities, to the Committee for the Defense of Human Rights (CODEH), and to national press media. Several public protests were held but no one has ever been brought to justice.

When the large-scale shrimp farm industry first appeared the farms were established on the seasonal lagoons and in the mangrove forests. The lagoons were surrounded by dikes and converted to large earth-walled ponds with barren borders. The large ponds spread across the coastlines for long distances, altering the hydrology and blocking access to the Gulf for fishermen and other traditional users. A significant amount of pollution was also produced. The mangrove forests were typically clear-cut, leaving stark wastelands that were made into shrimp farms.

This destructive incursion by the large-scale or industrial shrimp producers caused the local residents to lose food sources, incomes, access to firewood, loss of access to timber for construction; loss of access to traditional fishing places; loss of health of the coastal-marine ecosystems; and loss of personal security with the shrimp companies employing armed guards and bringing in outside workers. This was a violation of the human rights of these local people. The sudden incursion of shrimp farms and the destruction of the productive mangrove and lagoon ecosystems on which they depended destroyed the quality of life for thousands of people who had no voice in what was done to them.

The spread of the industry across the coastal wetlands of the Gulf of Fonseca does not even mean there was an increase in the efficiency of production. Shrimp farming is a destructive industry subject to frequent onset of diseases among the farmed shrimp and often declining productivity over a relatively short period of time as the quality of the environment declines. Increases may be obtained in the short term through territorial expansion into new farms, the increased use of chemical inputs and improved cultivation techniques aimed at improving production, but over the long-term, aquaculture is profitable and therefore sustainable only if the environment is preserved. But, without planning for sustainable development the shrimp industry tends to degrade its productive environment and to cause social problems as well.

A. *Violation of Existing Laws to Protect People*

These concerns about violations of peoples' human rights are not based on a need for Honduras or the international community to create new laws. Honduras already has laws reflecting the human rights of its people. The problem is a lack of enforcement of existing laws. The Honduran Constitution provides in Article 59, for example, that the human person is the supreme purpose of the society and the State. Everybody has the obligation of respecting and protecting the person. Article 61 states that the

Constitution guarantees to the Honduran people and foreigners resident in the country the right to the inviolability of life, individual security, liberty, and equality before the law. Article 65 sets out that the right to life is inviolable. Article 66 forbids the death penalty. Article 83 requires the State to appoint attorneys for the defense of poor people. Article 84 states that anyone found infringing the law can be apprehended by any person and taken to the appropriate authority. Article 90 concludes that no one can be judged except by a judge or a competent court with all the formalities, rights and guarantees Honduran law provides. Even if some of the fishermen who have been killed near the shrimp farms had been engaged in the taking of the farms' shrimp—and no one knows this to be true—if they were killed by the producers' security guards the Constitutional protections were violated by the imposition of summary capital punishment by private interests without any arrest or trial or the opportunity to be represented by a lawyer.

B. Violation of Laws to Protect Property

The Constitution of the Republic of Honduras created in Decree 131, January 11, 1982, provides in Article 107 that the lands of the State located in the bordering zone to the neighbor states, or at both seas littoral, on a extension of forty square kilometers to the inside of the country, only will be owned at any title by Hondurans by birth, by societies created by Honduran people and by state institutions, under the pain of the respective act or contract being declared null and void. The bigger aquaculture companies of Honduras, such as Sea Farms Inc., Granjas Marinas San Bernardo, Cumar and Acuacultura Fonseca have many investors and owners from the United States, as well as Culcamar from Ecuador. These ownership laws are ignored. But there are numerous other laws that are also ignored without consequence to the violator. For example, the law concerning fisheries provides for peoples' freedom for fishing and for the use of the beaches. Article 12 of the General Law of Fisheries provides that in no case will there be conferred rights that make it difficult to fish or obstruct access to fishing for the purpose of domestic food consumption of a region's inhabitants. Shrimp aquaculture produces almost exclusively for export purposes and clearly interferes with the food security rights of local people. Article 23 requires that the owners of lands contiguous to a beach will be not permitted to erect fences or construct or cultivate within 50 meters from the high tide line. Such land users are required to leave adequate space for fishing. Shrimp farms commonly violate this law.

C. Denial of Access Rights

The establishment of shrimp farms on areas that included mangrove forests, lagoons and tidal zones not only deprived local residents of their food, income and sources of wood for heating and cooking due to the cutting of the mangrove forests on which they depended, it also deprived them of the ability to have access to fishing sites. Along with this many people were expelled from the temporary houses they had constructed for provisional shelters, *rancherías*, at the edge of the estuaries and near the mangroves where the shrimp farms were established.

D. Pollution and Destruction of Livelihood

Article 50 of the Fisheries Law strictly forbids the discharge of industrial wastes into the sea, rivers, streams, and gullies. It also prohibits the deposit of such wastes in places that might erode, channel or filter wastes to those protected water sources. Along with this is a ban on the discharge of any other waste, substance and detritus that could cause damage to fish and their hatchery areas. At present more than 16,000 hectares of shrimp farms discharge their polluting wastes directly to estuaries without any treatment. When the shrimp are harvested, all the waters used in the shrimp farming, which contain thousands of tons of detritus and chemical substances that are used by the shrimp producers to prevent and fight diseases or fertilize ponds also go directly into Honduran estuaries. All the shrimp farms and a major part of the shrimp packing companies pour their wastes directly into estuaries. As a result the Gulf of Fonseca is polluted with pathogenic microorganisms, many of them from other countries. This includes the Taura Virus from Ecuador and the White Spot Virus from Asia. There are frequently legal denunciations of the massive deaths of fish and crustaceans that are caused by these discharges.

The violations of Honduran law are not confined to the Constitution and Fisheries Law. Honduras also has a General Environment Law that was effective May 27, 1993 pursuant to Decree 10-493. Article 32 forbids the discharge into continental or maritime waters where the State has jurisdiction, any kind of polluting wastes, solid, liquid or gaseous wastes capable of harming human or aquatic life, degrading water quality or disturbing the ecological balance in general. Article 66 requires that the solid and organic wastes coming from human activities will be treated to prevent alterations in rivers, lakes, lagoons and in waters in general.

Article 106 follows the "polluter pays principle" and requires in theory that the person who contaminates the environment and harms the ecological systems by failing to obey the requirements of the environmental law and other relevant laws will assume the cost of the environmental recovery to remedy such action or omission. That has of course not occurred and no one has been held financially liable for their actions. Article 52 of the General Fishery Law provides for the protection of mangroves, lagoons, estuaries, and biodiversity conservation. Article 52 forbids the cutting of mangroves and other trees at the river banks and their mouths, in estuaries, lagoons, at the edge of the sea edge and other places that can serve to fish and oysters as refuge (Fishery General Law: Decree 154, May 29, 1959). The mangrove destruction by shrimp farmers has been widely documented, but no one has ever been punished or required to pay for the damage.

Article 78 requires the preparation of an Environmental Impact Assessment (EIA) by people such as shrimp farmers whose activities represent a significant alteration of the environment. While several companies have presented Studies of Environmental Impact Evaluation (EIA), none has fulfilled the recommendations about mitigation measures to protect the environment.

The Declaration of Natural Protected Areas (Decree 5-99-E January 20, 1999) places ten Natural Protected Areas in the Gulf of Fonseca under legal protection. Seven of the sites contain significant amounts of mangroves, lagoons and coastal wetlands. These seven areas are designated by the Honduran government as "Ramsar Site 1000" in the Ramsar Convention for Wetlands Protection. On April 3, 2000, Coddeffagolf denounced internationally the destruction of legally protected wetlands in order to construct shrimp farms in three of the Natural Protected Areas. Nothing has been done to protect the areas and the illegal shrimp farms remain.

Conclusion

The Constitution of the Republic of Honduras and the laws that relate to protection of coastal natural resources and conservation of the Gulf of Fonseca have been violated with total impunity. The systematic institutionalized failure to apply a nation's laws justly is a violation of the human rights of its people. Nor can it be expected that the Honduran legal system can correct the violation—because it is a contributing part of the violations. The problem is that the judicial power in Honduras works in favor of small groups of favored people that have economic power and that are indifferent or opposed to the concerns of poor people. International financial organizations and development agencies have only been concerned with the immediate economic benefit from large-scale "industrial" shrimp production. This has caused them to ignore and even appease those who have violated the country's laws and caused environmental degradation, and the loss of the traditional quality of life of local communities. This serious disruption has stimulated the emigration of Hondurans to the countries of the North, including particularly the United States. The financial organizations must reevaluate their policies and the conditions of loans to include responsible measurements of citizens' participation, social equity, and conservation. International financial and development organizations are not considering the concerns of equity, social participation and environmental protection in the projects they support. Nor is the situation in Honduras exclusive. The same situation, or an even worse state of affairs, exists in many other countries in which the shrimp industry has taken over the coastlines.

© Jorge Varela Márquez and Ashgate Publishing Company 2001. Jorge Varela Márquez is director of a community-based, grassroots organization named the Comité para la Defensa y Desarrollo de la Flora y Fauna del Golfo de Fonseca (CODDEFFAGOLF) in Honduras.

12 Human Rights Education for Social Transformation: Innovative Grassroots Programs on Economic, Social and Cultural Rights

SHULAMITH KOENIG

My Name is Shulamith. In Hebrew "Shulamith" means: a woman of Jerusalem, a woman of peace. The Biblical Jerusalem was called Yru'shalem, the people will see wholeness, synonymous with peace—Shalom. A woman of Jerusalem is called Shulamith.

I speak of my name because it has a deep meaning to the commitments I have made to promote human rights education at the community level worldwide. Having lived in the outskirts of Jaffa, my parents had owned jointly a metal foundry with an Arab family. I used to play with their children, which was quite unusual at the time and unfortunately it is still unusual today for Jewish Israeli children to play with Arab Israeli children. Having had this experience I was very uncomfortable with what I was taught at school that the Jews are the "The Chosen people." "What about our Arab friends?" I asked my father who was a talmudic scholar. "Yes—he said—you are *chosen* for social responsibility—for Tikum Olam" (mending the world).

In the early fifties, I had the honor to accompany a group of young Jesuit students to a meeting with Martin Buber. One of them, after listening to this wise man said, timidly: "Professor Buber, allow me to ask you a stupid question: When will there be peace in the world?" Smiling, Buber answered: "There are no stupid questions my son, only stupid answers. Allow me to give you one: If one morning every women and man alive will say to the first person they meet that day 'Good Morning' and mean it, this will be the first morning of peace."

Holistic Learning about Human Rights

These are several of the narratives, from many years ago, that inform my world view and the commitments I have undertaken to energize, organize and facilitate transformative, holistic learning about human rights at the community level—using the narratives of struggle and hope as a powerful tool for learning, reflecting and acting; for people to become agents of change and achieve social justice, equality and full participation—of women and men alike—in human, social and economic development.

The Biblical narrative was very important to our education in Israel. Especially the "forty years in the desert" where Moses and Aaron, guided by the commitment to "Kdushat Ha'chayim"—the sanctity of the life of all human beings—appointed judges and established courts that through the processes of litigation enunciated egalitarian laws in the spirit of the Ten Commandments and as relevant to people's daily lives. Unfortunately these laws considered mostly men—ignoring half of humanity. Yet, this is a story of building a nation of law and justice in the desert—guiding people in how to move from slavery to freedom with social responsibility. This story became my guiding light, illuminating a fundamental principle: law without freedom is tyranny and freedom without law is anarchy and the fine balance between law and freedom is sustained and energized by human rights to enable us to break through the vicious cycle of humiliation.

In the mid 1980s, coming to live in the United States after being called a traitor in Israel for promoting a two-state solution to the Arab-Israeli conflict, I established the People's Decade for Human Rights Education, recently renamed: PDHRE, People's Movement for Human Rights Education. I made this commitment to fulfill the promise Israel made to the world but had so tragically neglected

I am convinced that through learning about human rights as a way of life, people develop systemic analysis and are empowered to take action and insist on fully participating in the decisions that determine their lives. Since 1998, PDHRE has been introducing transformative, holistic human rights education in more than 60 countries at the community level. I am very proud to say that as part of this process I was instrumental in the UN declaring a Decade for Human Rights Education, for the period 1995—2004.

Being convinced that imposed ignorance is by itself a human rights violation, I argued that fundamental change can be brought about only if every person alive will know that he or she are owners of human rights—

that all must become human rights educators, human rights monitors and implementers from generation to generation.

Being in Community in Dignity with Others

In the last two years, to achieve the objectives we had set for ourselves, PDHRE has initiated a historic development: the establishment of "Human Rights Cities." To date there are seven cities that have joined this effort. PDHRE is also developing four Regional Learning Institutions for Human Rights Education in South Asia, Asia Pacific, Latin America and Africa, guided by the prophetic statement of Nelson Mandela: "We need to develop a new political culture based on Human Rights." Through workshops, seminars and dialogue we hope to contribute to a new vocation: human rights education. The goal is to stimulate and train community leaders and educators who will join our commitment to influence a new generation to assume political leadership and be guided by the holistic human rights framework as a viable political ideology for the 21st century.

In that context human rights comprise the guideline and framework for social responsibility—being in community in dignity with others. I must stress here that I do not agree with a perspective that seems to me to be an artificial division between two kinds of human rights: individual rights and community rights. I feel very strongly that this odd separation is a left-over from the Cold War, which contributed to the statement of many in the South who often say: "human rights promote western values that are imposed on us!" Indeed, all human beings in every culture are individuals, but we all live in communities of one kind or another. It is this "living together"—the life of every individual living *in community*, which human rights define, promote and protect. Equality, discrimination, violations and realization, all happen for better or worse *in community*—in the relationship between people and amongst groups horizontally and vertically.

For this very same reason and to make sure that learners understand human rights as a holistic framework and a way of life, I insist of speaking on "the human rights to..." rather than "the rights to..." In my experience, using the words, "human rights" rather than "rights," informs the learners that human rights are the birthright of all humanity, as Professor Upendra Baxi says: human rights are the right to be human. With this inclusive vision we accept human beings—women, men, youth and children alike—as whole beings, endowed with the tools of justice, i.e. human rights. Furthermore, speaking of "human rights" rather than of "rights" enables the learner to understand the indivisibility, interrelatedness and interconnectedness of civil, cultural, economic, political and social human rights. The insight gained by the learners is invariably followed by advocacy and actions for gender equality and economic and social justice—be it with their governing bodies or within their communities "free of fear and free from want".

A Universal Value System Protected by Law

Human rights inform a universal value system protected by law. In this context it is important to call attention to the fact that the two major human rights instruments are called "Covenants!" In my perception they are *covenants with morality*, advocating a higher state of being in community, in dignity, with trust, or if you wish, with unconditional love.

We are all aware of the fact that human rights reflect the aspirations and hopes of humanity from its early beginning. So do the prophecy and teaching of most religions. The downside is that all religions are in essence patriarchal, which is a perspective that human rights attempt to change for women and marginalized groups—the "unwanted" others. It should be therefore understood that human rights do not deny religion but simply widen and enrich religion by recognizing women, the excluded and subordinated "others" as equal members of humanity.

In the last fifty years the struggles of people for economic and social justice fueled and invigorated the development of international human right law. This included women who were fighting to eliminate discrimination. They were insisting on the right to participate as equals in the decisions that determine their lives; the advocacy to change harmful conditions in which children grow; the endless shameful discrimination and racism throughout the world; and the criminal acts of torture. These were carefully attended to in various and detailed human rights conventions, each reflecting the spirit of the Universal Declaration of Human Rights and the two covenants.

These enunciations of human rights are not always perfect. They are often not detailed enough, but they are perfect in their call for justice—for a world guided by human rights. Even if from today on no new convention or resolution is added to this excellent overarching body of international law and we attend only to the implementation of human rights as encoded to date—and if from today on we demand that our governments stand by all the commitments they have made and the obligations they have undertaken in the international arena—we will be close to having a perfect world.

To achieve this dream it is our responsibility first to take action to have all people know human rights and have them join in "reminding" governments, and if necessary shame them—by holding them accountable to the many "Plans of Action" they have signed on to, the Conventions and Covenants they have ratified, undertaking a clear obligation for human rights to become the law of the land.

What is tragic in my eyes is that the people in struggle for whom the human rights were encoded and whose oppressions, impoverishment and pain the system of human rights is meant to alleviate, do not know that human rights exist nor do they understand the power and meaning of human rights for their lives.

In the hope of changing this unfortunate and very sad situation we made the commitment to develop a movement for human rights education. In essence human rights education is about hope and learning about justice. It is about people transforming systems in which differences are liabilities into systems where differences and diversity bring joy and richness to our lives. But mostly, human rights education is political education that leads to people taking active part in their own economic and social development.

Connecting Human Rights with People's Lives

Human rights education must not be theoretical, but relevant to people's daily lives. People learn from their own narratives to conceptualize human rights and work towards their fulfillment. Only then can we become agents of change.

In our workshops we ask people to define human rights and all they say is written on large sheets of paper, which are hung along the walls. The results are amazing. They reinvent the Universal Declaration of Human Rights. Their wording is often better and less abstract. Through play—acting they obtain insight into the relationship between men and women and are frequently embarrassed about how they participate directly and indirectly in strengthening systems in favor of the privileged and against the underprivileged. When we work with children and speak about the human rights to education we first point out that by having a school their human rights are being realized—but if they do not have enough books or the roof of the school is leaking, this is a human rights violation that must be corrected. We try always to first discuss human rights realization followed by analyzing human rights violations. We believe that this contributes to people moving from being victims to becoming claimants of human rights.

In our human rights education workshops we try to bring up to par the participants' understanding about economic, social and cultural human rights with political and civil human rights. The facts we share with villagers that food, housing, education, healthcare and the opportunity to have work at livable wages are human rights have them jump with joy. Almost instantly they start planning how to claim these human rights as a necessary and integral consequence of the development process. People have told us in many words that poverty is a human rights violation; that not only freedom fighters imprisoned by their government are political prisoners but that those who live in economic degradation are political prisoners as well, i.e. "prisoners" of bad political and economic management and destructive decisions.

PDHRE's Human Rights Workshops

Allow me to share with you several short stories about human rights education. The imperatives of our methodology is drawn from the teaching of the famous Brazilian education theorist Paulo Freire's *The Pedagogy of the Oppressed.* From their own narratives of oppression and struggles people learn what actions they must take to transform their lives and the life of their community.

A. *Costa Rica*

In a workshop we held in Costa Rica women were introduced to the fundamental concept of human rights as protecting and prompting theirs and insisting on the dignity of others. We then asked the women to each share with the group one human rights violation and one human rights realization which they have experienced in their lives. A woman, 53 years old, said: "First I want to speak about a violation. I was 13 years old and I was made to marry the man who raped me." You may know that in several Latin American countries if the man agrees to marry the woman he raped, he is exonerated. She continued: "I am now 53 years old and I just went back to school to finish my studies. I am now realizing my human rights." In those two sentences she analyzed her life within a human rights framework. We knew right then and there that she had learned to examine her life from a human rights perspective and that she will continue to do so for the rest of her life and teach it to her grandchildren.

Introducing the holistic vision of human rights in our workshops we discuss Article 30 of the UDHR, stating in our words its important message: No one human right can be used to justify violating another human right. We have people then identify the human rights of others that may potentially come into conflict with their rights. When asked "how can these conflicts be resolved?" we answer "all conflicts must be resolved within a human rights framework."

B. *South Africa*

Outside Durban, in South Africa, we invited 10 families from the Zulu community, 10 men, 10 women and their teenage children, to help us learn how to introduce human rights in their communities. First, my colleague and I, she is a local community activist who has been trained by PDHRE, held a discussion about dignity and how the new democracy is effecting change in their lives. I then took the 10 men out to a close by road and asked them to stand on the road, facing, in their "memory," the white policemen who used to come to the village. I asked them to talk about how they felt and what were the human rights violations inflicted on them by the whites. Together, we defined the human rights violations that were inflicted on them because of the color of their skin, and proceeded to write them down one by one on large sheets of paper. "Now," I said, "when apartheid is over what kind of relations do you want to have with the whites who are coming down your streets?" At this point we were defining the expressed hopes in terms of human rights realizations, continuing to write them one by one on white sheets of paper.

We then returned to the room where the women and the children were learning about human rights as it relates to their lives. We pasted the sheets of paper on the wall face down. I asked the children to go with my colleague to another room to discuss how human rights help secure and enrich the lives of children. I asked the men to sit on one side of the room and the women to sit across the room, facing them. I then asked the women to tell the men about the human rights violations they suffer because they are women, and proceeded to ask: "what human rights do you hope to fulfill in the relationship with men?" As the women spoke, one—by—one, we filled up new blank sheets of paper with the descriptions of their struggles and hopes, writing what they said in a human rights language. The embarrassment of the men became quite apparent. The women's pain was the same as the men's. The women's hopes for fulfillment were also strikingly similar to the men's. The insight men had gained when we asked them to uncover what they wrote and show it to the women was obvious and often funny, accompanied with a giggle. If they could, the men would have gladly become invisible. The beauty and power of this lesson is that nothing further had to be said by us to the men. They had said all that was necessary. It was all there on the wall.

We asked the children to join us and asked them the same questions as to their relationship with their parents. The parents recognized their own voices in the narratives of their children, listening to the desires for respect, equality and partnership in dignity.

It became obvious to all the participants that the vicious cycle of humiliation can be broken if they learn about human rights and mentor others to demand equality and to eliminate discrimination. Someone said that human rights are all they have hoped for. Others spoke of trust and being human with one another, women and men alike.

C. Senegal

The practice of FGC—female genital cutting—is indeed a gross human rights violation. Much work has been done to stop this practice, without any significant result. TOSTAN—a Senegalese grassroots organization, has worked for many years with women in the villages introducing them through separate modules to: democracy, literacy, health, participation, etc. There was, however, no real breakthrough and meaningful discussions on ending the practice of FGC did not take place.

I met Molly Melching the Director of TOSTAN in Germany at a UNESCO conference on adult education. Hearing her story I suggested to her to consider introducing the human rights framework through *all* the modules. Within a few days of my return to my office our researchers faxed to Senegal quotations of commitments and obligations regarding the issues of health and women. These were introduced and discussed with the men and women in the village of Malikunda. Very soon after they integrated all the pieces, which they had already learned over the years, they declared an end to FGC in their village, saying: "If our culture violates our human rights, we want a human rights culture."

French television came to interview the people of the village. A little girl was running in front of the cameras. Her mother called out to her: "Sensen, Sensen. Come here!" "What does Sensen mean?" the Cameraman asked. "Human Rights" answered the mother with pride. "Why do you call her human rights?" the cameraman asked again. "Because she is the first girl in the village that was not circumcised" the mother answered. Men and women alike declared an end to FGC in front of the camera, quoting the language of human rights from the materials we had sent to them, translated into *woolof*—the local language—which empowered them. Pride accompanied their recognition that the international community had also acknowledged what they believe to be decent and correct. These are norms and standards that they now accepted as their own.

The very same women in the village of Malikunda came several weeks later to their husbands, requesting parcels of land to grow vegetables. They said to their husbands: "Land is a human right" and they got the land. This is the result of internalizing human rights as belonging to all, which provides *the safe ground for negotiation* and is the only way we can relate to one another.

In both these cases it was evident that the men fully understood that to protect their human rights they must protect the human rights of women. I like to describe the reaction and action people take after learning that they and all others are owners of human rights as *moving power to human rights.*

Human Rights Cities

Human Rights Cities, which we have initiated, are developed by us and our colleagues from around the world. The goal is to use these experiences to create and ensure a multiplier/ripple effect in larger communities, i.e., The Human Rights Cities and the Regional Learning Institutions for Human Rights Education where learners will work to proliferate the development of such Human Rights Cities.

To date, seven cities are pioneering the development of Human Rights Cities through mass education in human rights. These cities are: Rosario, Argentina (Pop. 1,000,000, program is in its 3rd year); Nagpur, India (pop. 2.8 million, program is in its second year). It named itself a human rights sensitive city. Thies, Senegal (pop. 300.000, including 10 human rights villages, is in its 2nd year) Kati, Mali, (pop. 50,000, program inaugurated on Dec. 10, 2000), Dinajpur, Bangladesh, (pop. 100,000, to be inaugurated in the coming few months); Graz, Austria, whose City Council voted recently to declare their city a human rights city, the first in Europe; and, soon to be chosen, is an Indigenous Human Rights City in the Philippines.

The African Regional Institution was established in Bamako, Mali in November 2000. The South Asian Regional Institution will be inaugurated in August 2001, in Mumbai, India. Plans are now being drawn to establish the Latin American Regional Institution in Rosario, Argentina, and the Asia Pacific Regional Institution in Manila, Philippines toward the end of 2001. At the outset the institutions will engage in extensive research and curriculum development with its future faculty, and the adaptation of the necessary materials to local languages and regional concern. Thereafter, the institutions will hold six-week seminars including: in-depth training of trainers; development of methodology and strategy; and capacity building for implementing human rights education programs for social and economic transformation.

Learners will participate in intensive studies about human rights, political economy, sociology, and community development. The conditions for their participation will include a commitment to undertake the development of human rights education in their countries and collaborate to reach ever-wider constituencies—to weave a new political culture based on human rights.

In a human rights city a process is set for citizens to examine the laws, policies, development resources and the ongoing relationships in their city, horizontally and vertically. Argentina, Senegal, Mali, Bangladesh, India and Austria, where human rights cities are being developed, all ratified most of the Covenants and Convention with very few reservations. But most of the people in these countries do not have the vaguest idea of the obligations governments undertake when ratifying human rights treaties and how, if implemented, they can make a difference to their lives, the life of their community and of future generations. Thus, in each of these cities its citizenry learn and examine the laws and policies, continuously monitor them and take actions to see that their judicial system abides by the human rights framework. As part of this process a documentation center is created to map the human rights realizations and violations in the city, which then informs their action, demanding changes in laws and policies and developing an alternative budget for the city. In every city one can find groups that may fight to improve the healthcare in the city or the educational system, or the delivery of clean water, etc. The alternative budget comes to replace compartmentalized activities of one group or another. It consolidates and unifies actions through lobbying for a budget to fulfill the human rights needs of all the people.

We believe that this is the best form of participation contributing to the understanding of people why economic, social and cultural human rights cannot but be realized progressively. This process makes people responsible partners in the development of their city and to short and long-term allocation of funds.

Last but not least is the creation of "relationships." This relationship-building manifests itself in the change of attitudes toward religious freedom, police behavior in the community, and greater acceptance of marginalized groups, to mention just a few. Groups, as well as individual and various other stakeholders work to create an atmosphere of communication—overcoming fears, xenophobia, and homophobia.

In a visit to Rosario I met with the head of the Police Academy where policemen and policewomen were participating in intensive human rights workshops. They learn about their human rights as well of those they are to police. With much satisfaction of the evident results in the attitudes to and of the police, he said: "These workshops convinced me that there is no other option but human rights." Later in the year I shared this statement with the Governor of Thies, Senegal. His response was, "I will put up this statement in my office and all over the city." The activities and actions taking place in each of the Human Rights Cities can be found on our website: *http://www.pdhre.org*.

There is much more to share in promoting the cause of human rights education, as an imperative for women and men participating in assuring the sustainability of human rights, economic development and social justice. However, if human rights learning does not result in a systemic analysis and viable actions we educators will be known as well—meaning people but not as people who are making a difference in the real world.

To make this difference through human rights education in post-war situations where tragic violations have been committed within countries, any negotiation must include a clear statement about the dignity of both sides who participated in the conflict and the negotiated statement must be used to set the guidelines for resolving future differences before they flare up into new armed conflicts. Wars are a terrible part of the human experience. It is our hope that sharing the human rights vision actively and proactively, as it is reflected in international law, we may take the first step for dealing with conflicts in a different way.

Conclusion

To sum up what human rights education for social transformation represents, I will say again: *It is political education that holds within it a spiritual mission. It is recognizing that the root of all human rights violations in all societies is the absence of equality between women and men and non-discrimination.* It may sound very simplistic, which I pride myself on being, when I say that women and men alike, born into and living in a prevalent Patriarchal system, take for granted that it is "normal" and "human" for some people to be more privileged than others, and some to enjoy power and deny equality to others. In short, they come to accept injustice as justice. Moreover, people are ready to exchange equality for survival. Learning about human rights as a holistic way of living with others in a condition of equality and lack of discrimination is the first step towards changing a system that inherently advocates discrimination and leads to oppression and gross human rights violations.

To end this long discourse in arguing the imperatives of human rights learning, I would like to share with you two experience: One with 300 children in Rosario, Argentina, and the second one in a village in Tamil Nadu, India.

In Rosario, at the outset I asked one boy and one girl to be "cars on the road." I asked another boy and girl to be "pedestrians on a crossroad." I told them: "When I say go! You all go forward." "Go!" I cried out. They moved vigorously and bumped into each other, falling down while all the other children were clapping and laughing. "What happened?" I asked. "You didn't tell us to watch the green and red lights." "And what was the result?" I asked. "They were all hurt and maybe killed" they answered. "Did it matter if the driver was a boy or a girl—or if the pedestrians were women or men?" I asked. "NO! NO!" they all cried out. "Why do we need traffic regulation?" I asked. "Because we need to know when we can go and we need to stop... so we don't get hurt" one of the girls said. "This is why we need laws," I said, "these laws are called human rights which enable us to move from place to place without being hurt or hurting others."

I then asked them if they wanted to try and say what are the human rights we need after such an accident happens and for other children not to be hurt. I got amazing answers. Here are some of them: "We need Hospitals to take the people who were hurt."—"A house to get to once we get tired or it starts raining;" "Medicine and food to get well," "Our parents need to work so they can build a house and buy us food," "We need education so that we can read the traffic signs," "It doesn't matter if you are a boy or a girl. We are all equals" etc. etc. They have succinctly enumerated their wishes for moving in the world without being hurt. They created a holistic human rights framework and an understanding of the need for human rights laws to protect their lives and allow them to move in the world as equals.

In a village outside Chennai (formerly Madras) a group of fifty women and men welcomed me with flowers in a room smaller than your office. I didn't speak much and had them tell me what they know about human rights, the caste system in India, and their hopes for social and economic transformation. The issue that emerged most potently was the lack of good education in the village, which is so necessary, as they say, to overcome the vicious cycle of humiliation in which the Dalit people are trapped. They did talk about the efforts of their government and State through the "positive discrimination" act, enacted to meet the educational needs of the Dalit people. They felt, however, that they were not being consulted and that the process is bad.

In a moment of truth I had an insight and asked: "How many people are in the village?" I was told: "One thousand." I then asked them if it will be possible for each one in the village, young or old, to contribute just *one rupee* a day towards the improvement of their educational facilities and to hire better teachers. The response was unanimous "YES!" We did the calculation and realized that in one year they would have 360,000 rupees! "Could this help?" I asked and suggested: "you can request from the local authorities to cofinance the effort." With us in the room was my host, a Dalit lawyer who introduced himself to them and offered to help in this effort. Before leaving we all chanted together: "*We want our human rights! We want education for our children!*"

By next morning a delegation from the village appeared, unannounced, at my friend's office in Chennai, requesting from him to incorporate an association of the village to start this effort. And more, they had told him that they are going to reach out to fifty additional Dalit villages in the area to do the same and contribute one rupee a day for the human rights needs in their villages, and possibly collaborate to create better education and health care for all of these villages.

I must stress that during the one hour village meeting we spoke about patriarchy and the double discrimination Dalit women suffer in their own communities. We talked of how they can work together to overcome the discrimination against women, which will contribute towards Dalit men achieving their human rights realizing human rights for the village. This was accepted very well with very interesting comments about equality, the difficulty of being a Dalit man, and the issues of the "differences" between women and men in general.

I hope that I was able to argue successfully the importance of human rights education for social and economic transformation. If those who read this chapter actively join in the activities of this movement I believe we can make a difference and we can be instrumental in changing the world. It is indeed a human rights violation of huge dimensions if women, men, youth, and children around the world do not know the meaning of human rights to their lives.

I know that as human rights and humanitarian law experts and activists we are forced by the horrendous situations to try and eradicate the symptoms of violence, hate and deprivation. Indeed, human rights violations must stop today! However, working on symptoms we create human solidarity but adding to our work the examination and analysis of causes we stand a chance to create social change. This examination and analysis must take place among the people for them to move from being victims of human rights to become active claimants of their human rights. After all it is for the people that human rights were enunciated. In this work we must bring up to par the understanding of economic, social, and cultural human rights with political and civil rights. It is important to repeat: *It is high time that we all agree that people who live in dire poverty are political prisoners, and children who are hungry are on death row.*

I implore all human rights experts, academic human rights scholars, and human rights advocates: as you continue to do your extremely valuable work make a commitment to give several weeks a year to live in villages in the South and facilitate the learning about human rights with communities who need it the most. Human rights are the banks of the river within which life can flow in freedom and dignity. As a Jewish sage once said: "The material needs of my neighbors are my spiritual needs."

© Shulamith Koenig and Ashgate Publishing Company, 2001. Shulamith Koenig is Executive Director of PDHRE.

13 Appeal to Self-Interest in Human Rights Education for the Military: A Self-Defeating Strategy?

ERIC STENER CARLSON

Two Views of Human Rights Education—Self-Interest vs. Altruism

At a recent conference, I participated in a discussion on the Human Rights and International Humanitarian Law Course taught at the United States Army School of the Americas (USARSA), Fort Benning, Georgia.[1] The central question was whether human rights educators should appeal to a soldier's self-interest, as the instructors at the USARSA advocate, or whether they should appeal to his sense of altruism. In concrete terms, should our final objective be the same as the USARSA's Lesson Plan #2031, to "describe the reasons and advantages why complying with human rights is essential in order to have a successful military operation,"[2]— because it "focuses the mission; maintains discipline; reduces enemy resistance; [retains] support of the public; and [leads to] restoration of the peace"[3]—or should our goal be to persuade soldiers that the rights of captured belligerents and other *hors d'combat* must be respected, for no other reason than that protecting a human being's dignity, enemy or otherwise, has a value in and of itself? It must be noted that the Lesson Plan *does* state at the outset that the soldier's "personal duty to obey the law is sufficient reason to adhere strictly to the Law of War and human rights," but then it goes on to enumerate the many benefits listed above.[4]

The participation from the audience of educators, advocates and legal scholars was rich and varied, but, within that discussion, two blocs began to clearly emerge, representing, to my mind, the division I have often witnessed in discussions among my colleagues on this same topic. Therefore, I shall take this opportunity to briefly outline these two positions, framing my current exploration of self-interest within this ongoing, vibrant debate.

Before I begin, however, I feel I must address the sensitive nature of the subject matter. Any discussion of the School of the Americas is affected by the debate over whether it should be closed for having trained a number of soldiers who took part in death squads and led *coups d'état*,[5] and because of allegations that its instructors have taught torture. While I recognize the importance of this debate, I must clarify at the outset that my goal is neither to defend nor to denigrate the USARSA, but, rather, to isolate and to discuss one element of the School's human rights program, which I feel can be used to improve other human rights programs for soldiers at other institutions. Let me further clarify that my position is by no means neutral, as I am totally opposed to torture and to extra-judicial killing. But I shall not address the closing of the School of the Americas in this chapter because I do not want this important pedagogical question regarding self-interest to be swept up in this continuing and highly-politicized debate.

Returning to the topic at hand, the first of the two positions I identified holds that we cannot appeal to a soldier's self-interest, because it is immoral to do so. Obviously, there were gradations of support for this position among the audience. At the extreme was an advocate for social justice in Latin America who would not even entertain the idea. As an absolute pacifist, she believed the process of human rights education (HRE) was anathema to the profession of organized violence. Moreover, she argued that because soldiers in Latin America are primarily trained to defeat internal "insurrection"—which may include peaceful opposition to a brutal regime—and have historically protected the interests of oppressive élites, HRE for the military can only and always be a sham and to talk of improving this education by appealing to self-interest is to more deeply participate in this sham.

A bit farther down this continuum of opposition, was an educator who seemed to be more open to the idea of transmitting human rights values to soldiers. However, she was united with the absolute pacifist in her disdain for political scientists over-intellectualizing what she saw as a purely normative issue and characterized my use of the term self-interest as "evil."

Moderating the position even further, but still opposed, was a social worker. Taking into account how difficult it is to convince abusive men to stop beating their partners, because often neither altruism nor threat of legal sanction seems to work, she thought that, potentially, the most effective strategy would be to tell the husband, "If you don't beat your wife, she'll get more housework done." And this social worker concurred that the same strategy could work with soldiers: "Do not burn down the village, or you will lose your peasant base." However, she could not bring herself to adopt this strategy, because it seemed to undermine the morality of what she was trying to do, and to lessen the importance of respecting the battered woman's dignity.

Among the other bloc that favored an appeal to self-interest was an educator who trained women judges to more effectively promote human rights. She recognized that, as advocates, we are always making "Faustian deals," convincing people to uphold human rights by whatever way we can, by threatening punishment, by appealing to their honor or by manipulating their self-interest, because it is the goal that matters. In other words, her position was, "Whatever works." Joining her on this point was an international lawyer who was also a self-described Machiavellian: while he recognized a moral dimension to this argument, he felt that many times in human rights advocacy, "the end justifies the means."

In the next several pages I shall explore the positive and negative implications of the "moral" opposition to self-interest. Then I shall do the same for the "practical" support of it, and finally I shall examine a possibility for the confluence of the two, a point where morality flows into practicality, and where this debate may find a degree of resolution in the future.

The "Moral" Opposition

As I have previously observed, "That the [School of the Americas] provides one moral reason to five tactical ones for respecting rights should come as no surprise to [human rights] advocates, because militaries are generally goal-oriented in their approaches to war, while advocates are mostly concerned about the process."[6] While not surprising, however, many of my human rights colleagues have told me they find the School's approach morally unacceptable. For some, this is because their position on the human rights program is so bound up with their antipathy towards the School (for the reasons mentioned above) that they cannot distinguish between the two. For others, I sense there is a deeper, less contextually-bound reason. When my colleagues oppose an appeal to self-interest on moral grounds, they are tapping into a tradition that pre-dates the modern human rights movement by several thousand years.

We can roughly trace the rejection of self-interest to Plato's *Republic*, in which Socrates holds, "[N]o ruler of any kind, *qua* ruler, exercises his authority, whatever its sphere, with his own interest in view, but that of the subject of his skill. It is his subject and his subject's proper interest to which he looks in all he says and does."[7] What Plato gives voice to is what has often been called the *self-other model*, in which "an action has no moral worth unless it benefits others—and not even then, unless it is motivated by altruism rather than selfishness."[8]

This dichotomy is also present in the Judeo-Christian tradition that cherishes the well-being of the other and measures an act's value according to the purity of its motive. We can see this clearly in the parable of the Good Samaritan (Luke 1.25-37) in which a priest overlooks a robbery victim in order to avoid defilement. Though technically legal, his action lacks merit because it is based on self-interest. It is the Samaritan who is the protagonist in the parable, because he saves the wounded man, not for reasons of self-interest but because "his heart was filled with pity."

Both the Greek and Judeo-Christian conceptions of morality blend into the modern regime of human rights. We can see this in the preamble of the *Universal Declaration of Human Rights* that states "recognition of the inherent dignity and of the equal and inalienable rights of all members of the human family is the foundation of freedom, justice and peace in the world."[9] That is, recognition of the other's rights, the other's worth, with no reference to the self. This is precisely what a human rights educator recently wrote to me when responding to my query regarding self-interest on the Global Human Rights Education Internet listserv.

Self-interest is pragmatic and elevates me above all other human beings, makes me more important, worthy of prime consideration, makes me look inwards at myself. Human rights are not essentially pragmatic, but are only so in so far as civilisation values them. And what they do—essentially—is put all humans on an equal level; not for some utilitarian end such as that "it will be better for all of us in the long run" but (surely?) because we cannot do otherwise, since all humans are indeed equal.[10]

Therefore, to the human rights advocate who subscribes *absolutely* to this philosophical tradition, who defines a "successful" human rights education program as one that bases itself upon an other-interested, purely-moral position, then an appeal to self-interest *has* to be self-defeating.

In attempting to play the devil's advocate against this extreme moral position, I find I cannot provide traditional "proof," empirical or anecdotal, because it is not a question of logic but a question of faith. If someone truly believes that motives matter more than results, then no argument to the contrary will persuade her. However, there are few among us who toe such a strict moral line, and so, for those, including the social worker I mentioned above who is leaning more towards a results-oriented approach but cannot quite bring herself to employ self-interest, I offer the following "hard case" counterfactual story.

Let us assume the Samaritan in the parable takes another path, so the only one who approaches the wounded man is the priest.[11] And let us assume, furthermore, that there are two angels—omniscient but forbidden to directly intervene—sent to convince the priest he must tend to his unfortunate brother. They inform the priest it is his moral obligation to act. But the priest scoffs at this suggestion. After all, he has nothing to gain; in fact, he has a great deal to lose. Not only does he risk defilement, if the man is actually dead, but also there is the question of time and energy spent in binding the man's wounds, and then there is the money he must pay to put the man up at the local inn. He becomes tired of the angels' moralizing and is about to walk away.

At this point, the first angel—let us call her Amy—who adheres to the extreme moral position outlined above, considers threatening the priest with damnation, but that would promote self-interest. She also considers suggesting that, if the priest acts today, then some other day on these brigand-filled roads, someone will follow his example and help him when *he* is the victim, but that would be self-interested too. So she decides she must let the wounded man bleed to death.

Before the priest turns away, however, the second angel—let us call him Alistair—who has a less-stringent interpretation of morality, decides to engage the priest's preexisting world-view to the dying man's advantage. He suggests to the priest, that, if he binds the man's wounds and brings him to the inn, then the townspeople will praise the priest as a holy man, and they will give him expensive gifts, more than making up for his expense in bandages and medicine and the risk of defilement. The priest is convinced by Alistair's appeal and saves the wounded man.

The obvious question is, "Which angel made the right decision?" The answer is, "That depends on whether one values the means—adherence to an abstract moral code—or the ends—saving the life of another human being."

The same question faces human rights educators for the military and so does the same answer. In any given classroom, there will be a number of soldiers who will not be swayed to respect human rights for reasons of morality. (This, I shall explore below.) Thus, if they are not given self-interested reasons—that they need to treat the peasants well to prevent them from joining the guerrillas; that it is better to take advantage of the existing infrastructure than to build their camp from scratch. . . etc.—and, if they are so disposed, then they will torture, rape and burn down villages unless some external force stops them from doing so.

I find little to convince the absolute pacifist in the audience that the angel Alistair is right and the angel Amy is wrong, because, for her, morality is all that matters, and it is undercut by an appeal to self-interest.

But if she stands by her decision, I feel she should realize the costs implicit in it, for this is no longer a parable, no longer a morality game involving priests and angels, but, rather, a real scenario involving soldiers, educators and potential victims. For the pragmatist willing to make "Faustian deals," the pacifist's moral dilemma is more imagined than real. After all, the success of human rights education, is counted, not in saved souls, but in saved lives. However, as I shall explore in the next section, self-interest does not always work in the ways that the pragmatist may imagine, and, as Faust himself learned, when the devil makes a deal, there is always a price to pay.

The "Practical" Response

While the "moral" rejection of self-interest is based upon a philosophical commitment, one that is not connected to physical circumstances, but to ideal goals, the "practical" acceptance of it is very much related to the specific context of the classroom in which HRE takes place, primarily to the attitudes educators perceive soldiers hold regarding human rights. From discussions with civilian and military educators who promote self-interest, I have identified two attitudes, the existence of which, according to them, lessens the likelihood a direct appeal to altruism will be effective.

A. Waging War or Upholding Rights: A Perceived Dichotomy

First, some soldiers have come to see an either/or relationship between the practice of war and the maintenance of legal norms, including human rights.[12] That is, either a soldier uses all means possible to attain victory—including torturing and illegally detaining the enemy—or he respects his enemy's rights and risks defeat. It is often difficult for human rights educators to rearrange this way of thinking, to convince soldiers that these "civilian" and "military" goals are not necessarily at odds. As Colonel Glenn Weidner, Commandant of the School of the Americas, concedes, there may be soldiers who attend the human rights course at the USARSA who come from Armed Forces with a history of committing massive human rights abuses, who will not incorporate newly-taught values and who could rationalize future atrocities. This is because they perceive themselves as scapegoats, feeling forced to do a "dirty job" their society tacitly expected and still expects them to do and for which they are consequently vilified.[13]

According to Roland Hammer, a fifteen-year veteran of the human rights dissemination program of the International Committee of the Red Cross, audiences such as police and especially armed forces are very tough audiences; historically they always have been special institutions, quite hermetic with their own socializing mechanisms. They are the depository of legal force in the state and how often are defense questions considered above or beyond the law because they concern the "vital" interests of the State?[14]

Some of these "socializing mechanisms" are tacit, inherent in the process of *growing* a soldier within the military environment. The soldier may begin to observe, as John Hillen has said, that: "The civil culture of a liberal democracy pulls the military one way, while the hierarchy of values needed to succeed in the unnatural stresses of war pulls it another way"[15] and may come to believe he has to make a choice between the two. There are also overt mechanisms, by which the military inculcates in soldiers the belief that maintaining human rights is antithetical to their goals. Kaufmann writes, "[W]e have to acknowledge that in many cases among the ranks HRE may produce some cognitive dissonance with previously accepted values and perhaps concurrent courses that tend to stress aspects of the 'national security doctrine' (often antithetical to HRE)."[16]

B. Association of Human Right Advocacy with the Enemy's Goals

The first attitude mentioned above feeds directly into a second: not only does respecting human conflict with the soldier's "true" mission, but it also promotes the enemy's goals. This attitude has much to do with the recent history of human rights advocacy in Latin America, which saw right-wing military dictatorships criticized by what they perceived as left-leaning, fellow-travelers of revolutionary opposition groups.[17]

Viewed through these dictatorships' Manichean lenses, anyone calling for the elimination of "disappearances," death squads, and torture centers, was not promoting a universal standard of treatment for human beings, but, rather, mobilizing sympathy for terrorist organizations. In late 1950s Argentina, such linking of social justice/human rights issues with the "enemy's" goals was expressed by Manrique Miguel Mom, when he wrote, "We find the work of [Communist] dissolution and regrouping everywhere, in the national and international organizations, in different churches, in the 'progressive' or 'liberal' media, in the public and private administrations, in the unions, in the student organizations, etc., etc."[18] In 1980s El Salvador, it was much more succinctly put: "Be a patriot, kill a priest."

Even today, such thinking among Latin American militaries persists. Advocates who call for the self-determination of indigenous peoples in Guatemala are seen as promoting rural insurgency, and mothers in Argentina, who are searching for their disappeared children twenty years after their deaths, are branded as apologists for left-wing subversion. Thus, when an educator steps in front of a classroom full of soldiers and says,

"Respect human rights," the message that is sometimes perceived is "Respect the rights of terrorists, anarchists and radical communists."

Antipathy and Apathy: Twin Challenges of the Classroom

Given the two attitudes mentioned above—that human rights are incompatible with mission goals, and, moreover, that they work to the enemy's advantage—the classroom environment for the human rights educator can be a daunting one. The audience is often primed to distrust the educator and feel affronted by her message, ready to turn off the moment they feel criticized or their core values denigrated. Russell Ramsey, an instructor at the USARSA, gives voice to this distrust in his recent book, *Guardians of the Other Americas: Essays on the Military Forces in Latin America*. Ramsey quite vehemently opposes what he terms "[s]pooning out generic morality sermons to the developing world's best military professionals in the human rights arena." According to him, "Latin American leaders will eventually refuse to send their military professionals to be scolded ceremonially over the sins of the Salvadoran Army and the South American 'Dirty Wars.'"[19]

The comments of Major Jeff Palmer, a human rights educator with the U.S. Air Force, suggest that, even when the audience is not aggressively opposed to HRE and even when the educator manages to present human rights without offending their sensibilities, the success of the human rights course is far from assured. Palmer describes soldiers who have reluctantly participated [in human rights courses] to merely tick a box on the long road to improving their human rights record. This is particularly true in parts of South America, where, in many instances, EIMET [Expanded International Military Educational Training] participation is linked to other U.S.-funded programs. There, I have personally witnessed an audience full of "extras"—like some movie set—not there for any meaningful experience but rather to occupy a chair and not jeopardize other U.S. aid/loan programs.[20]

What Ramsey and Palmer describe is what Sonnier calls the "difficult challenge" that "[m]ilitary instructors have long been faced with" and that is, "the individual's presence may be commanded, but his attention cannot be forced."[21] Given this challenge, it is clear why "practically-oriented" educators do not package HRE for soldiers in terms of altruism. If helping the other hurts yourself (an other, who is, moreover, undeserving) or, at the very least, does nothing for you, then why help? Given the soldier's worldview, "selling" altruism to him is even more difficult than selling it to the priest in the parable, for not only do we have to justify the expense and time lost in caring for the wounded man (upholding his human rights), but we also have to deal with the fear that, when the wounded man is well, he will place a bomb in the soldier's house.

But if we appeal to the soldier's self-interest, we do not have to try to undo his antipathy towards the "enemy," we do not have to rework his vision of the world. Indeed, if we assume, as many of the social and natural sciences do that "people actively and single-mindedly pursue their self-interest, whether it takes the form of reproductive fitness, utility maximization, reinforcement or the pursuit of pleasure"[22] then self-interest seems to be the path of least resistance. This is precisely what Major Antonio Raimondo, human rights instructor at the USARSA believes and points to an example in international relations in which all parties involved acted self-interestedly, and yet this self-interest ended up promoting human rights: "When the European Union rejected Turkey and denied its entry into the EU for having a poor record on human rights, it did so not for altruistic reasons but for the selfish reasons of not wanting a bad neighbor, a bad and unreliable economic partner. In turn this selfishness forced Turkey to rethink its record on human rights. Self-interest works not only in a market economy, but in the area of human rights as well."[23]

According to this way of thinking, we just have to convince the soldier that respecting human rights is good *for him*, and everything else will fall into place. Michael Hinkley, who taught HRE through the Defense Institute of International Legal Studies, believes such a move is possible.

A theme emphasized during the "Law of Armed Conflict" presentations and discussions, for example, is that following "the law" in protecting against human rights abuses is not only easy (and, of course, right), but also makes good common sense: why, as a military leader of troops, would you waste time, money, and effort destroying civilian structures, pursuing or harassing noncombatants, and allowing your troops to plunder villages, when all these activities use up valuable time, squander supplies or ammunition, cause hate and entrenchment in the civilian populace, heap international scorn on your activities, and lead to a breakdown in unit discipline as your soldiers become more interested in lining their pockets with loot than in your mission accomplishment? When phrased in such terms, heads begin to nod in agreement: to the military commander, this makes sense, and helps him.[24]

The Negative Consequences of Appealing to Self-Interest

Before we can accept what Hinkley says as true, that an appeal to self-interest "makes sense" to the commander and that it helps him convince his troops to respect human rights, we should have empirical proof. If the world were a laboratory, then we could test comparable HRE programs, among comparable militaries, merely flipping the toggle switch on the motivation variable from altruism to self-interest. That, obviously, is not possible, although I *can* envision several case studies that attempt to prove this point in the non-clinical environment that is the world, and I hope this current discussion may spur on other scholars to do so. However, my point here is not to graph how much more effective self-interest than altruism is, but, rather, to draw out the potential consequences of each. So far, the scoreboard apparently favors self-interest, if outcome and not purity of motive is what matters most. Nevertheless, there are a number of problems with the self-interested position, both essential to its reasoning and potential in its application.

Self-Interest's Role in Human Rights Violations: Same Motivation, Different Results

Self-interest may go a long way towards reducing a soldier's animosities towards HRE and may even convince him to protect civilians' lives, but, as Ishtiyaque Haji asks, "[W]hat about those special situations where an immoral act seems advantageous and where duty fails to have 'the visage of a sweetie or a cutie'? Does it not in these situations pay to be immoral?[25] Indeed, I see the rationalization of committing human rights violations as the dangerous flip-side to promoting the "Whatever works" approach to HRE for soldiers. As I have cautioned elsewhere, "[T]he basis for using more humane [counterinsurgency] techniques can never rest solely on the argument that they are more effective than the inhumane, for, in a given situation, torture, disappearance, unlawful detention . . . etc. may all achieve the desired military objective."[26]

Bearing in mind the comment of the self-described Machiavellian lawyer I mentioned above, if we consult the source of his inspiration, *The Prince*, we see how violating rights can actually be preferable, *if* self-interest is the primary criterion by which we define a military mission's success:

I say that each prince should desire to be held merciful and not cruel; nonetheless he should take care not to use this mercy badly. Cesare Borgia was held to be cruel; nonetheless his cruelty restored the Romagna, united it, and reduced it to peace and to faith. A prince, therefore, so as to keep his subjects united and faithful, should not care about the infamy of cruelty, because with very few examples he will be more merciful than those who for the sake of too much mercy allow disorders to continue, from which come killings or robberies.[27]

Machiavelli's self-interested logic has proven to be seductive to soldiers for thousands of years, and armies have successfully violated human rights in order to: "focus the mission, to maintain discipline, to reduce enemy resistance, to retain popular support, and to restore the peace."

History is replete with such examples, from Herod's men massacring all infants in Bethlehem, in the hopes of murdering the one Messiah who threatened the existing political order, to U.S. soldiers in W.W.II executing surrendering Japanese soldiers in the Pacific islands campaign, because they could not—or so they rationalized—secure the beachhead and deal with prisoners of war at the same time. In these instances, soldiers followed the logic advanced by HRE "pragmatists" but came to a decidedly different conclusion: "Human rights violations work."

Reinforcing Tendencies Contrary to Human Rights and Civil Society

Even if an appeal to self-interest does not lead a soldier down the path to committing human rights violations, it can reinforce unhealthy attitudes, such as the belief that human rights protection and mission goals are at odds, even when the price of protecting those rights was incredibly low. We can see this in the case of Captain Lawrence Rockwood who was part of the multinational peacekeeping force (MNF) in Haiti in 1994. Captain Rockwood, a counterintelligence officer in the U.S. Army, was court-martialed for having investigated human rights abuses at the Haitian National Penitentiary. Believing human rights abuses were being committed at the prison and that it was his duty to act, he went against orders, traveled a short distance from the MNF compound to the prison and interviewed inmates there. Even though his actions were, arguably, in consonance with a soldier's obligations under international law and that there were, in fact, abuses occurring throughout Haitian prisons at the time, the Army characterized Rockwood's actions as having "personally creat[ed] a dangerous and unstable incident [sic] between the U.S. government and the government of Haiti during a period when the U.S. government attempted to maintain a stable relationship with the de facto government of Haiti to avoid unnecessary violence."[28]

This example is as hard a case for the "pragmatist," as that of the Good Samaritan above is for the "moralist." According to the Lawyers Committee for Human Rights, "the tragedy of the *Rockwood* case is that the MNF, in unquestionable control, with overwhelming force, facing a subordinate rather than adversarial foreign army, and serving under a mandate to rectify military abuse in preparation for democracy, would not authorize a six-kilometer trip to a downtown prison to investigate serious abuse."[29] If one of the most professional armies in the world, with the international media watching, can conclude, in the words of the Lawyers Committee, that "Self-protection, but not rights protection, was the priority for the U.S.'s overwhelming array of forces in Haiti,"[30] then what are we to expect from the developing world's militaries, who have often shown a tendency to violate human rights in order to promote some "greater good?"

A self-interested approach may also aggravate the marked division between military and civilian spheres that exists in many countries. As Marc Howard Ross has observed, "Cultural mobilization builds on fears and perceived threats that are consistent with internalized worldviews and regularly reinforced through high in-group interaction and emotional solidarity. Such worldviews are expressed in daily experiences as well as significant ceremonial and ritual events that effectively restate and renew support for a group's core values and the need for solidarity in the face of external foes."[31] In Latin America, the military's "external foes" have historically been the civilian population.[32] Because of this, an appeal to self-interest may play the role of restating and renewing this dangerous world-view, such that "civilian" concerns for democracy and the rule of law are further disregarded, and cleavages within the society increased.

Human Rights of the Soldier, Moral Development and Other Heresies

At the closing session of the conference that originally sparked this chapter, I announced that I would like to write a book one day entitled *Human Rights of the Soldier and Other Heresies*. What I meant by this was that one usually hears a great deal at such conferences about the human rights of the traditional "other," the civilian victim of abuse, but not about the human rights of that other "other," the soldier. The reason why this is a "heresy" is that soldiers are usually the ones abusing the rights of civilians, not vice versa, and soldiers in many countries have already demanded so many special entitlements that to talk of providing them more sounds absurd, even dangerous. Nevertheless, I would like to suggest that, by enlarging our vision of soldiers as human rights bearers and not just potential abusers, and encouraging soldiers to do the same, we may be able to foster a sense of empathy, even community, and, thus, lessen the potential for future abuses. Indeed, I see this as a possible way to bring together the apparently irreconcilable "moral" and "practical" positions regarding self-interest.

The Soldier: "A Fellow Human Being First"

Early last decade, at the Council of Europe's Meeting of Directors and of Representatives from Police Academies and Police Training Institutions, Türker Soukkan suggested, "[I]f we don't want. . . 'the servant of the public' to remain just empty words, perhaps we ought to embrace the notion of the role and an ideology of training, that would consider the individual police officer a fellow human being in the first, a citizen in the second and guardian of the law only in the third place. To me it is evident, that the police officer is both 'of the people' and 'for the people.'"[33]

This is Kaufman's position, who adds: "It could be argued that the best way for becoming aware of the rights of the other (civilians) is to be empowered in the demand of their own (law enforcement agencies) rights in a democratic society."[34] This would not necessarily (indeed, it must not, if we are to preserve the notion of equality) mean giving soldiers *more* rights than civilians but *equal* rights. Kaufman envisions such rights as those of the military to organize and unionize, as other workers do, to vote and to receive just compensation, although he recognizes emerging democracies may be loathe to do so, because of recent military abuses.

At the same Council of Europe meeting at which Soukkan spoke, John Anderson added, "It hardly needs to be said that police officers themselves, their families and friends also benefit from [human rights] laws."[35] But I believe it does need to be said that state agents, too, should enjoy human rights, and it should be said more often, if we are to deconstruct this unhealthy dichotomy of soldiers'/abusers' goals and civilians'/enemies' rights.

Self-Interest and Moral Development: A Possible Confluence

But from a Kohlbergian perspective, however, such a move is hardly a solution, because we are still giving the soldier reasons that have to do with his own well-being and not the other's. For moral educators who share this perspective, an educator who appeals to a soldier's self-interest, undercuts his moral development, inducing him to remain at the "preconventional level," specifically at the second stage or "instrumentalist-relativist orientation," far from his potential as a human being.[36] John Wilson, for example, believes "self-considering" is one of the many "wrong (unreasonable, inappropriate) ways of thinking about morality."[37]

But I suggest it is only inappropriate if we retain the traditional "self-other paradigm" on which morality is based. Recently, Kelly Rogers has questioned the assumptions inherent in this paradigm and has concluded that one can be both moral *and* self-interested. To demonstrate this, Rogers uses the example of a Vietnam veteran who has struggled against disability to receive a college education and to graduate at the top of his class. Rogers writes, "It is not *despite* the fact that he is pursuing his best interest that we admire his courage, determination, and integrity, but precisely in virtue of the fact." Therefore, "to assume, in advance, that a person's efforts at self-realization, or flourishing, must be at variance with morality, is manifestly false."[38]

Building on Rogers' example and adapting it to the battlefield, the moralist can hardly consider the soldier immoral who does not torture a captured civilian because he views the whole human community as benefiting from his restraint, a community of which he sees himself an integral part. And the pragmatist can hardly object to such a move, because it works. Or, rather, it has the *potential* to work, a potential that human rights researchers should investigate further. Human rights educator Frans Limpens recently supported this position when he wrote, "We can only really advance in HRE if we're able to convince the other part[ies] that human rights in the long run is also 'better' for them and their families. If this were not true, something would be wrong [with] human rights."[39]

Therefore, I suggest that through a process of folding self-interest (defined in terms of a greater, human community and not merely by demands of the military mission) into morality we have the potential to motivate the soldier to do the right thing, for himself *and* for the other, with the added benefit of not providing him with reasons to violate human rights in the future.

That is, however, a possible solution for only the long term. In the short term, given the current relationship of the soldier with the topic of human rights and the dynamic between him and the educator, we must decide whether the potential, "practical" benefits outweigh the immediate "moral" dilemma of appealing to the soldier's self-interest.

Notes

© Eric Stener Carlson and Ashgate Publishing Company, 2001. Eric Carlson is pursuing his Ph.D. in Political Science at the University of California, Santa Barbara, where he is a Doctoral Scholars Fellow. He is currently based in Geneva, Switzerland, where he works for the International Programme for the Elimination of Child Labour as an official for the International Labour Organisation (United Nations ILO).

I would like to express my gratitude to the following individuals without whom this project would not have been possible: Dr. Alan Liu, for his insightful comments on earlier drafts and for advocating an inclusive approach to political science; Dr. Aaron Belkin, for his keen insights on several drafts and dedication to mentorship; Dr. Herb Spirer for his continued guidance in this and other projects and for his steadfast support of human rights issues; Dr. Thomas Schrock for his insightful comments, and Dr. Peter Digeser for having encouraged me to incorporate political theory into my work. Also, special thanks go to Dr. Benjamin Cohen, who, as my graduate advisor, played a crucial role in supporting my research, and to David Barnhizer for coordinating the recent conference at the Cleveland-Marshall College of Law at which I presented my preliminary research. In the same vein, my appreciation goes to the International Society of Political Psychology for inviting me to present this article in its current form at their 23rd annual meeting in Seattle, Washington and to the many participants there who both challenged and supported me in equal measure. Thanks also to the Political

Science Department and the Graduate Division at the University of California, Santa Barbara for funding my fieldwork at the United States Army School of the Americas. And, of course, my deep appreciation goes to all those who consented to be interviewed for this research project, civilians and soldiers, whose diverse views have enriched this ongoing debate on self-interest in human rights education for the military.

1   Effective Strategies for Protecting Human Rights, Cleveland-Marshall College of Law, Cleveland State University. April 13-15, 2000.

2   Lesson Plan #2031, "Slide 3," dated January 10, 1999. From the USARSA website, http://www.benning.army.mil.

3   *Id.*, "Slide 49."

4   *Id.*

5   Christina Nifong, "Trial Will Highlight Military School Controversy," The Christian Science Monitor, March 2, 1998. According to Nifong, the School of the Americas "names among its graduates Gen. Manuel Antonio Noriega, Panama's former leader now in jail in the US for drug charges; Raoul Cedras, head of the Haitian coup that ousted elected leader Jean Bertrand Aristide; and 19 Salvadorans accused of murdering six Jesuit priests, their housekeeper, and her daughter in 1989."

6   Eric Stener Carlson, "Giving the Devil His Due: Transforming the Human Rights/National Security Dialogue in Argentina," *Low Intensity Conflict and Law Enforcement* 7.3 (Winter 1998): 25. N52.

7   Plato, *The Republic*, trans. Desmond Lee (London: Penguin, 1987), 342e. 83.

8   Kelly Rogers, "Beyond Self and Other," *Social Philosophy and Policy* 14.1 (Winter 1997): 1.

9   Center for the Study of Human Rights, *Twenty-four Human Rights Documents* (New York: Columbia University, 1992), 6.

10 Ellie Keen, HRE Consultant for Central and Eastern Europe, Amnesty International. Communication with the author. May 18, 2000. Interested parties can view logs of the ongoing debate at hr-education@hrea.org.

11 We must remember the Levite also encounters the wounded man, but he is of little consequence for this analysis.

12 Obviously, there does exist a variation in attitudes within and between militaries. These are generalities but generalities often repeated by HRE educators that "prove," for them at least, the necessity of appealing to self-interest.

13 Interview with the author. April 23, 1999.

14 Communication with the author. August 10, 1999.

15 Williamson Murray, "Does Military Culture Matter?," *Orbis* 43.1 (Winter 1999): 56.

16 Edy Kaufman, "Human Rights Education for Law Enforcement," in George J. Andreopoulos and Richard Pierre Claude, *Human Rights Education for the Twenty-First Century* (Philadelphia: University of Pennsylvania Press, 1997), 286.

17 For an exploration of this topic, *see* "Giving the Devil His Due," *supra* n. 6.

18 Manrique Miguel Mom, "Guerra Revolucionaria: El Conflicto Mundial en Desarrollo," *Revista de la Escuela Superior de Guerra* 331 (October-December, 1958): 656.

19 Russell Ramsey, *Guardians of the Other Americas: Essays on the Military Forces in Latin America* (Lanham: University Press of America, 1997), 242. Originally appearing in "Forty Years of Human Rights Training," *Journal of Low Intensity Conflict and Law Enforcement* (Autumn, 1995).

20 Communication with the author, August 16, 1999 [Palmer's comments do not necessarily reflect the official position of the Department of Defense or the United States Air Forces.]

21 David L. Sonnier, "Quality Learning: A Key to Military Training," in *Affective Education: Methods and Techniques*, ed. Isadore L. Sonnier (Englewood Cliffs: Educational Technology Publications, 1989), 106.
22 Dale T. Miller and Rebecca K. Ratner, "The Disparity Between the Actual and Assumed Power of Self-Interest," *Journal of Personality and Social Psychology* 74.1 (1998): 53.
23 Interview with the author. USARSA, April 21, 1999.
24 D. Michael Hinkley, "Military Training for Human Rights and Democratization," in *Human Rights Education for the Twenty-First Century*. 303.
25 Ishtiyaque Haji, "Escaping or Avoiding the Prisoner's Dilemma?," *Dialogue* 30 (1991): 153.
26 Carlson, "Giving the Devil His Due," *supra* n. 6, at 16.
27 Niccolo Machiavelli, *The Prince*, ed. Harvey C. Mansfield (Chicago: University of Chicago Press, 1998), 65-66.
28 Lawyers Committee for Human Rights, *Protect or Obey: The United States Army Versus Captain Lawrence Rockwood* (New York: Lawyers Committee for Human Rights, May 1995), at 2. [I draw on *Protect or Obey* to describe this case above.]
29 *Id.* 12.
30 *Id.* 1.
31 Marc Howard Ross, "Culture and Identity in Comparative Political Analysis," *Comparative Politics: Rationality, Culture and Structure*, ed. Mark Irving Lichbach and Alan S. Zuckerman (Cambridge: Cambridge University Press, 1997), at 66.
32 As a general statement, Latin American militaries have historically focused on responding to an internal threat and not a foreign enemy, although many of these militaries in a process of transition.
33 Türker Soukkan, "Aspects on Policing/Police Training and Human Rights: General Issues and Recent Development in Sweden," *Proceedings of the Meeting of Directors and of Representatives from Police Academies and Police Training Institutions Organised by the DH-ED*, ed. Council of Europe, Committee of Experts for the Promotion of Education and Information in the Field of Human Rights (Strasbourg: Council of Europe, 1991), 121. [While Soukkan spoke specifically about education for police, I believe his remarks are equally applicable to that of soldiers.]
34 Kaufman, *supra* n. 16 at 285.
35 John Anderson, "Police Training—What Are the Needs?," *Proceedings of the Meeting of Directors and of Representatives from Police Academies and Police Training Institution*, at 99.
36 Lawrence Kohlberg, "The Claim to Moral Adequacy of a Highest Stage of Moral Judgment," *The Journal of Philosophy* 70.19 (October 25, 1973).
37 John Wilson, *Practical Methods of Moral Education* (New York: Crane, Russak and Company, Inc., 1972), 29-30.
38 Rogers, *supra* n. 8, at 6.
39 Communication with the author. April 11, 2000.

14 Enforcing Human Rights through the External Use of Local Public Opinion

ILIAS BANTEKAS

This chapter seeks to identify public opinion as a political tool against the human rights abuses of a governing body, albeit within the context of international law. More specifically, it is concerned with situations of gross human rights violations within a given state, and the ability of the international community to remedy such violations through the "manipulation" of that state's public opinion. In this sense, we are viewing this "manipulation" as an alternative to the unavoidable human cost that humanitarian or other forceful interventions entail.

To make the case clearer, it is useful to utilise the example of the Federal Republic of Yugoslavia (FRY), under the leadership of its President Slobodan Milosevic. A year after the signing of the 1995 Paris Peace Agreement (otherwise known as the Dayton Agreement),[1] which formally ended the Bosnian civil war, the state of the Serbian economy resulting from President Milosevic's isolationist politics had outraged the Serbian people to such an extent that mass, daily, fervent demonstrations against his regime were expected to force him into abdicating his grip on power. Notwithstanding these developments, whether because public pressure was not sustained long enough or because it was not sufficiently supported, the Milosevic regime failed to topple. Instead, it remained in power after the dawn of the new millennium, even sparking a major armed conflict in the heart of Europe; the Kosovo conflict. More interestingly, although the Serbian people in their vast majority were negatively predisposed to their leadership, during the Kosovo affair and subsequent NATO bombing they supported Milosevic's actions and saw themselves as targets of the international community. This popular affection to an undemocratic government can hardly be the result that both NATO and the

United Nations wanted to convey, both to the world at large and the Serbian people in particular. Irrespective of the shortcomings of the ensuing armed conflict, which now seems to have created substantial instability in the wider Balkan region, would not it have been preferable were the Serbian people to remove Milosevic on their own, install a democratic government, and avoid heavy human and material losses? It is evident that, at the time at least, decision-making was hardly dedicated to pursuing an avenue whereby the international community's influence and support of the Serbian people would ultimately lead to a peaceful transition to democratic rule.

The aim of this chapter is to ascertain the possible modalities of such an exercise by the international community. It focuses on two types of governmental structures in order to premise its paradigm: illegitimate regimes originating usually through a *coup d'etat*, as well as legitimate bodies, albeit with undemocratic aims or practices. Although this study addresses questions relating to human rights violations in general, it is hoped that its suggestions and general strategies can find application with regard to varying human rights and related problems.

Democratic Governance and Public Participation

It has been very strongly advocated in the recent past that democratic governance has attained the status of a rule of international law.[2] However, despite the efforts of western nations to enhance and promote this notion, political expediency prevails in some cases, thus decreasing somewhat the credence of this rule. Hence, while democratic governance was demanded and sought in the cases of Haiti (1994) and Panama (1989) by the United States, the same has not been demanded from the military regimes of Pakistan and Turkey.[3]

Notwithstanding these observations, the concept of democratic governance should be a visible target for the community of nations. If one explores its historic origin, it will easily be discovered that it has not come about as a "gift" from the governing to the governed. On the contrary, it has risen to its current state as a result of popular participation in the affairs of the state. Demand for such participation has always been constrained by the various power structures, because the greater public participation is in state affairs, it is less likely that the governing will trespass on the prerogatives of the governed.

To put matters into a practical perspective, the fundamental question posed is how to bring about and guarantee popular participation in the political evolution of states. In this study we have identified five essential elements. These include democratic elections, protection of civil and political rights, transparency of government affairs, education, and international co-operation and scrutiny. The first three usually constitute an integral part of a domestic Constitutional arrangement, and are defined within a context of civil and fundamental rights. The same is not true of education and international scrutiny. The former is a positive right, which a state may claim that it is not in a material position to satisfy, while for the latter the classical sovereignty rhetoric usually demands no further justification. The proper functioning of each of these five elements requires a high degree of interdependence among them. It has far too often been the case of eloquent and lofty Constitutions containing a wide range of fundamental rights guarantees, which in fact remained void of any practical significance.

For our purposes, the function of international co-operation and scrutiny is served in large part through individual or inter-state access to international institutions, including human rights bodies, the state obligation of submitting analogous annual reports, and the investigation of human rights issues by such international bodies.[4] However, and despite the customary nature recognized to most rights, these machineries initiate procedure for taking preventive or remedial action only in the event that the "accused" state grants its consent.

Similarly, impartial, quality, and widespread education is not high on the agendas of oppressive regimes, since they recognize that knowledge is itself a form of empowerment. It is established that the development of rights has evolved through increased mass participation in public life, and this has in turn shaped the content of constitutional rights, and has been the instigator of rights legislation and other implementing state action. Such popular participation would not have been possible without an informed participant movement.

Since it is clear that each of the five enumerated elements constitutes part of an inseparable whole, when it is claimed by a particular government that only one of these is not fully observed for whatever reason, none of the others can reasonably be observed either. Further below we shall assess how these elements may be implemented through an international procedure, as well as through the efforts of regional and global organizations in order to enforce them in third countries.

The Violation of Fundamental Rights by Undemocratic Regimes

The basis of power for any authoritarian regime is its perceived dominance over a given populace. This is subject to specific territorial and spatial considerations. Such dominance is attained through subjugation to military or police force, which itself may be legitimized on either religious or other ideological premises. It is evident that force alone is not capable of sustaining constant abuse of rights and freedoms, since there does exist a clear threshold point of tolerance, even by a people perceived to be submissive to the dictates of its leadership. Hence, further legitimization is sought by the oppressive government, which although fostering some degree of discontent among the governed, serves to portray the regime's force as deriving from a healthy and deserving source, thus decreasing the impact of the abusive behavior.

In many cases the governing hierarchy might well utilize part of its population, usually a majority group, to attack another group, thus pretending to follow or simply "allowing" the will of the people to prevail. A maneuver of this kind may serve to defuse a specific situation by turning the peoples' focus on a new issue. Examples of such action are abundant even in contemporary political practice. Before the outbreak of Bosnia's civil war in 1992, the leadership of the Bosnian Serbs was engaged in the use of nationalistic ferment against other national or religious groups so as to wield support among local Serbs in order to materialize its campaign of annihilation of non-Serbs. Similarly, stringent *Sharia* regimes, such as that of the Afghan Taliban and, to a lesser extent, of the Gulf states, curtail fundamental rights and freedoms through the use of internal force on the basis of their purported adherence to *Sharia* principles. The main characteristic in both cases is the creation of an "enemy"—portrayed either as a threatening minority, or as violators of moral principles—threaded and supplemented around prevailing community perceptions of insecurity. Community values can easily be manipulated, especially where the freedom of expression is curtailed and opposition to such values is labeled as an act of apostasy.[5] Education likewise, in oppressive regimes, does not allow any form of dialogue or criticism; rather, it strives to preserve stiff government rhetoric, which is used to infiltrate the media and education channels in order to maintain and serve its purposes.

Remedies and Aims

A. *Human Rights and National Sovereignty*

The traditional concept of sovereignty is the product of the European era associated with the emergence of the contemporary nation state following the Peace Treaty of Westphalia of 1648. This was premised especially on the principle of legal equality of states, but the 1648 Treaty itself did not prohibit the recourse to armed force. It was clear, nonetheless, that to the extent which a state could defend or maintain its territorial integrity, it was not susceptible to any kind of external interference on matters relating to its internal affairs.

Despite reference to human rights in the Charter of the United Nations, signed in 1945, there was no attempt, at least at the inter-state level, to alter the traditional concept of sovereignty. This was confirmed both in article 2(7) of the UN Charter, which prohibits interference in the domestic affairs of states by the Organization, and also by General Assembly resolution 2625 (1970), which proclaims the duty not to intervene in matters within the domestic jurisdiction of states, either by individual states or groupings of them.[6]

The invocation of domestic jurisdiction as a bar to external intervention does not apply to action authorized by the Security Council under Chapter VII of the United Nations Charter, or to any acts that are incompatible with the Charter. However, since the Charter is the product of the bloody aftermath of World War II, drafted with the purpose of prioritizing international peace (and avoidance of armed conflicts) over maintaining a sense of international justice,[7] any construction of the Charter under this light would not today serve the purpose of human rights. Things have evidently and for good reason moved on since 1945. The contemporary political agenda undoubtedly seems to prioritize human rights above the traditional concept of sovereignty, a fact which does not indicate a shift from the Charter paradigm of peace over justice, but a promotion of a balance between the two. This development belies a contemporary notion of sovereignty within the context of an interdependent international society, where internal matters have been expressly determined as directly affecting international peace and security.[8] This is obviously the case with human rights and such has been the practice of global and regional international organizations, especially following the collapse of the cold war.

B. Legal Justification for External Non-Forceful Intervention

The purpose of this thesis is to suggest strategies in order to prevent and remedy violations of human rights without recourse to the use of force. It moreover supports the view that the only legitimate source of armed force is that which is authorized by the Security Council of the United Nations, or that which is consistent with the principle of self-defence in accordance with article 51 of the UN Charter. It is true that external influence of the local public opinion of a third state would constitute a violation of the principle of non-interference in the domestic affairs of states. We have noted, however, the gradual erosion of the absolute character of this principle in the human rights era, and the consistent intrusion of international organizations in matters otherwise thought to be the exclusive domain of individual states.

If external intervention is to acquire any degree of legitimacy, it is necessary that it originate from a collective source, specifically under the auspices of an international organization. Increasingly, this model has been applied outside the United Nations, as was recently the case with the European Union's stance to Jorg Heider's far right Freedom Party participation in Austria's coalition government.[9]

Three alternative legal avenues have been identified to address the question of external public opinion influence, in such a way as to be at balance with the principles of sovereignty and the protection of human rights. Firstly, the decision regarding a nation's form of government, and its subsequent practice in the human rights sphere constitutes the basic ingredient of a people's right to self-determination; more specifically, this comprises the internal aspect of self-determination. Undoubtedly, internal self-determination cannot be imposed externally, as this would not differ much from the illegitimacy of the local government. Nonetheless, if the collective right to self-determination is to have any substance, it requires that its addressees have sufficient access to information, fair elections, impartial judicial institutions and the freedom to exercise their civil and political rights. If this is not the case, the right to internal self-determination is seriously impaired and cannot be exercised. In this case, the addressees of the right should be able to seek alternative means of enforcing it, and the use of external support legally justifies their plight.[10]

A second feasible legal avenue might appear by attempting a hierarchy of international norms. More specifically, by viewing the norm of democratic governance above that of invoking domestic jurisdiction as a bar to international scrutiny. This allows for the use of all those means that facilitate democratic governance against the dictates of the target state, albeit in conformity with international law. In the present scenario, this would involve respect of the rule prohibiting the use of force,[11] unless authorized by the Security Council,[12] and strict adherence to human rights standards. The preceding analysis amounts to a viable solution only if democracy is proven to constitute a rule of *jus cogens*, a peremptory norm of international law. Contemporary political practice is highly hypocritical in this regard,[13] and the present author is of the opinion that, insofar as the sources of international law allow us to make any conclusions, democracy has not yet been elevated to a *jus cogens* status.[14] Nonetheless, it is also visible that sovereignty and democracy stand at a delicate balance.

Finally, the Security Council is in a position to take positive action in the human rights sphere. It has indicated its willingness to authorize Chapter VII and other action in such circumstances by treating on a number of occasions gross human rights violations as threats to international peace and security.[15] Certainly, the Council is more inclined to act when a serious armed conflict is imminent or is in progress, or when there is no willingness by the culprit government to conform to United Nations resolutions, than when these elements are missing. A Council resolution authorizing action falling below the use of armed force,[16] is not simply more desirable, it is also far easier to attain. Any such action, however, involves complex political decisions, and any determination on the use of public opinion has to be filtered through a variety of channels, principally satisfying the members of the United Nations that the Council is not exceeding its powers. It is important, therefore, that the delicate balance between democracy and sovereignty as explained above, tips in favor of the former, so that the Council, or indeed other UN bodies, may find ample support in pursuing the influence of public opinion in human rights issues.

Next, we propose to explore certain tools in order to materialize the target of human rights protection through the use of local public opinion.

Tools For Influencing Public Opinion

It should be made clear from the start that the methods instituted by various domestic bodies in order to influence public opinion within the exclusive domain of a particular state, do not constitute appropriate precedent models, where the source of influence from our perspective is geared from international political bases. A simple example is the promulgation of a favorable domestic tax statute by a state's constitutive organs, which aims at appeasing popular unrest regarding pressing social or political problems. The United Nations is obviously unable to pass such statutes or resort to analogous action, and hence has to adhere to other means in order to attract popular attention.

In order for the United Nations to persuade a particular population to stand against an abusive government it is essential it discerns a core target of influence, upon which to impress an appropriate plan of action. This should ideally be a mass, informed and coherent movement. This means that it must be composed of a dynamic core movement embracing large segments of the population on account of their wide and non-extremist ideological advocacy, which has the capacity to enjoy a long-term, majority local support. Groups with narrow ideological bases cannot sustain long-term or majority influence and should not receive international support.

The movement must also be fully aware of its aims, objectives and the means with which to attain them. This would certainly require an intellectual nucleus ensuring that the movement maintains realistic targets and remains unaffected by political or ideological rhetoric used by the government to prevent expansion of the core to the wider masses. This is particularly true of those governmental and societal structures based on religious tradition, such as the Gulf states, where both public and private life is regulated on the basis of the holy *Qur'an*. In such cases the intellectual core would propagate an interpretation of holy Scriptures free from the repressive and abusive application of the political and clerical elite.

Once the appropriate movement, as discussed above, is identified, depending on the severity of human rights violations and the intransigence of the government, it may be expedient to impose either a number of sanctions or resort to vehement condemnation of its practices. International condemnation through the various organs and procedures of the United Nations has the potential to become effective only if it is kept on the agenda long enough and receives sufficient political consensus.[17] It is the combination of condemnation and UN sponsored sanctions that provide evidence of such a political consensus; however, this is difficult to obtain. Unfortunately, states with a poor human rights record but endowed with geopolitical or financial significance, such as a large number of *Sharia*-governed countries and China, have not been widely criticized by the United Nations—except through thematic reports undertaken by UN Special Rapporteurs—nor have they been subject to any regime of sanctions. On the other hand, so called "pariah states" such as Sudan, Iraq, Libya and Afghanistan have received the wrath of the international community and have suffered as a result of harsh sanctions, sometimes only to the detriment of the local populations.[18]

Notwithstanding the politics of the international system, sanctions have the capacity to be effective. South Africa abolished its long-standing policy of racial segregation (apartheid) after sustained sanctions that crippled its economy and left the country in financial ruin. Similarly, despite its many shortcomings, the Sudanese military government did at some point in the late 1990s agree to hold a referendum on the question of the secession of South Sudan and has allowed access to humanitarian organizations throughout the territory of that country.[19] Furthermore, it was the devastating financial effect of UN sanctions against the Federal Republic of Yugoslavia (FRY) that urged its leadership to reach an agreement on the termination of the Bosnian civil war. Effective and strict observance of these sanctions by the authorities of third countries can only serve to enhance their general effectiveness.[20]

Following civil unrest in the FRY province of Kosovo in 1999, a severe sanctions regime was imposed against the FRY by the United Nations and the European Union[21] because of that government's poor handling of the situation and the subsequent undemocratic stance of its political leadership.[22] This led to renewed pressure from large segments of the Serbian population through the staging of daily demonstrations and other campaigning, urging the government to resign.[23] Eventually, the combination of harsh sanctions and foreign aid to dissident groups[24] paved the way for a popular uprising against President Milosevic, whose regime was toppled through force by the Yugoslav people following his refusal to surrender power after losing the September 2000 elections. Sanctions are an indirect mean by which the international community strengthens the internal movement because the lack of goods raises dissatisfaction among the local population while it also enhances a feeling of isolation. These should be supplemented with other direct means. Firstly, the international community is in a position to control mass media and the transmission of information through radio, television and the Internet.[25] This capacity should be utilized to prevent the flow of inciteful or false propaganda messages. Such broadcast jamming is fully compatible with international law, and in particular with article 20(2) of the 1966 UN Covenant on Civil and Political Rights (ICCPR), which holds that:

Any advocacy of national, racial or religious hatred that constitutes incitement to discrimination, hostility or violence shall be prohibited by law.[26]

International law further specifically empowers the Security Council, under article 41 UN Charter, to take any measures not involving the use of armed force, including inter alia "complete or partial interruption of ... telegraphic, radio and other means of communication...." The 1994 genocide of the Tutsi population in Rwanda was instigated mainly through radio broadcasts to that effect by a governing Hutu regime.[27] These public broadcasts advocated powerful messages of hate, calling on the entire Hutu population to participate in a campaign of extermination not only against all Tutsi but also against moderate Hutus. One author has suggested that the United Nations had the capacity to jam these radio broadcasts, and had it done so the large scale of the massacre may have been prevented.[28] It is submitted that radio jamming is useful not only for preventing unlawful broadcasting, but also for informing populations at a mass level.

Measures directed at preventing abuse of mass media and communications can be effective both in the case of developing nations, in situations of urgency such as that of Rwanda, but also with regard to developed nations, such as the FRY.[29] This differentiation is crucial for the foregoing analysis. Less developed states have a low standard and access to education and hence are more susceptible to governmental manipulation than are people with a high degree of literacy. It is necessary therefore, when seeking to influence public opinion, to approach both cases in a different manner; developing nations on a long-term basis, while developed nations even on a short-term basis.

Strategies for Developing Nations

Developing states are encouraged to promote and protect human rights through a number of effective avenues. Among these one can list their participation in international organizations or specialized agencies with human rights agendas, as well as their ratification of mutual co-operation and financial assistance agreements with human rights caveats. These caveats are inserted as so called "conditionality clauses" in multilateral or bilateral aid treaties, and their aim is to ensure that the aided state adheres to certain principles as laid down by the aiding/co-operating parties. These principles usually concern human rights protection and an obligation to respect democratic values.[30]

The European Communities have promoted such agreements from the early 1970s, and have since invigorated this process by providing that conditionality clauses form an integral part of all such agreements.[31] Although the content of these clauses is an especially welcome development, as is the possibility of suspending recalcitrant states, these human rights provisions lack specificity and enforcement. More specifically, there is no requirement as to how the various rights need be implemented, or how the aiding/co-operating states might offer specific assistance in this respect. It serves no practical purpose reiterating the wording of rights that the participating states have already ratified as part of other international agreements. Implementation and efficiency should be the goal of the international community, through the assumption of specific negative and positive obligations. Furthermore, without doubting the indivisibility of human rights, it is an essential element of any democratization process that the right to education be positively materialized and specifically catered for in these agreements. The lack of reference and commitment to education is at least suspicious. The question arises as to whether the developed world really wishes to promote a developing world through the means of mass education, especially since developed economies are rapidly turning their financial interest to the services sector rather than strengthening their manufacturing industries. Expensive labor and rising economies in Europe and North America means that production of most material goods is no longer economically viable in these areas of the world. Hence, industrial corporations are manufacturing their products in developing countries where labor and raw material is cheap. The establishment of sound and universal educational systems in the developing world runs counter to the interests of the various corporations, since labor would eventually cease being cheap.

Finally, one readily observes that the enforcement machineries governing these agreements, at best, reserve a right to suspend states breaching their human rights provisions. The financial significance of these agreements for developing states should be used by their counterparts to secure a monitoring obligation in accordance with pre-arranged plans and procedures. These would set out in advance both positive and negative obligations and the mode by which they would be implemented, under the guidance and supervision of a supervisory commission. This commission would also ensure that the money allocated for the promotion of various rights would be appropriately used. It is imperative therefore that the aided state agrees to be monitored by an independent international human rights commission, which oversees human rights projects and related expenditures.

Private and inter-governmental institutions are increasingly inserting human rights and environmental clauses in investment and loan contracts with developing nations.[32] However, the same problems identified above with regard to inter-state development/aid treaties are existent also in investment and loan contracts. Any quasi-judicial bodies established by the World Bank or the IMF function only after a report or complaint has been filed by an interested party, and there is no independent monitoring body charged with verifying the terms and human rights aspects of the contract.[33] It would be highly desirable if such bodies were established as integral aspects of these contracts, as would also be the promulgation of legislation in developed states to the effect that private corporations heavily investing in developing countries establish analogous mechanisms.

Strategies for Developed Nations

As already explained, public awareness in developed nations is at a much higher level in comparison to developing nations, on account of the increased educational level and the flow of and access to information. This does not, however, prevent the manipulation of public opinion by governing power structures in these states. This was sadly manifested in the 1999 Austrian crisis with the participation in government of an extreme right wing party, and also the strict Sharia application in a large number of Moslem-majority countries. In Austria and FRY-type situations, two targets have been identified; firstly, the reversal of that portion of public sentiment sympathetic to the violating party, and secondly, the avoidance of assimilating entire groups with the violating party.

The first of these targets refers to statements, acts or wilful omissions, resorted to by governments or other power bases with which they intend to manipulate various problems or perceived problems within a community. The manipulation occurs by inventing or exaggerating a "problem," and subsequently creating a nucleus of community support against the usually small portion that is accused of being the "troublemakers." This was the case with Nazi Germany against Jews and other minorities during the inter-war years, in FRY the "problem" was the ethnic Albanian community in Kosovo (1999), in Austria it was the immigrants that were targeted (1999), and more recently in Zimbabwe the wrath of the government was unleashed against white farmers (2000).[34] The common feature in each of these case studies is the existence of minority groups under an initial severe verbal attack, followed by physical attacks on a small or large scale. Furthermore, the initial verbal attack, which is grounded on the exploitation of domestic issues, is linked to a very specific aim of the attacking party. Hence, Nazis attacked the Jewish minority, taking advantage of popular discontent over high unemployment, with the aim of establishing a unified and socially supportable racist strategy that would justify resort to a global war and excuse brutalities. The same language was used by the Austrian Freedom Party against immigrant workers, albeit with more limited aims. Similarly, in the case of both the FRY and Zimbabwe, incitement to violence against Kosovar and white minorities respectively was aimed at preserving in power the two ailing governments by inventing an "enemy," thus turning public focus from a deep resentment of its government, and securing community support in combating the newly invented "enemy."

The second crucial target for the international community is to disengage the local population from the rhetoric of the violating party. The latter will in many cases seek to portray any attack on itself as an attack against the entirety of the local population, and specifically against its ethnic, national, religious or political identity, when in fact it is only the policies of the governing power that are under fire. In such situations, it should be made abundantly clear that the local population is in no way conceived to be assimilated to the culprit party, even if to a large degree it has succumbed to the latter's indoctrination. This attitude was not followed in the case of the Bosnian Serbs with regard to the Bosnian civil war between 1992-95. More specifically, this ethnic group was assimilated in the world press and official documentation to that very small part of Serbs that planned and committed horrendous atrocities during that country's civil war. This only succeeded in marginalizing them and creating a deep feeling of victimization, which subsequently evolved into a popular and widespread spirit of animosity against the United Nations and anything non-Serb. The same mistake was unfortunately repeated during the Kosovo campaign, although that time there were no references assimilating the Serbian people to their President. However, there was a direct attack on their cultural and national pride, which forced them to turn against NATO and the United Nations, even though prior to the bombing raids public opinion was strongly opposed to the Milosevic regime. It should not, therefore, have been a surprise seeing television reports of Serbs during the bombings wearing target placards on their chests, indicating that they alone were the real targets of the NATO raids. Hence, thanks to the efforts of the international community, Milosevic lost the war, but rallied an overwhelming domestic popular support that succeeded in keeping him in power far longer than he should.

In situations such as the one just described, the most appropriate course of action would be to take full consideration of the various sensitivities of the targeted local population, whether national, cultural or religious. These sensitivities should be fundamentally respected by the international community. It should be made clear that the only institution under attack, preferably non-forcefully, is the abusive party through its illegal actions or policies. With this attitude, any action subsequently undertaken by a global or regional organization would receive the support of the local population. Since late 1999, a large segment of the international community initiated a direct campaign of appeals to the Serbian people to rid themselves of their President, promising, *inter alia*, to alleviate them from years of financial suffering and isolation as a result of sanctions.[35]

Finally, some mention should be made of those states asserting their opposition to the allegedly western concept of human rights, at least in terms of content, hierarchy and enforcement, on the basis of their cultural differences with the drafters of such human rights instruments.[36] Efforts thus far to impose a "western"-type human rights regime in these countries has attracted only a theoretical debate, focusing on the argument that human rights are universal and not subject to cultural relativism. From the prism of the preceding analysis, this theoretical debate would be redundant if the populations in relativist states were to adopt a universalist viewpoint of rights. Very simplistically, this would be achieved either by rejecting the religious, ideological or cultural link-elements which binds a given social group, or, and more preferably, by interpreting these elements in a way which coincides with the universalist concept of rights, but still reflecting the distinctive identity of the group. Furthermore, and far from solving the dispute, are the proponents of the universality theory, on their part, willing to accept that through a democratic process the people of a particular country may in fact decide to adhere to relativist principles?

It is true to say that in general Moslems living in Islamic states are to a large degree satisfied with the Qur'anic legal order and the penetration of religious doctrine in the regulation of daily life. There is of course some dissent to such regulation, both external and internal, but internal dissent seems to be a minority call. As a system of meaning, the Islamic world constitutes a network of internal communication among its members, through which these persons, *inter alia*, identify themselves. According to Luhmann, since the various systems use different procedures for validating and comprehending external reality, as opposed to a uniform procedure that is readily agreed with regard to their internal reality, social systems are not able to communicate the same meaning to one another. In this sense social systems are closed, but reproduce within themselves their version of the external environment.[37] If this argument is correct, the West should primarily strive to become an observer of the Islamic system in the same way as any of its members understand the coding and messages communicated within that system. Thus, the West must be able to comprehend and convey the exact same messages that a Moslem comprehends and conveys to other Moslems. The aim of this procedure is to merge the western and Islamic systems, at least in their common understanding of the Moslem internal reality. When this process is completed, the second step is to communicate within that internal channel an appropriate human rights message, whose content will take consideration of the previously observed Moslem internal reality. There is no guarantee that this too will be commonly understood or appreciated similarly within both systems. This is however a crucial test for this strategy, since if the Western model is seen by the Moslem observers as a suitable option, Moslem public opinion will have shifted from its previous position on the Western concept of rights. This is, nonetheless, a strategy that is long-term, costly, and imbued with political risk, but it is also void of academic legal jargon and takes account of popular demand.

Some Lessons for Capital Punishment Strategists

The death penalty is a sensitive issue on the political and social agendas of those countries where it is in force. Abolitionist states generally oppose the practice of retentionist jurisdictions by prohibiting the extradition of individuals to such countries, not only where it is known that capital punishment exists, but also where there exists a real risk of being subjected to it.[38] In recent years the capital punishment debate has moved on from the realm of bilateral relations to international fora, and more specifically the United Nations (mainly the General Assembly and Human Rights Commission) and the Council of Europe.[39] Despite the failure of the abolitionist movement in the General Assembly to reach global agreement even on a moratorium, the mere presence of the death penalty on the international agenda has had some impact. Turkey, a member of the Council of Europe and a retentionist, will not be enforcing capital punishment against the captured Kurdish PKK leader, Abdullah Ocalan. This decision was obviously linked to Turkey's bid in joining the European Union, and this gesture demonstrated some adherence to human rights in accordance with the principles underlying the Council of Europe, of which Turkey is a member. It is doubtful, however, whether the Turkish military regime would have adhered to such principles had it not been for the demand of its substantial wealthy middle class—and its rapidly growing industry—for closer economic and cultural union with Western Europe.[40] Hence, a strong catalyst for change in the preceding case was a potent form of external intervention, albeit with substantial benefits for the target state.

A variation of this model may serve capital punishment strategies in other Moslem or Christian retentionist countries. Moslem states assert their authority to impose the death penalty on provisions of the *Quran* and Islamic tradition. However, some Christian majority states apply it also, so it cannot be said that the call for its abolition is a matter connected exclusively to Moslem tradition and influence. Vehement opposition to capital punishment in the Islamic context by abolitionists can only serve a limited purpose if it does not also take into consideration the popularly perceived Moslem viewpoint. Moslem public opinion can only reach consensus on abolition if the weight of the West's argument is centered on an Islamic interpretation of abolition. A Western view, even one based on existing international human rights jurisprudence, has been and will be rejected in any future attempt. The "core" that is capable of investigating a new religious interpretation of capital punishment is a combination of Moslem clerical and intellectual elite. A possible reconstruction could be based on a temporal interpretation of Islamic sources, resulting in the redundancy of the death penalty in light of contemporary advances in sentencing and the effectiveness of such mechanisms in general. This could be initiated through *Ijtihad*, which represents a method of juristic reasoning in search of answers where the primary sources of Islam are silent.[41]

In the USA, a society with strong secular and religious adherents, public opinion is to a large extent influenced by mass media. Popular perception has been nurtured to believe that a rising criminal rate, however that may be defined, can be curbed by strict punishment, and is thus not generally opposed to the imposition of capital punishment, or a majority at least is indifferent as to its imposition or not. Any future strategies have to target the amendment of this popular perception by way of self re-examination, either through the press or other institutions. One such institution is the Church, which is itself opposed to capital punishment, and is in a position to convince and positively influence its members as to the righteousness of this cause.

Conclusions

Human rights strategies, foremost, require appropriate international support, simply because such strategies involve some form of intrusion in the internal affairs of states. This interventionist model seems to be followed in the post cold-war era, albeit on the basis of political criteria and not at a uniform level. Within the strategies pursued by individual states and international organizations, it would perhaps be useful if public opinion in the states of abuse was utilized to persuade the culprit government to resign or change its policy. This "manipulation" of local public opinion is far from being considered in this essay as a method with a settled content or form, but it is a first forum for discussion and elaboration for the future. It is hoped that more scholarly work will emanate with application in all fields of human rights, giving substance to my primitive ideas.

Notes

© Ilias Bantekas and Ashgate Publishing Company 2001. Ilias Bantekas is Senior Lecturer and Director, International Law Unit, School of Law, University of Westminster, and Barrister.

The author is grateful to Dr. Elias Zafiris, Imperial College London, for illuminating discussions on this topic.

1   General Framework Agreement for Peace in Bosnia and Herzegovina, reprinted in 35 *International Legal Materials*, 1996, p. 75.
2   T. Franck, "The Emerging Right to Democratic Governance," 86 *American Journal of International Law*, 1992, p. 46.
3   *See* I. Bantekas, Z. Ibrahim, "International Law Implications from the 1999 Pakistani Coup d'Etat," *ASIL Insight*, 1999.
4   *See* D. McGoldrick, *The Human Rights Committee*, 1994; P. R. Ghandi, "The Human Rights Committee and the Right of Individual Petition," 57 *British Yearbook of International Law*, 1987, p. 201; D. J. Harris, M. O'Boyle, C. Warbrick, *Law of the European Convention on Human Rights*, 1995; Murray, "Decisions by the African Commission on Individual Communications under the African Charter on Human and Peoples' Rights," 46 *International and Comparative Law Quarterly*, 1997, p. 412.
5   The Baha'is in Iran have been persecuted since their split from Islam in 1863, and this has continued to the present day. See Report of the Special Rapporteur of the Human Rights Commission, UN Doc. E/CN.4/1987/20 (28 Jan. 1987); in 1985 the Nimeiri regime in Sudan ordered the public hanging of a Sudanese intellectual, Mohammed Mahmud Taha, on the grounds of apostasy for his personal interpretation of the Quran. See A. A. An-Na'im, "The Islamic Law of Apostasy and its Modern Applicability: A Case from the Sudan," 16 *Religion*, 1986, p. 197.

6   G.A. Res. 2625 (1970), Declaration on Principles of International Law Concerning Friendly Relations and Co-Operation Among States in Accordance with the Charter of the United Nations.

7   A. C. Arend, R. J. Beck, *International Law and the Use of Force*, 1993, p. 34.

8   See Security Council Resolution 770 (13 Aug. 1992) determining that the Bosnian civil war constituted a threat to international peace and security; a similar situation was determined to exist in Resolution 794 (3 Dec. 1992) on the basis of the magnitude of human tragedy caused by the internal conflict in Somalia.

9   I. Bantekas, "Austria, the European Union and Article 2(7) United Nations Charter," *ASIL Insights*, 2000.

10   Principle IV of G.A. Res. 2625 (1970) makes it clear that the denial of the right to self-determination constitutes a violation of fundamental human rights and the UN Charter. Cassese argues that in cases of internal self-determination third parties are allowed under international law to lend economic, financial or political assistance to the rebellious group. A. Cassese, *Self-Determination of Peoples: A Legal Reappraisal*, 1995, pp. 154-55.

11   Art. 2(4) United Nations Charter.

12   As was the case with S.C. Res. 940 (31 July 1994), where the Council authorised the use of force under Chapter VII to restore democracy in Haiti.

13   This is especially true, since countries such as Turkey, Pakistan and the Gulf Emirates, to name a few, are favorably treated by western states, despite their lack of democratic government and abhorrent human rights records.

14   In accordance with the Democratic Peace theory, which builds on the ideas of Kant, a world of democratic states is *ipso facto* a peaceful world, because democracies do not go to war with each other. See F. R. Teson, "Collective Humanitarian Intervention," 17 *Michigan Journal of International Law*, 1996, p. 323, at 333.

15   *Supra* note 9; furthermore, although not in the context of Chapter VII, it is worthwhile noting that in January 2000 the Council, at its 4086th Meeting, held a debate on the impact of AIDS on peace and security in Africa. See Press Release SC/6781 (10 Jan. 2000).

16   Art. 41 UN Charter.

17   The investigation of particular countries' human rights records in accordance with ECOSOC Res. 1235 (1967) procedure exercised intense international pressure on some investigated states, resulting in gradual amelioration of their overall human rights situation. See A. H. Robertson, J. G. Merrills, *Human Rights in the World*, 1994, pp. 78-84.

18   S.C. Res. 1214 (8 Dec. 1998) and subsequent Council resolutions have called on Afghan factions to put an end to discrimination against women and girls, but the author could not find any other Council resolution demanding the same from other wealthy Arab states.

19   Art. 10 Chap. VII of the Khartoum Peace Agreement, signed 21 April 1997 between the Sudanese Government and seven warring factions from Southern Sudan, guaranteed a right to self-determination for the people of South Sudan. The Khartoum Agreement was incorporated in the Sudanese legal system via Presidential Decree No. 14, 10 April 1998 (unreported, on file with author). This was followed by a resumption of activities by the International Committee of the Red Cross through an Agreement on 22 January 1998. *However, the Peace Agreement has failed to materialize due to non-participation of the major rebel entities.*

20   *See* US sanctions against UNITA rebels in Angola, 64 Fed. Reg. 51419 (23 Sep. 1999); US sanctions on Afghan Taliban for support of Bin Laden, 64 Fed. Reg. 36750 (7 July

1999); in similar conformity with a stringent sanctions regime, the US 5th Circuit Court held in *Paradissiotis v Rubin*, 171 F.3d 983 (1999), that regulations dealing with sanctions against Libya apply not only to transactions that benefit Libya directly, but also to those that profit individuals who represent Libyan interests.

21 EU implementation of petroleum embargo, 1999 O.J. (L 108) 1; freezing of Yugoslav funds abroad and bar of future investment in Serbia, Council Regulation No. 1294/1999, 1999 O.J. (L 153) 63 and Council Decision 1999/424/CFSP, 1999 O.J. (L 163) 86.

22 On 22 May 1999, the Prosecutor of the International Criminal Tribunal for Yugoslavia (ICTY) issued an indictment against Milosevic, the President of Serbia, the Chief of Staff of FRY, as well as the Interior Minister for offences committed by FRY forces in Kosovo. ICTY Press Release JL/PIU/403-E (27 May 1999).

23 "Protest Movements Began by Ordinary Serbs," *The Times*, 27 May 2000.

24 To encourage opposition activities in Serbia, the Clinton administration, through the U.S. Agency for International Development, spent $25 million in 1999. Nearly half of the money, $11 million was spent on helping unions, media organizations and civic associations.

25 This could fall within the ambit of information warfare (IW), which seeks to exploit the use of the enemy's high-technology civilian and military infrastructure. This option was raised regarding the Kosovo conflict, but ultimately rejected by NATO command. See W. Church, "Information Warfare," 82 *International Review of the Red Cross*, 2000, p. 205.

26 6 ILM, 1967, p. 368.

27 In *ICTR Prosecutor v. Ruggiu*, Case No. ICTR-97-32-I, Judgment of 1 June 2000, paras. 47-50, Trial Chamber I noted in particular the very powerful and extremely influential role of the media in inciting the Rwandan massacres.

28 J. F. Metzl, "Rwandan Genocide and the International Law of Radio Jamming," 91 AJIL, 1997, p. 628

29 S.C. Res. 837 (6 June 1993) strongly condemned "the use of radio broadcasts, in particular by the USC/SNA, to incite attacks against UN personnel" in Somalia; similarly, S.C. Res. 918 (17 May 1994) imposed an arms embargo on Rwanda, stating as one of its reasons the incitement of annihilation advocated through mass media.

30 On 29 May 1995, the Council of the EU adopted a political guideline to insert into every forthcoming treaty with third states two clauses, one relating to human rights and the other to democratic principles. See EU Bulletin, May 1995, p. 1, and M. Fouwels, "The European Union's Common Foreign and Security Policy and Human Rights," 15 NQHR, 1997, p. 291; similarly, in *Portuguese Republic v Council*, Case No. C-268/94, [1996] ECR I— 6177, the European Court of Justice (ECJ) held that respect for human rights and democratic principles is an essential element of co-operation agreements under the then Art. 130(u) EEC Treaty.

31 *See* Art. 4 African, Caribbean and Pacific States (ACP)—European Economic Community, IV Lome Convention, 29 ILM, 1990, p. 783, which made general reference to civil, political, and socio-economic rights. Arts. 5 and 366a of the 1995 Revised IV Lome Convention incorporated the 1995 EU Guidelines and a non-fulfilment clause. These clauses enabled the EU to suspend development aid to a number of states violating human rights.

32 *See* B. Kingsbury, "Indigenous Peoples in International Law: A Constructivist Approach to the Asian Controversy," 92 *American Journal of International Law*, 1998, p. 414.

33   The Inspection Panel of the World Bank—established by IBRD Res. 93-10 and IDA Res. 93-6, 22 Sep. 1993—operates a grievance redress mechanism, available to private parties of the borrowing state, who must show actual or possible material damage as a result of a serious failure by the Bank. A. Qureshi, *"International Economic Law,"* 1999, p. 354.

34   "Mugabe Stokes up Anti-White Campaign," *The Times*, 17 April 2000.

35   "Power of Milosevic cannot Last says Solano," The Times, 5 October 1999; "West Changes Tactic to Ease Out Milosevic," The Times, 6 November 1999; "EU Urges Serbs to End the Reign of Milosevic," The Times, 25 March 2000.

36   *See generally*, C. Cerna, "Universality of Human Rights and Cultural Diversity," *16 Human Rights Quarterly*, 1994, p. 740; R. Higgins, "Human Rights—Some Questions of Integrity," 52 *Modern Law Review*, 1989, p. 1.

37   For further reading, *see* N. Luhmann, "The Representation of Society within Society," 35 *Current Sociology*, 1987, p. 101; M. King, "The Truth About Autopoiesis," 20 *Journal of Law and Society*, 1993, p. 218, 220.

38   For example, Art. 11 of the 1957 European Convention on Extradition, 359 UNTS 273; in *Soering v United Kingdom*, Eur. Ct. H. R. Reports, Ser. A, No. 161 (1989), the European Court of Human Rights held that Art. 3 ECHR, which prohibits torture and inhuman and degrading treatment or punishment, prevented the UK from extraditing the accused to the state of Virginia where the death penalty was still available. This decision was based on the fact that prolonged subjection to the death row phenomenon amounted to inhuman and degrading treatment; the same approach was adopted by the Human Rights Committee, based on a violation of Art. 7 ICCPR, in respect to Canada's extradition of an individual to the state of California, in *Ng v Canada*, 98 ILR, 479. *See* generally, J. Dugard, C. V. den Wyngaert, "Reconciling Extradition with Human Rights," 92 *American Journal of International Law*, 1998, p. 187.

39   W. A. Schabas, *The Abolition of the Death Penalty in International Law*, 1997.

40   It is true that this pro-Europe model has inspired the Turkish military as a result of Ataturk's political thinking, since the fall of the Ottoman Empire.

41   Although a consensus evolved around the 10th century A.D. that *ijtihad* was no longer accepted, a number of modern Moslem jurists have argued that *ijtihad* was never abandoned, and that it may validly be exercised by respected Moslems. Nonetheless, there is clear consensus that *ijtihad* can never be allowed to contradict the Quran or the deeds and words of Prophet Mohammed (*sunna*). *See* J. Schacht, *"An Introduction to Islamic Law,"* 1964, pp. 69-75; W. B. Hallaq, "Was the Gate of Ijtihad Closed?," 16 *International Journal of Middle East Studies*, 1984, p. 3.

15 International Women Judges Foundation: Why Bother with Judicial Training?—Judicial Training Programs on International Law and Women's Rights

ANNE TIERNEY GOLDSTEIN

International law standards can give judges a fresh perspective on the hidden assumptions about men and women in their particular country's legal system. Making these assumptions visible is, in turn, the first step to changing them.[1] This chapter describes the *Jurisprudence of Equality Project* of the International Women Judges Foundation, and generally explores strategies for designing judicial training programs on international law and women's rights. The chapter particularly focuses on the Uruguayan law of sexual assault as a case study of how the abstract promises of international human rights law can be translated into the concrete reality of judges' daily workload.

Judges and Judicial Training

Within the human rights community, there are two competing images of judges. On the one hand, there is the courageous crusader, the maverick who bucks the system and not infrequently appears in the literature as a human rights victim. On the other hand, there is the faceless, robed representative of an oppressive system—a callous, indifferent, perhaps outright corrupt figure who is written off by human rights advocates.

Yet judges, like the rest of us, lead complicated lives and resist stereo-typing. Some judges may be stupid or for sale or both—but most judges are diligent, intelligent professionals, who went into the field of law because they cared about justice.

Even when judges are not the strongest proponents of human rights, advocates for human rights ignore them at their peril. Like it or not, these judges deal every day with some of the most vulnerable people in their societies—and quite simply, it is better to bring them into a discussion of human rights than to ignore them.

Training programs based on either of these competing images of judges—or, for that matter, on any stereotyped image of judges—will have limited impact at best. Only a small percentage of members of any profession, including the judiciary, will ever have the energy and inclination to be crusaders. On the other hand, a trainer who approaches training with the idea that the participants are scoundrels is hardly likely to garner their attention, let alone their respect.

To be effective, then, judicial training programs must be designed for judges with a range of interests, backgrounds and abilities. They must respond to the needs and concerns of the judges in a particular legal community, and they must build on participants' expertise and experience. They must be respectful. Participants must be accorded the presumption that they are intelligent and have integrity—a presumption that in some circumstances may seem naïve, but is in fact the opposite.

In other words, training programs must themselves embody human rights principles, starting with Article 1 of the Universal Declaration of Human Rights: *All human beings are born free and equal in dignity and rights. They are endowed with reason and conscience and should act towards one another in a spirit of brotherhood.*

A good training program will seek to empower judges who are already committed to human rights, and reach out to those who are not. It will focus on developing skills and changing attitudes, more than on simply conveying knowledge about the contents of international conventions.

The "Towards a Jurisprudence of Equality Project" of the International Women Judges Foundation and the International Association of Women Judges

The International Women Judges Foundation (IWJF) is the tax-exempt fundraising and education arm of the International Association of Women Judges (IAWJ). The IAWJ is a membership organization of judges from eighty-five countries around the world. As of April 2001, it had 4,394 members, including 215 from Argentina, 80 from Nigeria, 50 from

Bangladesh, 10 from Iceland, and 74 from Mongolia. Members meet every two years, by tradition in the home city of the president of the organization, which was Rome in 1994, Manila in 1996, Ottawa in 1998, and Buenos Aires in 2000 and will be Dublin in 2002 and Nairobi in 2004.

In 1994, the IAWJ committed itself to the "Towards a Jurisprudence of Equality Project, or "JEP." Through the JEP, the IAWJ and the IWJF develop and run judicial training programs on the use of international law in cases that come before domestic courts involving discrimination or violence against women.

All JEP programs are developed in partnership between the IWJF and national chapters of the IAWJ. In each instance, the national chapter sets priorities and identifies problems that the training program should address. Representatives of the national chapter are responsible for handling the logistics of the training program, and for identifying talented academics and judges who will become the in-country trainers. Those selected as trainers spend two weeks at JEP "Training the Trainer" Workshops. Working in two-person teams, the trainers each lead at least two three-day seminars for judges in different regions of their respective countries.

While most of the fundraising for the JEP is done by the IWJF, national chapters that elect to participate necessarily commit substantial financial and human resources. The ultimate goal underlying this design is that each project will be locally owned and self-sustaining.

Thus far, JEP training programs have taken place in Argentina, Brazil, Chile, China, Costa Rica, the Dominican Republic, Italy, Kenya, the Philippines, Romania, Uganda, Uruguay and the United States, and are currently being prepared in Ecuador, South Africa and Tanzania.

International Law and Women's Rights: Nondiscrimination, Equal Protection and Stereotyped Roles for Men and Women

International treaties and conventions offer women many promises, but for purposes of this overview, these promises can be summarized in one sentence: International law promises women protection from discrimination and from violence.

These promises sound somewhat distant, almost ethereal. Most of us do not think about international law as affecting our daily lives. Yet these promises can be translated into the reality of daily life in small town courts in the Philippines or Tanzania. The key is to use international law standards as a means to measure—and ultimately to change—local legal and judicial cultures.

International law can give judges a fresh perspective on the hidden assumptions of their particular country's legal system. Making these assumptions visible is, in turn, the first step to changing them.

The United Nations Convention on the Elimination of All Forms of Discrimination (also known as the Women's Convention or "CEDAW") requires States Parties to eliminate "discrimination" from their domestic laws. Both the International Covenant on Civil and Political Rights (in Article 26) and the American Convention on Human Rights (in Article 24) speak in terms of guaranteeing women the "equal protection of the law."

Equal protection and nondiscrimination in fact can be seen as two sides of the same coin. The question is what the coin is worth.

One could argue for days—academics have done it for years—over what "equal protection" means in the abstract. But the very abstraction of much of this debate stands in the way of seeing the concrete reality of discrimination.

Sexual assault, for example, is not a crime perpetrated by gender-neutral people who "just happen to be" men against other gender-neutral people who "just happen to be" women. It is overwhelmingly a crime perpetrated by men against women.

When it comes to resolving legal disputes about sexual assault, however, legal and judicial systems all over the world are structured in ways that simultaneously reflect and obscure this basic, gendered reality. Distrust of women and their testimony is built into legal systems in ways so deep that we have to make a conscious effort to see them.

JEP training makes this distrust visible, and encourages judges to find ways to end it. Training programs start with Article 5 of CEDAW, and the concept of "stereotypes" as a way of relating the abstract ideal of "equal protection" to concrete situations.

CEDAW Article 5 provides:

States Parties shall take all appropriate measures:

(a) To modify the social and cultural patterns of conduct of men and women, with a view to achieving the elimination of prejudices and customary and all other practices which are based on the idea of the inferiority or the superiority of either of the sexes or on stereotyped roles for men and women.

Early on in the training seminar or workshop, trainers show participants an overhead transparency of Article 5(a). They ask them, "What kinds of stereotypes do you think people have in your country about men and women?" Then the trainer makes a chart, using a flip chart or blackboard. S/he makes two columns, one for stereotypes about men and the other for stereotypes about women. As participants call out a stereotype, the trainer writes it down.

The resulting charts never vary significantly from one country to another. Women are weak/men are strong; women are nurturing, domestic, better with children. Men are aggressive, assertive, better at meeting the demands of commerce. Women are emotional and empathetic/men are rational and analytical. These stereotypes appear to be, if not universal, then at least so pervasive they might as well be.

Typically, judges like this exercise. They laugh and joke as they do it, because they have encountered these stereotypes in their own lives. Very often, a female judge will describe how she did not get a job or a promotion because of one of these stereotypes ("women aren't aggressive enough to be criminal court judges—you belong in juvenile court or in family court," etc.)

Then participants discuss what is wrong with stereotypes and why international law would try to ban states—and state officials, including judges—from relying on them. The reasons elicited from participants generally include some or all of the following:

- Some stereotypes are simply false. If a stereotype is false, then it is totally irrational to base government policy on it.

- Even if a stereotype is "true" in a statistical sense—meaning true "on the average" it will be false as to many individuals. As to those individuals, a policy or law based on stereotypes is irrational. This is the problem, for example, with laws that bar women from holding jobs that require the lifting of more than a certain amount of weight. It may be true that men, on average, are more capable of lifting heavy weights than women. But it makes no sense to bar *all* women from a job on the grounds that *some* women can't do it. Why not test directly whether the worker, male or female, is capable of doing the job?

- More broadly, legislating on the basis of stereotypes that are true "on average" disregards the *individual* at the heart of human rights law. Statistically, it is "true" that men commit the vast majority of violent crimes. But we do not lock up *all* men on the theory that *some* men are violent. People have the right to be treated as individual human beings, not as members of a statistical cohort.

- Finally, stereotypes have a tendency to become self-fulfilling prophecies. Consider the stereotype that men and boys are more analytical then women and girls. If this stereotype is widely shared by members of a particular culture, one would expect parents to select toys for pre-schoolers based on the stereotype, teachers to call on boys more often in science classes, guidance counselors to steer boys towards and girls away from math courses, and so on. (In the United States a few years ago the Mattel Corporation came out with a talking Barbie doll that told little girls over and over, hundreds of times, that "math is hard.") You would expect employers to avoid hiring women in jobs requiring analytical or math skills, since they are "less qualified." Finally, you would expect women to have less interest in such jobs and avoid training or applying for them, because of a perception that women are unwelcome in this line of work. In short, the stereotype creates and perpetuates its own reality.

Over the course of the seminar or workshop, judges consider the ways in which stereotypes are embedded—and perpetuate themselves—in hiring practices, sexual harassment law, custody determinations, domestic violence, etc. They look at laws and practices, and consider the hidden assumptions of legislators, policy makers and judges. Then they discuss how these assumptions can be changed.

Case Study: A Sexual Assault Trial in Uruguay

One of the JEP project's Uruguayan trainers told the following story at a 1999 "Training the Trainers" Workshop in Buenos Aires. The trainer in question was a criminal court judge from Montevideo, and shortly before the workshop she had been assigned to preside over a sexual assault case, in a small town outside the capital. The facts of the case, as she described them, were that three young men were drinking at a bar, when they met three teenaged girls, with whom they spent the next few hours drinking and talking. The young men were sons of prominent members of the community—in the phrase that kept coming back during the trial, they were "de buena familia" (of good family) while the young women were from the poorer end of town. The two groups of young people had not met before that night.

It grew late, and everyone said goodnight. The two groups left separately. Not long after, however, their paths crossed in the street, and the young men invited the girls to drink beer (they were already drunk) in the apartment of one of them. Two of the girls declined the invitation and the third accepted. The four young people went to the apartment, where, the girl would later testify, she was gang-raped.

The story came out the next day, after the girl's grandfather, with whom she lived, reported her to the police as missing. Later that day, she was found crying, curled up in a closet in her home.

The case received considerable attention in the community, little of it sympathetic to the young woman. Her two friends, along with virtually everyone else, concluded that she must have "wanted it," since, after all, the boys were de buena familia, and what kind of girl was she? She danced with one of them—and he was nice looking. A not guilty verdict was considered a foregone conclusion.

The rush to judgment troubled the judge who told this story. During the pre-trial skirmishes, she made some preliminary ruling or rulings in favor of the prosecution. Her colleagues made remarks to her—nothing threatening, really, just the kind of well-this-is-an-easy-case-what-do-you-think-you're-doing kind of remarks colleagues make to one another.

The victim had been examined, but in this small town there was no forensic doctor to analyze the evidence from the examination, and the police had not bothered to send the evidence to a pathologist in Montevideo. Under the rules, the judge had only 48 hours to make her decision. She herself had the evidence delivered to a forensic pathologist in the city, who found that there had been semen in the girl's vagina.

When the witnesses came to court, the girl told her version of what had happened. The defendants took the stand and confirmed her account, up until the point that the four had arrived at the apartment. Once there, however, the young men swore under oath—not that she had consented—but that nothing had happened. They never touched her, no rape, no consensual sex, nothing happened. The problem for the defendants, of course, was that the forensic examiner had certified emphatically and unequivocally to the presence of semen in the victim. In other words, the victim's testimony was consistent with the medical evidence, while the defendants' testimony was not.

Judges have the job of resolving credibility disputes. What often makes sexual assault cases difficult is that all the evidence is he said/she said. In this case, what she said was 100% consistent with the medical evidence; what he (here, they) said, 100% inconsistent. Accordingly, for the judge this became an easy case. The victim was telling the truth, the defendants were lying. Guilty. She wrote up her judgment and sentenced the defendants to four years in prison in accordance with the Uruguayan Penal Code.

The defendants' supporters in the community were outraged, and protested in front of the jail. One of the boys' fathers was a prominent political figure. Shortly after the sentencing, members of the Supreme Court and other government officials came to visit prisoners in this prison. A minister asked one of the young men why he was there. Naturally, the young men appealed the conviction.

Two months after they were sentenced, the Supreme Court pardoned all three defendants. The Court did not overturn the trial judge's findings of fact. Nor did it tell her that she had misinterpreted or misapplied any relevant law. Nor did it send the case back to her for further findings or explanation. It simply ordered the young men to be set free.

When she complained to one of her judicial colleagues about the way in which the appeal had been handled, her colleague tried to reassure her. He told her that she should feel satisfied that her opinion had been so well reasoned, and so analytically solid, that the Supreme Court could not overturn her through the normal legal rules. The only thing the Supreme Court could do with her decision, he said, was make it go away—and she "should feel *good* about that."

How Training Can Help Judges

The JEP is not going to teach this judge anything about the meaning of discrimination. She knows all about it. She also knows that she has made some political enemies—and perhaps harmed her own prospects for career advancement—simply by doing her job, by trying to dispense justice evenhandedly, without favor based on either gender or class.

The question, then, is whether and how a training program can empower such judges to be more effective at the job they are sworn to do. In other words, why bother with judicial training?

The answer is twofold. First, the fact that an international development agency or bank, or a national judicial college or ministry of justice thinks the issues are important enough (and mainstream enough) to warrant training is itself a victory. In countries where the government has a history of identifying human rights advocacy with one end of the political spectrum or the other, judicial training programs help de-politicize the subject. De-politicizing human rights in turn can encourage judges to deepen their knowledge of and increase their reliance on human rights principles.

Second, a judicial training program can be a way to encourage and support judges already committed to human rights, and persuade and convert judges who are not. Training can confer both professional status and practical skills. Both of these will be addressed in turn.

A. *Encouraging Judges Already Committed to Human Rights*

The Uruguayan judge perceived the mere fact of having been selected as a trainer to be empowering. She explained to the other workshop participants that it was a great honor to be chosen for an international project such as this one.

Subjectively, she believed that her professional standing with her colleagues had increased. Just before the workshop, she and the other judges on her court had agreed to get together once a month to discuss among themselves issues of common concern. The first meeting was supposed to take place while she was out of the country at our workshop, but her colleagues insisted on rescheduling the meeting after her return.

In many countries, for judges and academics, opportunities to take part in interesting professional programs are doled out based on seniority or political connections. In court systems or law schools where women experience either crude discrimination or "glass ceiling" issues, this predictably leads to fewer opportunities for women to take part in such opportunities.

In the JEP project, while national chapters have discretion as to the details of the selection process, the process they develop must be based on ability and demonstrated interest in and commitment to human rights. Moreover, since each trainer commits to running two seminars after his or her training is complete (which requires many hours of work) those without genuine interest in the subject have little incentive to apply.

Thus, in choosing trainers the project is designed to reach out to judges and academics who are not necessarily politically connected and who may not serve on the highest courts or teach at the most prestigious schools. Generally, the trainers selected are simply smart, decent, hardworking women and men. The fact that they have been chosen gives them a status and credibility with their colleagues that they may not previously have enjoyed.

B. Providing Judges with Analytical Tools: A Closer Look at Uruguayan Sexual Assault Law

At the time of the Uruguayan case study above, Uruguay's law governing sexual assault, like the law of several other South American countries, drew distinctions between chaste and unchaste victims. JEP trainers are encouraged to make transparencies of their own country's laws or a neighboring country's laws that draw this kind of distinction.

Uruguayan Penal Code: Crimes against Good Customs and Family Order[2]

- Article 266. (Abduction for sexual purposes of an honest widow, divorcee or single woman over 18.)

He who, with violence or threats, detains or restrains an honest single woman over 18, or an honest widow or divorcee of any age, for the purposes of satisfying a carnal passion or contracting marriage, shall be punished with between 12 months in prison to five years in the penitentiary.

- Article 267. (Married woman, or minor of 15 years or less.)

He who with violence or threats detains or restrains a married woman to satisfy a carnal passion will be punished with eight years in the penitentiary. The same punishment shall apply to he who sustains or restrains a minor of 15 years or less to satisfy a carnal passion or contract marriage, even if no violence or threats are used.

- Article 268. (Abduction for sexual purposes of a single honest woman over the age of fifteen and less than eighteen, with her consent or without it.)

He who, with any of the aims established in the preceding articles, detains or restrains an honest single woman, older than 15 but younger than 18, with or without her consent, will be punished with from three months in prison up to three years in the penitentiary.

- Article 269. (Impact of the goal of marriage or the dishonesty of the victim.)

A proposal of marriage or the dishonesty of the victim, shall constitute attenuating circumstances.

A JEP trainer could use this transparency in several ways. One possibility is to make a chart similar to the one in the exercise described above on the concept of stereotypes in Article 5 of CEDAW.

The trainer might start by asking participants about their understanding of an "honest woman," and writing the responses on the chart. S/he would then ask whether their perceptions of an "honest man" differed from their perceptions of an "honest woman." To date, JEP trainers who have tried this have obtained the same results: participants report that an honest man is a man of his word, a man whose word is his bond, a man you can trust. An honest woman on the other hand, is a woman who is not promiscuous.

The trainer could then ask participants such questions as, "How would you argue that this statute does *not* violate international law?" S/he might show them the 1998 report of the Inter-American Commission on Human Rights on the Status of Women in the Americas, calling on States to reform sexual assault provisions of this type.[3]

Participants then explore the options open to judges confronted with a statute that so obviously violates their country's international treaty commitments.[4] Can a judge invalidate a statute? Does it depend on the court on which the judge sits? If the judge lacks that power, can s/he refer the case to a constitutional court? Can a judge exclude evidence introduced to show a woman's "dishonesty" (i.e., lack of chastity) that would not be relevant to evaluating the "honesty" of a man?

The trainer might then lead a discussion on Uruguay's sentencing structure—why is the abduction of a married woman punished more harshly than the abduction of a single one? Could this have anything to do with historic notions of wives as property of their husbands? Why should a proposal of marriage attenuate the crime and lessen the sentence?

Throughout JEP seminars and workshops, trainers encourage participants to analyze different facets of their country's civil and criminal laws in this manner. In these discussions, international law is the standard against which domestic law is compared.

Postscript

Both formal and informal evaluations of the JEP program to date generally have been positive. I would like to conclude this chapter with the words of Judge Ana Lima of Montevideo, whose case study is featured above:

A few months after taking part in the Jurisprudence of Equality Project, I noticed the police were bringing me far more domestic violence cases than they ever had before, and that the other judges in my court were getting fewer of them. I asked one of the policemen why this was so, and he said to me, "It is because we know that if we bring them to you, they will not just be dropped. You will do something with them. You are like a lioness with these cases."[5]

Notes

© Anne Tierney Goldstein and Ashgate Publishing Company, 2001. Anne Goldstein has been the Human Rights Education Director for the International Women Judges Foundation since 1993.

1   This chapter is based loosely on what originated as a November 1999 "brown bag" presentation to officials of the Inter-American Development Bank on IADB-funded IWJF training programs in South America. Brief portions of this chapter have previously appeared in training manuals of the IWJF, and are used here with permission.

2   (Author's translation from the Spanish): *Código Penal de Uruguay, TITULO X, DE LOS DELITOS CONTRA LAS BUENAS COSTUMBRES Y EL ORDEN DE LA FAMILIA, CAPITULO III, Rapto Artículo 266. (*Rapto de mujer soltera mayor de dieciocho años, viuda o divorciada honesta) El que, con violencia, amenazas o engaños, sustrajere o retuviere, para satisfacer una pasión carnal o contraer matrimonio, a una mujer soltera, mayor de dieciocho años, a una viuda o a una divorciada, honestas, cualquiera fuera su edad, será castigado con pena de doce meses de prisión a cinco años de penitenciaría. 267. (Mujer casada o menor de 15 años) El que con violencias, amenazas o engaños, sustrae o retiene, para satisfacer una pasión carnal a una mujer casada, será castigado con penitenciaría de dos a ocho años. Con la misma pena será castigado el que sustrae o retiene para satisfacer una pasión carnal o para contraer matrimonio, aunque no mediare violencia, amenaza o engaño, a una menor de quince años. 268. (Rapto de soltera honesta mayor de quince y menor de dieciocho años, con su consentimiento o sin él) El que, con alguno de los fines establecidos en los artículos anteriores, sustrajere o retuviere a una mujer soltera, honesta, mayor de quince años y

menor de dieciocho, con su consentimiento o sin él, será castigado con tres meses de prisión, a tres años de penitenciaría. 269. (Influencia de la finalidad matrimonial y de la deshonestidad de la víctima) Constituyen circunstancias atenuantes, según los casos, el propósito de matrimonio del culpable, o la deshonestidad de la víctima.

3   The report urges states to classify sexual assault crimes as crimes against personal integrity, liberty and privacy rather than as crimes against decency and good morals. States are further exhorted to eliminate "any mention of the concept of decency, honor, and related notions. . . as extenuating circumstances." Report of the Inter-American Commission on Human Rights on the Status of Women in the Americas, OEA/Ser.L/V/II.100, Doc. 17, October 13, 1998, at 34.

4   Uruguay is a party to CEDAW, the American Convention on Human Rights, and the International Covenant on Civil and Political Rights.

5   Personal communication, reproduced with permission.

16 Reflections of a Global Women's Activist on the Use of International Human Rights Law

SUSAN BAZILLI

Over the last decade there have been a plethora of international human rights conferences, meetings, training sessions and workshops, United Nations sessions, and Beijing +5 Preparatory Committee meetings, etc. that were all designed to further the agenda of achieving equality and human rights for women. But in what ways does this international work actually further effective social, political, and economic change at the local level? And how would we know?

As the Beijing +5 review process draws near,[1] it is a good time for activists, academics and advocates to be self-reflective and self-critical at the international level as well as in our own backyards. I have had the privilege of working in many countries with feminist activists engaged in human rights work—from Bosnia to Russia, South Africa to Cameroon, Indonesia to Azerbiajan, Tanzania to Kyrgyzstan, and from the U.S. home to Canada. This chapter contains my reflections on the personal challenge of reconciling these contradictions, a challenge that I am posing to myself as well as to readers.

Global Women's Rights Activism and CEDAW

At the International Women's Rights Project[2] based at York University in Toronto, we have recently completed an evaluation in ten countries of the use of the Convention to Eliminate All Forms of Discrimination against Women (CEDAW).

The methodology we chose was a grassroots one. If global activists are going to organize and train women at the local level on the use of international instruments and mechanisms, the effectiveness of such work needs to be evaluated by the parties involved—the local women.

The study concluded that effective change in the status of women is dependent on the capacity of local women's NGOs to organize and mobilize members of their communities, to use their countries' reporting procedures, and to engage in dialogue with, if not influence, their governments. These are political organizing strategies of local women's movements and civil society as much as they are about the use of CEDAW or any other human rights instruments. CEDAW will only be effective if we can ensure that women at the local level have sufficient political power to force their governments to change domestic laws and policies in accordance with the Convention—but that obviously needs to be done only where the Convention is stronger than domestic law.[3]

The research reports on each country also illustrated the importance of the use of international human rights norms in domestic legislation. Many countries in transition and new democratic governments are attempting to ensure that their legislation and policy is congruent with international law and covenants. This has been true for much legislation that pertains to women's rights since the adoption of the Beijing Platform for Action by the majority of the world's governments. However, it would appear that this adoption has much more to do with the demands of the international donors to require conformance with the rule of law, rather than any real commitment to ensuring the creation of the economic and social conditions needed to realize the human rights of women. While CEDAW was referred to in many of the countries' domestic legislation, this mere reference did not ensure its enforcement. However, this and other studies are being added to the important methodology that is being developed by women to study the effective implementation and enforcement of women's international human rights.

As part of the critical monitoring process, we need a substantive equality analysis to use as a fundamental interpretive principle in assessing any compliance with international human rights law.[4] We do not need to simply find formal equality in the legislation and policy and assume that it is enough. Only with this analysis can we focus on the specific gendered character of poverty and violence, and of women's social deprivation and human rights violations against women. The development of such methodologies has been the ongoing practice of the women's movement for the last several decades.

Women, Globalization, and Trade Liberalization

It is critical that equality-seeking organizations participate in domestic as well as international policy debates and meetings that are informed and affected by globalization trends and the liberalization of trade.[5] When I was attending the Beijing Plus 5 Prep Com in Geneva in January 2000, I was struck by the fact that our efforts were going into a process that seemed to be a lot of smoke and mirrors. While the smoke was about to be blown away from the mirror the following week at Davos, with the advent of the first World Economic Forum meeting since the WTO's famous *Battle of Seattle*, nary a word was uttered at the Geneva meeting of Davos—and we were only a few hours away—by bus.

At this point the greatest barrier to progress for women lies in the reluctance of governments to commit the fiscal resources for essential programs required to address the fundamental rights to shelter, food, water, peace, education, and the disastrous effects of structural adjustment. For women in Canada, that would be our way of describing the need for anti-violence and anti-racism programs; job creation; equal pay; affirmative action; anti-poverty programs; health care; etc. Structural adjustment for us means the downloading and dumping of fiscal and other programs on local governments and structures by federal governments—rather than the acceptance of their responsibility by national governments. Such reluctance by governments the world over seemed to be the one unifying force at these Beijing Plus 5 meetings.

Mobilizing Women at the Grassroots Level

We hope that any losses by the women's movement at the international level are not attributable to a myopic focus on UN conferences and documents at the expense of building strong local women's movements that mobilize grassroots women to bring about concrete change. The most absorbing activity of the last two Beijing +5 Preparatory meetings was our fight against the roll-back of gains made in Beijing, whereby states have avoided commitments to allocation of resources or to any re-distributive agenda. This is clearly mirrored in our own national struggles. Governments around the world are subverting our agenda with their own political maneuvers in venues where we have little voice in the process. None of this is new within the UN system. With little in the way of enforceable documents or an effective means of implementation, and a process fraught with political intrigue not of our own making, what meaningful change can occur?

Excessive Dependency on Law

Academics, activists and advocates who work in the international women's movement—especially those of us in the subsidiary of the international human rights industry—need to question whether we have become too dependent on legal frameworks, part of the "human rights box" that seems to be becoming increasingly disconnected from integrated struggles for democracy engaged in by civil society. We may be twisting ourselves around the legal paradigm in artificial ways, disconnecting ourselves from our real agenda.[6] The narrow focus of a version of "find the bad guy" that is so replete in criminal justice systems, without a more comprehensive analysis of the conditions that perpetuate abuses, too often renders women as "victims." Creating the economic, social, and political conditions—the material conditions that will lead to the securing of rights is surely as important as is finding the violators and seeking redress. We all know that one of the fundamental aspects of the recognition of human rights is the principle that they are indivisible, interrelated and interdependent. The full recognition of the civil, political, economic, social and cultural rights of women, and the lasting progress of the implementation of human rights is dependent on sound effective national and international policies of economic and social development.[7]

The Undermining of Local and National Women's Movements

However, we need to ascertain whether the resources directed to the international level have drained funding for some of our national women's movements. This has been the case in my country, Canada, which the UNDP Human Development Index consistently awards the "Oscar" to Canada for being the best country in the world in which to live. The ranking is impressive, as long as you don't read the "scores" for the supporting roles of women and indigenous peoples. The fact is that women and children are poorer now in Canada than they have been in the past 20 years. Given the enormity and horror of the gross human rights violations of genocide, rape, and starvation throughout the world, Canada's plight may seem trite. This continues as long as you don't know about the tragic and genocidal treatment of indigenous peoples in our country of Canada. But the tragic irony is that Canada is one of the countries that could most easily remedy its own violations of human rights.[8] As Canadian anti-poverty activists have repeatedly pointed out, it is the overall affluence of Canada that makes the disparity and the extent of poverty and inequality such an egregious violation of human rights norms.[9]

The Domestic-International Human Rights Gap

Canada's behaviour illustrates the heart of the local/global dilemma. There is a growing gap between Canada's compliance with its international human rights obligations and its domestic policies and actions.[10]   Canada excels at international donor aid and provides expertise on democracy and human rights outside its borders, while seldom acknowledging its own complicity in abuse and oppression at home.   In fact, UN committees charged with monitoring major treaties, such as those on CEDAW, the International Covenant on Economic, Social and Cultural Rights (ICESCR), and the International Covenant on Civil and Political Rights (ICCPR), are increasingly finding Canada to be violating the fundamental rights of our most vulnerable citizens.   It is noteworthy that the Committee on CERD—the Convention on the Elimination of Race Discrimination— has not found Canada to be accountable for its institutional and systemic racism, as Canada has simply refused to comply with the tabling of reports to CERD.

Canada appears of late to choose to support participation in UN conferences and international work, rather than respond to its own civil society groups seeking to change existing Canadian policies that abuse human rights.   Such contradictory behaviour perpetuates the perception, especially among people in developing countries, of the image of an imperialist international human rights and development industry.   It provides a poor example for many countries trying to reconcile nascent democracy, development of the rule of law, and emerging civil society, under terrible economic conditions.

Conclusion

It is necessary to consider women's real social and economic conditions and to design laws, policies and programs that can address and ameliorate women's real inequalities.   There is no question that many women around the world are poor—many abjectly so—and that women are poorer than men in every society.[11]   Women's persistent poverty and economic inequality is caused by many inter-related factors—and we need to find just as many inter-related solutions.   Using the international human rights system is just one.

In Canada, we must enhance democratic participation and transparency in order to hold our government accountable.   If we cannot do it at home, in the HDI "Oscar" country, how can those of us who work at the global level hope to ensure the accountability of the governments for those who are the "victims" of human rights violations around the world?   The Canadian government adopted a plan on "gender equality"[12] to comply with its commitment to the Beijing Platform for Action, making a commitment to analyze the impact of its policies and legislation on women. However, since they have not actually done so and followed up on their promise, Canadian feminists have been able to successfully use the UN system to at least draw attention to the violations of human rights.

And perhaps more critical a question: to whom are we as global activists accountable? One of the uses of the international human rights system could be at the very least to articulate the hypocrisy of the North. But that is hardly enough!

We advocates and scholars seeking to broaden women's rights need to focus on closing the gap between the local and the global, while continuing to identify the pressure points wherever we find them. This is no less tall an order than the lifetime task of protecting and realizing women's human rights that we have set ourselves.

Notes

© Susan Bazilli and Ashgate Publishing Company, 2001. Susan Bazilli works with the International Women's Rights Project, York University, Toronto, Canada.

1   This paper was presented in April 2000; The Beijing Plus 5 United Nations General Assembly Special Session was held in June 2000.
2   Director, Marilou McPhedran, Centre for Feminist Research, York University, and co-author of *The First CEDAW Impact Study, Final Report*. IWRP. Dr. McPhedran presented the final report to the CEDAW Committee in June 2000, New York. For details of the IWRP *see* www.yorku.ca/iwrp.
3   *Confronting Violence Against Women: A Brief Guide to International Human Rights Law for Canadian Advocates*, Canadian Women's Studies, October 2000.
4   *Canadian Women and the Social Deficit: A Presentation to the International Committee on Economic, Social and Cultural Rights*, National Association of Women and the Law [NAWL], November 1998.
5   In Canada, one place we are doing this work is within FAFIA—the Feminist Alliance for International Action, an alliance of feminist organizations.
6   *See* Susan Bazilli, *Human Rights Dialogue*, Carnegie Council on Ethics and International Affairs, Summer 2000, Series 2 Number 3.
7   *Civil and Political Rights of Canadian Women*, National Association of Women and the Law (NAWL), March 29, 1999. International Committee on Civil and Political Rights.
8   *Judging Poverty: Using International Human Rights Law to Refine the Scope of Charter Rights*, Bruce Porter, 15 Journal of Law and Social Policy, 2000.
9   *The Ontario People's Report to the United Nations on Violations of the International Covenant on Economic, Social and Cultural Rights* submitted to the Committee by LIFT, Low Income Families Together and Josephine Grey. Geneva, November 1998.
10 NAWL op. cit.
11 LIFT op. cit.

12 *Federal Plan for Gender Equality and Gender Based Analysis: A Guide for Policy Making.* Government of Canada, 1995.

17 The Bureau des Avocats Internationaux, a Victim-Centered Approach

BRIAN CONCANNON, JR.

The Bureau des Avocats Internationaux (BAI) is a group of lawyers funded by the Haitian government that assists the judiciary with human rights cases, mostly from Haiti's 1991-94 *de facto* military dictatorship. The BAI's mandate is a general one: to do what it can to move human rights cases through the justice system. We use a "carrot and stick" approach: we help the system perform better through technical and material assistance, and we pressure it to do so by helping human rights and victims' groups advocate in the courtroom, on the streets, and in the media.

This chapter will discuss the BAI's experiences in the larger context of Haiti's struggle to establish accountability for past atrocities, and democratize the justice system.

Background

The *de facto* dictatorship ousted Haiti's first freely elected government in September, 1991. Over the next three years, the military and its paramilitary allies murdered an estimated 5,000 civilians, and beat, raped or otherwise tortured hundreds of thousands more. The justice system helplessly watched the terror from the sidelines, unable to intervene. When asked why, a prosecutor testifying in a recent human rights trial pointed to the still unpunished October 1993 assassination of Justice Minister Guy Malary, and invoked a Creole proverb: "Konstitisyon se papye, bayonet se fer" ("the Constitution is paper, bayonets are steel").

The *de facto* period was not the first time the justice system failed to protect the majority of Haitians. The entire system, from the police to judges to prosecutors and private lawyers, had always been unwilling or unable to curb the abuses of those with guns or money. Justice in Haiti is often described with the word "exclusion." the exclusion of the poor from the formal justice system, and the use of the system to exclude the poor from the country's economic, political and social spheres.

In addition to, and because of, its ideological deficiencies, the justice system suffered from acute technical deficiencies. Legal proceedings were theatrical and formalistic, with little attention paid to the presentation or analysis of facts. Lawyers were not adept at preparing cases for trial, and judges were not good at hearing them. Rigorous preparation was not deemed important where cases were decided by merits other than legal or factual ones. Formalism and shoddy practice also served to obscure the true bases for decisions.

The return to democratic rule in Haiti in October 1994, was an important victory for human rights in the country, but only the first step in establishing the rule of law. The legal system's historical exclusion of Haiti's majority, and its deep technical deficiencies made it incapable of functioning under a democracy without a fundamental overhaul. Change needed to be made in practices, but also in people and structures. Personnel throughout the system needed to be trained to perform at a higher level than before, and to perform in a way that respected the rights and interests of the majority. Replacements needed to be found for those who could not or would not change. The codes and the administrative structure needed overhaul as well. They are largely unchanged since the 1840s, and are ill-adapted for a twenty-first century caseload.

The BAI

The Haitian government formed the BAI both to help victims of the coup obtain justice and to assist the overall effort to improve the justice system. We view our work in the context of the larger democratic transition, and combine political strategies with legal ones. The linchpin of the BAI's strategy is its work with victims, which includes representing them in court proceedings through the "partie civile" (civil party) procedure, and helping them assert their rights in the courts, in the press, and on the streets.

The BAI's five core functions are: 1) representing victims in civil and criminal cases against violators; 2) assisting judges and prosecutors; 3) helping police locate and arrest suspects; 4) helping NGOs improve their human rights advocacy; and 5) promoting coordination among these actors. The office also has a training program for young Haitian lawyers, hosts interns from U.S. law schools, and collaborates with U.S. law school clinics working on its cases.

A. Representing Victims

The BAI's most important and visible core function is representing victims in civil and criminal cases against violators. In all of our cases, BAI lawyers represent the victims from the initial investigation through the trial, verdict, and recovery of civil damages. We start most cases by meeting with victims, usually through an organization. If the victims are willing to pursue a prosecution with our help, the BAI interviews the victims, conducts an investigation, and prepares a complaint.

Once a complaint is filed, our representation includes three components: a) traditional lawyering, b) advocacy outside of the courtroom and c) assisting the victims to advocate on their own behalf. Traditional lawyering by the BAI involves representing the victims at pre-trial, trial and post-trial hearings, preparing and presenting evidence, and preparing pleadings, especially responses to defendant appeals. Under the French system used in Haiti, a claim for civil damages can piggy-back on a criminal prosecution. A victim seeking damages is called a "partie-civile" and his or her lawyer is allowed to participate in most aspects of the proceedings. The lawyer can introduce evidence and examine witnesses and parties at trial, submit pleadings to the court, and argue legal issues relevant to the civil claim. In this role, BAI lawyers act as a backup to prosecutors where necessary. The BAI also helps victims obtain medical and other assistance.

The BAI's advocacy for the victims extends well beyond the courtroom. We meet regularly with national and local officials regarding particular cases and broader policy towards victims. This ensures that the officials understand the victims' perspective, and raises victims' concerns among the officials' diverse and sometimes conflicting priorities. BAI lawyers also communicate regularly with international organizations working on justice and human rights in Haiti.

The BAI also helps victims increase their capacity to advocate for themselves. We spend a lot of time, in both formal and informal settings, explaining the relevant legal issues and procedures for all of our cases. We involve victims as much as possible in strategic decisions, and work with them to analyze the different obstacles to their case. We advise victims and their organizations on specific initiatives, such as planning a press conference or writing an open letter to a government official.

Assisting victims to advocate on their own behalf may be the most important part of the BAI's representation. In the short term, it allows our cases to move forward. A well-timed and reasoned press conference, open letter or demonstration can compel official action where legal strategies or the BAI's lower-profile advocacy could not. Active involvement by the victims also encourages long-term changes in the judiciary. Once empowered, the victims we work with become more effective at demanding the broader democratization of the justice system. The system itself becomes habituated to working with the historically excluded, and their advocacy serves as a model for others insisting on judicial reform.

An example of this collaboration was the initiative to remove the chief prosecutor, or *Commissaire de Gouvernement* in the *Raboteau Massacre* case. Neither the victims nor their lawyers trusted him, but he was allowed to stay in office for over a year of pre-trial preparations. Although the two Ministers of Justice over that span acknowledged the prosecutor's shortcomings, he was not replaced because of his political connections, and the difficulty of finding a better replacement. The BAI protested the *Commissaire*'s original nomination, and privately urged his replacement, in both written and oral communications with officials. When that failed to work, the BAI raised the issue with victims and human rights groups, who also urged the government to replace him. Eventually, the victims in the *Raboteau* case made their complaints public, with the BAI's help, through open letters, denunciations on the radio, and, finally, street demonstrations. The demonstrations worked, as the *Commissaire* was removed, and replaced by another prosecutor who performed well at trial.

B. *Assisting Judges and Prosecutors*

The BAI's second core function is assisting judges and prosecutors. Although many people in the judiciary support human rights prosecutions, most lack the training and resources to do it well. The BAI helps judges and prosecutors rise to the task in their cases by providing technical and material support, and by advocating for the officials' needs at the national level. Technical support includes legal and factual research and analysis, consultation on strategic issues and assistance in preparing documents at the pre-trial, trial and appeal stages. Material support includes obtaining national and international legal materials, providing typing and other support services, and purchasing office supplies and equipment when necessary.

The BAI's judicial assistance complements and supplements other efforts, such as Haiti's Ecole de la Magistrature (Judicial Academy). While these programs attempt to raise the performance of a large number of officials to minimally acceptable levels, the BAI concentrates on helping a select few perform at a high level in complex, high profile cases.

The BAI also encourages judges and prosecutors to work closely in partnership with victims. "Professionalism" in Haiti has traditionally meant that officials ask crime victims narrow questions and expect narrow responses, and that prosecutors spend little time explaining their actions and strategies to victims. BAI lawyers use their own experience as an example to officials of how close collaboration with victims can enhance the "technical" preparation of the case, and how empowered victims can help with many aspects of the case, from tracking down suspects to advocating for a judge's transportation needs. BAI assistance to judicial officials has generated substantial results. The written work done by judges and prosecutors, from indictments to appeals briefs, is usually among the best of its kind ever produced by the justice system, and is used as models for other cases. As officials see these results, judges and prosecutors are increasingly interested in working on human rights cases, and with the BAI.

C. Helping Police Locate and Arrest Suspects

The BAI's third core function is helping police locate and arrest suspects. Two teams of the *Brigade Criminelle*, a special investigative unit of the Haitian National Police, are assigned to BAI cases. As with judges and prosecutors, the BAI provides police with technical and material assistance. We meet with the investigators most days, and every week, to help plan strategy, not just for arrests and investigations, but also for obtaining resources and other cooperation from the government, and for working with judges, prosecutors and victims.

One 1997 arrest illustrates both the initiative of the *Brigade Criminelle*, and why they sometimes need a boost from the outside. The suspect was a former soldier, believed to be armed and possibly dangerous. The *Brigade* assembled a good file on him, including a description of his car and the location of his house. Along with the BAI, the police were trying to plan an arrest away from his home, to minimize resistance and interference from family and neighbors. One day a *Brigade* member burst into our office, breathlessly demanding the keys to the office's car. He blurted out that the suspect was just up the street, stuck in the usual Port-au-Prince traffic.

As we handed over the keys, we asked if they had the numbers and firepower for the potentially dangerous mission, and were shown a shotgun which supplemented the service revolvers. The police caught up with the suspect in the borrowed car and made the arrest. The suspect did not resist, fortunately, as there was no ammunition in the shotgun. That arrest was number twenty-one for the case, which was, at the time, one more than the total number incarcerated in connection with the Yugoslav War Crimes Tribunal.

D. Helping NGOs Improve Their Human Rights Advocacy

The BAI's fourth core function is helping Haitian NGOs improve their advocacy strategy. BAI has two initiatives in this area, one for newer organizations and another for more established ones. In general, the BAI provides information to NGOs about its cases, consults on issues regarding organizational structure, helps with advocacy strategy, and provides material assistance.

Haiti has experienced a blossoming of grassroots organizations along with its democratic transition. Most of these groups, however, are underfunded and have limited organizing capability or experience. The BAI helps them develop their capacity by providing materials and contacts on organizational issues, lending them meeting space, computers and access to communications, and putting NGOs in touch with victims.

A good example of this collaboration is the Fondation 30 Septembre (FTS), which started in 1997 and is now Haiti's largest victims' group. Despite its success in organizing, the group does not yet have the funds for a permanent office. It uses BAI's facilities for meetings, telephone calls, word processing, and Internet access. The BAI and FTS meet frequently to exchange information and strategy ideas, and collaborate on initiatives of mutual interest. Partly through its collaboration with BAI, FTS has raised its profile in Haiti and abroad, to the point where it can now apply for funding to open its own facility.

The BAI also works with more established groups, helping them better engage with the government and advocate on issues related to human rights prosecutions. As governmental institutions make the transition to more democratic practices, civil society needs to make similar transitions in its strategies and engagement. The traditional denunciation by press release, although still valuable in some situations, needs to be supplemented with less confrontational, more nuanced strategies. The BAI helps with this transition by explaining its cases to NGOs "from the inside," to help them understand the real obstacles to progress, and allow them to better target their critiques. We also help them plan their strategy, and coordinate our own initiatives to maximize their impact.

For example, a coalition of established human rights organizations complained to us that judicial authorities never seemed to listen to their recommendations regarding one of the BAI's cases. A week later, a Ministry of Justice official complained that the same groups always denounced problems, but never offered any solutions. Seeing an opportunity, the BAI proposed, then facilitated a series of meetings between the groups and the Ministry. We met with the coalition beforehand, to provide information and discuss strategy. We also helped them produce written materials, some of which were distributed to the press. The meetings were a success, as the coalition effectively advocated for several improvements in the prosecution, and established at least some ongoing relationship with the Ministry.

E. Promoting Coordination

The BAI's fifth core activity is promoting coordination among the various actors involved in its cases. As discussed above, there has traditionally been poor communication between judicial officials and either victims or NGOs. There has also been poor communication within the justice system: prosecutors do not always speak with investigating judges, both often neglect to listen or talk to police, and all three usually failed to coordinate with the prison system. The BAI has tried to bridge these gaps, by holding coordination meetings, serving as a conduit for information, and encouraging closer collaboration.

BAI Training Programs

The BAI is helping train a new generation of human rights lawyers through its programs for Haitian law graduates and U.S. law students. In our experience, the lack of trained lawyers willing and able to do high quality human rights or public interest work is the largest single problem with the justice system. Existing lawyers and institutions have shown their unwillingness to change this situation, so the BAI is creating a new structure to train a corps of new lawyers willing and able to change the system.

The main cause of this human resources problem is a training system that: a) does not train lawyers to prepare a quality, fact-based case, and b) perpetuates a legal culture that reinforces existing injustices. Law school in Haiti is theoretical, with no practice classes or clinics. Once a prospective lawyer completes law school, he or she must write a *"memoire de sortie,"* or master's thesis, then complete a two year apprenticeship, or *"stage"* with a licensed lawyer. Both the *stage* and the *memoire* serve as numerical and ideological filters, preventing progressive students from becoming progressive lawyers. Both also miss opportunities to properly train law school graduates.

Although the *memoire* affords an opportunity to gain expertise and produce useful research in human rights issues, in practice it almost never does so. Technical support and guidance for the *memoire* are not integrated into the curriculum, so a graduate must find a lawyer to "godfather" it, and must pay for this service. Less than twenty-five percent of graduates ever clear this hurdle. Those who do are channeled down the well-worn paths, as existing lawyers are not interested in graduates and topics that either challenge the structure that supports them or are outside their professional experience.

The *stage* is the largest squandered opportunity to prepare lawyers to work on human rights cases. Practical training replicates the habits of the practitioner, which in Haiti means the habits of someone neither ideologically nor professionally qualified to prepare high quality human rights cases. As lawyers in Haiti have always sided with those able to pay or intimidate them, there are few people who can and will train young lawyers to cross the line to assert the rights of the poor or powerless. The experienced lawyers' own emphasis on procedure and theater at the expense of the presentation and analysis of facts precludes them from being able to train an apprentice in the rigorous preparation of a case.

The BAI provides free assistance on the *memoire* to graduates willing to do research on a topic of interest to the program. The most promising of these then enter the office to complete their *stage* through supervised work on the office's cases. Upon completion, some of the newly licensed lawyers will continue at the BAI, while others will enter the system as prosecutors, judges and private lawyers. The BAI will stay in contact with the graduates, and work to place them where motivated, trained candidates are needed for important judicial posts.

The BAI also trains law students from the U.S. We host interns from U.S. law schools each summer and most winters. More recently, we have established relationships with clinical programs at DePaul, Harvard and Yale universities to work on our cases. This program exposes U.S students to real "developing world" human rights cases, with all their attendant promise and frustration. Interns in Port-au-Prince work closely with victims, and are consequently exposed to a very different economic, social and political reality.

Conclusion

The BAI's system has already produced results. The *Raboteau* trial was completed in November of 2000, and is considered by far the best legal proceeding in Haitian history. Sixteen of the twenty-two defendants in custody were convicted, as well as thirty-seven *in absentia* defendants, including the dictatorship's top military and paramilitary leaders. National and international observers agreed that the case provided justice for the victims, while respecting the rights of the accused. The BAI's system of preparation is being copied in other high profile cases.

The *Raboteau* trial has also changed the way victims and officials alike view justice. The victims now believe that the system can respond to their demands, and expect it to provide high quality justice, at least in important cases. Judicial officials as well have started believing in the system, and have recalibrated their own expectations. The BAI's largest impact, however, may eventually come from its training program. If the office can add three to six well trained public interest lawyers to the bar every year, it will change legal training and the way lawyers relate to their clients forever.

Index

Entries preceded by I. refer to the companion volume: Effective Strategies for Protecting Human Rights: Economic sanctions, use of national courts and international *fora* and coercive power

Institutions and Organizations,
NGOs

Institutions and Organizations, Governmental and Multilateral

Cases

General